THE BORDER COUNTRY

A Walker's Guide

by
Alan Hall

CICERONE

2 POLICE SQUARE, MILNTHORPE, CUMBRIA LA7 7PY
www.cicerone.co.uk

All photographs by the author.
Quotations carry the author's name if known.

A catalogue record for this book is available from the British Library

Dedicated to Greta

Acknowledgements

Special thanks to Greta my wife, who travelled with me every step of the way, from the book's conception to its completion – a shared journey that enlarged the pleasure and enhanced the outcome. Also included is our son Kevin, with his unbounded enthusiasm and energy for the entire project. His knowledgeable company c   Hector Innes for
his expert .   ryside Rangers,
Scottish Bc   ny friends who
unearthed   d, and finally to
hill walker   heir time in the
Borders. I c   uragement, and
to all lover   lates you all to
travel just t

Front cover: Smailholm Tower, Walk 19

CONTENTS

Advice to Readers

Readers are advised that while every effort is taken by the author to ensure the accuracy of this guidebook, changes can occur which may affect the contents. A book of this nature with specific descriptions is more prone to change than some – waymarking can alter, for example, and new buildings go up or old ones disappear. It is advisable to check locally on transport, accommodation, shops, etc., but even rights of way can be altered and paths eradicated by landslip, forestry work or changes of ownership. The publisher would welcome notes of any such changes for future editions.

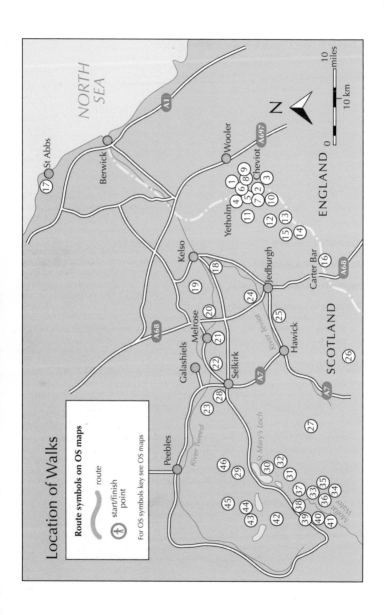

Location of Walks

Route symbols on OS maps

~~~ route

⊕ start/finish point

For OS symbols key see OS maps

INTRODUCTION

Grey recumbent tombs of the dead in desert places,
Standing stones on the vacant wine-red moor,
Hills of sheep, and the homes of the silent vanquished races,
And winds, austere and pure.

R L Stevenson

THE BORDER HILLS AND SOUTHERN UPLANDS

Between England and Scotland lies the solitude of an upland area which, though neglected by rambler and mountain walker alike, offers to both a wealth of adventure. Although linked to the north of England and the Lothians of Scotland, this area has, because of its geographical seclusion and its history and tradition, retained its own distinct identity. The Borders region of Scotland (comprising the districts of Berwickshire, Roxburghshire, Ettrick and Lauderdale, and Tweeddale) and the northern fringes of Northumberland constitute the landmass known as the Borders covered in this guide. The population is around 120,000, the majority of whom reside in small towns and villages of which only 14 have more than 1500 inhabitants. This makes the area the second most thinly populated part of Scotland and certainly the most thinly populated part of England. The average space per head in the Borders is one person for every 11 acres, compared with an overall average for Scotland of less than four acres per person.

The fertile farms in the straths (valleys) of the Tweed and Teviot have fostered a fine arable and stock tradition, while the surrounding hills have a reputation second to none for breeding and feeding sheep, proudly producing named breeds such as the Cheviot and the Border Leicester. Allied with the agriculture are twin spin-offs: quality textiles (the shrinking mainstay of the local economy) and food processing. In recent years the industrial base has widened to include industries such as plastics, chemicals, paper production, health care and electronics, all of which has, fortunately, led to the reversal of the population drift and, in the last 15 years, increased the numbers residing in the area. The Borders is also renowned in the field of sport, particularly rugby union.

This Borderland has a character of its own, manifest not only in the green and rounded hills, the glens and bubbling burns, but also in Border legend, poetry and music. It is a subtle character, one that may not be fully understood by a single ascent of Cheviot or a walk in Ettrick Forest, yet as certain as the seasons.

9

Teviotdale and Hawick from Rubers Law (Walk 25)

The region offers 68 mountains and tops in excess of 2000ft (610m), the highest being Broad Law 2754ft (839m), with only a smattering of rock climbs and several scrambles on scree or in rocky gullies. The highlights of the area, however, are the many long and exhilarating ridge walks, although some include the notorious peat hags of the upper Cheviots. No matter what your tastes, there are walks in this guide to suit all pedestrians and lovers of the countryside, whatever your abilities and secondary interests.

CLIMATE AND WEATHER PATTERNS

The number of hours of sunshine depends to a certain extent on the height above sea level, in particular in the vicinity of Cheviot, Hart Fell and Broad Law, whose summits attract precipitation and cloud. Lower Tweeddale, the coastal plain and the more sheltered valleys enjoy up to 50 per cent more sunshine than the hills over 2000ft (610m), especially those in the west of the region.

SUNSHINE												
Daily Average Hours of Bright Sunshine												
Jan	Feb	Mar	Apr	May	Jun	Jul	Aug	Sep	Oct	Nov	Dec	**Annual total**
Ettrick Head												
1.3	2.2	2.9	4.5	5.3	5.5	4.6	4.3	3.3	2.5	1.8	1.2	**1198**
Lower Tweed												
1.7	2.7	3.7	5.3	6.0	6.6	6.1	5.4	4.3	3.4	2.3	1.6	**1493**

TEMPERATURE		
Daily Average at Sea Level (°C)		
	Maximum	Minimum
January	6.0°	0.0°
July	19.5°	10.5°

The lapse rate, a reduction of approximately 3°C for every 1000ft (305m) increase in height above sea level, allows a simple calculation to be made in relation to the Border walks. However, sheltered inland valleys can be colder than the summits during the winter months, as cold air tends to drain into the valley floors and form frost pockets, while the converse is true during the summer.

Visibility

The Borders enjoys very good visibility, situated as it is well away from industrial pollution and heavy traffic. Evening and night fogs, should they occur, are formed from water droplets, and as such they invariably clear during the day with the increase in temperature. Sea haars (cold mists or fogs) can be experienced along the Berwickshire coast and may occasionally affect Walk 17 from April to September.

Wind

Based on readings taken at 1000ft (305m), the prevailing wind pattern governing the Border hills and the Southern Uplands is from the south-west – winds blowing from between south and west are at least twice as frequent as from any other point on the compass. Wind speeds for 85 per cent of the year are between 1½ and 18½mph, plus 5 per cent below 1mph (graded as calm). Records show that sustained wind speeds never exceed 46mph, although occasional gusts may do so. April to October are the calmest months to walk the Border hills, with January to March being the coldest and most windy. During the winter months the uplands can be sterilised by cold northeasters that ride in from the Arctic or the continental steppes on the edge of high pressure systems.

Precipitation

With the prevailing wind pattern from the southwest, and influenced by its journey over the Atlantic Ocean, it is the west of the area that receives most rain. The western bastion of the Tweedsmuir Hills has an average annual fall of 89in on Lochcraig Head, 85in on Hart Fell, 83in on Gameshope Loch and 82in on Garelet Dod. The eastern Cheviots (including the Cheviot plateau) by comparison only attract 45in, with the lower western tops receiving on average 36in, emphasising how dry this area is when compared with the annual deluges of 125in occurring in the more 'fashionable' areas of the Western Highlands and the English

PRECIPITATION

By month

	Driest in Year	Wettest in Summer	Wettest in Winter
Cheviots	Mar Apr June	Aug (wettest in year)	Nov Dec Jan
Tweeddale	Mar Apr June	Aug (wettest in year)	Sept Nov Jan
Ettrick Forest	Mar Apr June	Aug	Nov Dec Jan
Moffat Hills	Mar Apr June	Aug	Oct Nov Dec
Manor Hills	Mar Apr June	Aug	Oct Nov Dec

Lakes. At the lower levels in Tweeddale and Teviotdale and on the Merse of Berwickshire the annual rainfall ranges from a mere 26in to 30in. (To convert inches to centimetres multiply by 2.540.)

With showers in mind the peaks and troughs for walking in the Borders are as follows.

The incidence of summer thunderstorms and hail showers in Scotland as a whole, and the Borders in particular, is low, much less frequent than in parts of England. In Edinburgh such phenomena appear on average 7 times a year, in areas of England on average 15 to 20 times a year.

Snow in winter very rarely impedes the walker, even at heights in excess of 2000ft (610m). Any coverings that occur invariably enhance the scene and provide just that little extra challenge.

Evidence from the weather patterns cited above, i.e. from records compiled over the last 20 years, would suggest that the month of June provides the Border walker with the brightest and driest days, the best walking temperatures, little or no wind, good visibility and, of course, long days and short nights. June is closely followed by April, May and July, with only a small reduction in either temperature or hours of sunshine, or an acceptable increase in precipitation. All in all, a very pleasant climate in which to walk.

SNOW

Average Number of Days per Month
(with snow lying at 0900 hours, alt. 1000ft (305m))

Jan	Feb	Mar	Apr	May	Jun	Jul	Aug	Sep	Oct	Nov	Dec
10	9.6	4.7	0.7	0	0	0	0	0	0	1.9	5

Heatherhope Valley from Philip Shank (Walk 13)

FLORA AND FAUNA

Upper Heaths and Moors

This type of terrain dominates the Cheviots, Ettrick Forest and the Tweedsmuir Hills, where the dry heaths on the steep upper slopes change gradually into peat bogs on the flatter summits and plateaux. Such heathland contains heather (ling), cotton grass (Scotsman's heids), and cross-leaved heath, all of which grow happily on the wet and acidic peat. Bilberry (blaeberry) and bell heather prosper on the drier slopes, while on well-drained summit ridges cloudberry, crowberry and dwarf cornal grow, and on the highest hills the rare alpine foxtail may occasionally be found. Grasses that thrive on the Border hills are mainly mat grass (which turns vast areas of the upper Cheviots white in late summer) and wavy hair grass, while in areas of water percolation tussocks of purple moor grass (molinia) make walking difficult. In poor visibility the varying vegetation at higher levels acts as a guide, giving indications of altitude, and warnings of wet and potentially dangerous conditions underfoot.

Sixteen types of bird utilise this habitat to hunt, feed, nest and breed. This area remains one of the last strongholds for species such as the peregrine falcon (in the crags), the

13

merlin (hunts over the heather), the hen harrier, dunlin and golden plover. On the higher craggy hills and gullies, such as Blackhope Glen and the Hen Hole, ravens may be found, although in small numbers, whereas carrion crows (the moorland scavenger) are much more common. Few if any animals and reptiles inhabit the summits and the tops, though summer visits may be made by the fox, the blue mountain hare (with its distinctive white coat in winter), and feral goats. Domestic sheep are to be found at all levels in the Border hills.

Lower Slopes, Ridges, Cols and Open Moorland

These are blanketed by bent grass, fescues and bracken (becoming a great threat) and, growing in the less acidic soils, patches of red fescue. Colour is provided by blaeberry, catspaw, wild thyme, heath bedstraw, rockrose (food for the rare northern brown argus butterfly, Walk 17) and the yellow mountain pansy. Any wet and badly drained areas are clearly indicated by an abundance of rushes and sedge – home to snipe, lizards, slowworms and frogs (newts prefer the lower rocks and burnsides). The shy adder, although venomous, is not classed as a highly poisonous snake and can occasionally be seem in the Cheviots basking on a warm rock before slithering off to hide in the bracken.

Sounds that are music to the hill walker's ear are provided by two fascinating moorland birds. The distinctive curlew (whaup), with its curved beak and plaintive cry, together with the clown of the fells, the peewit (green plover), are both evident in satisfying numbers. Another interesting inhabitant of the heather moors is the short-eared owl, which sleeps at night and hunts for voles during the day.

With the encroachment of fast-growing pines, larch and spruce, the deer population has greatly increased in recent years, as has the number of stoats, weasels, feral mink and, thankfully, woodpeckers.

Lochs and Coastline

Three natural lochs, St Mary's Loch, Loch of the Lowes and Loch Skeen, together with the reservoirs of Talla and Megget, are stocked with trout and inhabited by seabirds. The many burns provide a regular diet for the stately heron and fine sport for anglers, and are home to the ring ouzel and the cheeky little dipper. Three lochans on the northern edge of the Cheviot range also act as staging posts for huge numbers of migratory birds and wintering wildfowl, such as greylag and pinkfooted geese.

The cliffs of St Abb's Head are home to thousands of fulmers, common gulls, razorbills, kittiwakes, shags and puffins, and the clifftops support a carpet of interesting plants. Further and more specific details can be obtained from the information boards displayed on the walks and from local tourist information centres.

Physical

BC	Significant Events Affecting the Area
500,000,000	*Silurian Era:* A huge earth movement joined the land masses bearing Scotland and England.
400,000,000	*Devonian Era:* Red sandstone and Cheviot lava.
350,000,000	*Carboniferous Era:* Calciferous sandstones as found in the Merse of Berwickshire; volcanoes, e.g. the Eildon Hills.
12,000–10,000	Retreat of the ice sheets.
9000	Invasion by trees and shrubs, moss and lichen, and other open-ground vegetation. Tundra conditions.
7000	Significant rise of the North Sea, with the land bridge to the continent severed, forming raised beaches.
6000	Forests of broadleaved woodland and areas of scrub grew below 2500ft (762m), reducing and replacing areas of coniferous forest.
4000	Elm tree decline, allowing infiltration by ground vegetation into forest clearings.

River Tweed to Caddonfoot overlooked by Neidpath Hill (Walk 22)

15

Human
BC

6000–3000	*Mesolithic Period:* Penetration of settlements along riverbanks, e.g. Rink Farm near Galashiels, Kalemouth and Springwood near Kelso.
3500–2500	*Neolithic Period:* Saw the introduction of a basic form of agriculture.
2500–2000	Development of a hierarchical society in which ceremonial objects such as polished stone axes and maces were made.
2000–1250	Introduction of new types of ceremonial sites such as beaker burials, individual burials in cairns and cists (stone coffins). The erection of stone circles and standing stones, e.g. Five Stanes Rig, Ninestane Rig and Threestone Burn.
1750	Bronze Age technology introduced into the Borders.
1500–700	An age of open settlements and field cultivation together with hilltop meeting places, e.g. the Eildon Hills and the heights surrounding the glen of Heatherhope.
700–500	Iron Age technology, ring ditches, horseshoe houses with palisaded settlements, e.g. Hownam Rings.
500–200	Iron Age fortifications, with the development of arable and livestock farming, e.g. Glenrathope and the Street.

AD

80–105	Roman occupation of the Borders – Flavian's cohorts established at Trimontium, Melrose.
140–180	Antonine occupation of the Borders – HQ remained at Trimontium, Melrose.
205–212	Severan's Roman campaigns.
400–550	With the Roman withdrawal a period of tribal warfare, followed by early Christian crusading by the Celtic communities, e.g. the Yarrow Stone.
550–1015	Northumbrian political and religious domination of the eastern and central Borders. Monastic settlements established at Jedburgh, Old Melrose and Coldingham.
1015	Battle of Carham; Berwickshire and Teviotdale incorporated into the kingdom of Scotland.
1128–1140	The four great Border abbeys of Kelso, Melrose, Jedburgh and Dryburgh were completed in the reign of David I of Scotland.

Derelict fort at Yeavering Bell (Walk 1)

1124–1603	Continuous conflict between England and Scotland, during which the Borders were trampled underfoot by the armies of both sides. When they had passed through, the reivers (fighting families) on both sides of the Border were at each other's throats. The reiver had no loyalty save that of a blood relationship. Reiver strongholds were the pele towers such as those at Smailholm, Newark, Dryhope, Kirkhope and, the bloodiest of them all, Hermitage.
1603	The Union of the Crowns, after which there was a 100 year period of pacification before peace and prosperity came to the Borders.

PUBLIC RIGHTS OF WAY

This is a grey and troubled area, and it is not within the remit of this guide to go further than state the four criteria needed to establish and maintain a public right of way.

1 It must have been used by the general public for a continuous period of 20 years.

2 It must have been used as a matter of right.

3 It must connect two public places.

4 It must follow a route more or less defined.

The law of trespass differs in England and Scotland, especially with Scotland's 'Right to Roam Law' imminent at the time of this edition's update, and this guide is not qualified to lead the walker through either maze. The author suggests that a serious and courteous enquiry to the landowner, farmer or shepherd regarding the feasibility of a certain route makes life much easier for all concerned. To show concern for others' property and privacy, as well as the environment, is to show concern for the entire countryside.

Two publications are recommended:

Public Rights of Way in the Borders Region, Scottish Borders Council, Newtown St Boswells, Melrose, TD6 0SA

A Walkers Guide to the Law of Rights of Way in Scotland, Scottish Rights of Way Society Ltd, 24 Annandale Street, Edinburgh, EH7 4A. Tel: 0131 558 1222

ACCESS

Rail Links

Two main lines pass through the Border hills and the Southern Uplands, stopping at Berwick-upon-Tweed on the east coast Intercity line, and Carlisle on the west coast Intercity link between Glasgow and the western areas of England and Wales (Carlisle station is connected to the central Borders by the Scottish Borders Rail Link bus).

Frequent Intercity services stop at Berwick-upon-Tweed each day, with several slower stopping trains supplementing this service. Carlisle is served from Glasgow, the west of England, Wales and London. Timetables, tickets and fare details are available from Scottish and English railway stations, and travel agents. The telephone numbers of the two stations serving the area can be found in Appendix 3, Useful Information.

Road Links

The A1(M) and the M1 lead north to Tyneside from the eastern half of England, and from there the A1 continues north to Berwick-upon-Tweed. Scenic routes from Newcastle upon Tyne are the A697 to Wooler and Coldstream (Chapter 1), and the A68 directly through the Cheviots via Jedburgh to Teviotdale and Tweeddale (Chapters 1 and 2). For southbound travellers four roads lead from Edinburgh direct to the heart of the Borders, the A703 to Peebles (Chapter 4), the A7 to Selkirk (Chapter 3), the A68 to Melrose and Jedburgh (Chapters 2 and 1), and the A697 to Kelso and Wooler (Chapters 1 and 2).

To reach the Borders from the southwest of England and Wales, take the M5 then M6 motorways north to Carlisle, then travel northeast on the A7

Borders scenic route to Langholm, Hawick and Selkirk (Chapter 3). From Glasgow use the A74 to Moffat, then northeast via the A708 road to St Mary's Loch and Selkirk (Chapters 3 and 4).

When a car is used to reach the start of a walk and parking space is limited, care should be exercised to make sure that your parked car does not restrict access and passage for those who live and work in the area.

Bus Services

Long-distance City Link express bus services from 29 major cities and towns (including four airports) in England and Scotland pass through the eastern Borders, stopping at Galashiels, Hawick and Jedburgh. Western fringes of the area are served with long-distance buses from the west of Scotland, England and Wales, calling at Carlisle and Moffat.

Local Services

As in the majority of wild and lonely areas, the Borders are not particularly well served by local bus services. School buses can be used in some areas, as can the post bus (remember that many remote areas have only one delivery or collection per day). To supplement these services from July to September (inclusive) the Harrier Bus is routed to call at the tourist parts other buses do not reach. The majority of walks in the guide can be reached by a local bus service of one type or another, though not always at times to suit the walker, nor can the return trip

be guaranteed. Bus timetables are available from the Scottish Borders Council, bus stations, the Scottish Borders Tourist Board and its tourist information centres, and contacts for bookings, etc., can be found in Appendix 3, Useful Information.

ACCOMMODATION

The walks are arranged in geographical groups with one base covering several walks, thus reducing the need to be continually hunting for overnight accommodation. A wide and varied selection of accommodation is available in the Borders to suit all tastes and pockets. To assist the walker in finding the most convenient place to stay, all walks descriptions list the nearest village or farmhouse providing accommodation.

Accommodation details and booking arrangements can be obtained from tourist information centres and youth hostels, details of which are given in Appendix 3, Useful Information.

USING THE GUIDE

Aims

The overall aim is to produce a guide that is both comprehensive and as easy to understand as it is to carry, that is both graphically explicit and verbally inspiring, thus enabling the walker to traverse the Borderland with confidence, enthusiasm and enjoyment.

The 46 walks in the guide have all been walked several times, and a few special favourites many times. The journeys, a fraction of the walks available in the Borders, have been planned to suit all tastes, whether they are those of the committed mountain walker or the leisurely valley stroller.

Layout

The area is divided into four – Chapters 1 to 4 – each one self contained and geographically different from its fellows. Chapters 1 and 4 cover the mountainous and hilly sections and obviously contain a high proportion of hill walks, while the walks in Chapters 2 and 3 are of a more gentle nature.

Chapter 1 covers 16 walks in the Cheviot range of hills, lonely and isolated and unchanged over centuries. Chapter 2 describes 11 walks in the romantic valleys of the Tweed and its largest tributary, the Teviot, while Chapter 3 follows in the footsteps of the literary giants of the Borders' past, with nine walks in the Ettrick Forest. Chapter 4 comprises 10 walks in the massifs of the Moffat and the Manor Hills.

In Chapter 5 there are five long-distance walks that pass through, or start or finish within, the region. These are the final and the toughest 29 miles of the Pennine Way; the final section of the Alternative Pennine Way; the eastern section of the Southern Upland Way; the first half of St Cuthbert's Way from Melrose through the Cheviot Range; and the Borders Abbeys Way linking the ecclesiastical Border towns

of Kelso–Jedburgh–Hawick–Selkirk–Melrose–Kelso. Also included in this chapter are details of seven town trails – walks and strolls of pictorial and historical interest through and round the principal towns of the Borders.

To quickly and easily identify a special interest with a specific walk, refer to the Special Interests Table that follows this section.

At the end of the book are four appendixes. Appendix 1 is a glossary of local dialect words and names relating to the area, together with local pronunciations. Appendix 2 is a bibliography, Appendix 3 (Useful Information) lists addresses for accommodation, transport, various relevant organisations and weather forecasts, and Appendix 4 has a summary of the walks.

Structure of Chapters 1 to 4

Each chapter introduces the area with a portrait of the landscape, followed by a thumbnail description of each of the numbered walks. The individual walks descriptions begin with an information box summarising the hard facts under the headings Distance, Height Gain, Start/Finish, Grade, Walking Time, Maps, Accommodation, Parking. This is followed by a short paragraph summarising that walk, and then a description of the route itself with strategically placed boxes describing items of interest along the way. (These boxes describe places or things encountered en route, and are completely distinct from the route description, so that they can easily be skipped over and returned to at your leisure.)

The route descriptions have easy-to-read maps showing the suggested way, accompanied by a blow-by-blow account of the way itself (with six-figure map references and compass bearings if necessary). Instructions to turn left or right are usually accompanied by a further instruction, e.g. east or west.

The walks are timed using the established formula of W W Naismith. For each 3 miles (4.8km) of linear distance allow 1 hour, and should an ascent be made in that distance add 30 minutes to the walking time for each 1000 feet (305m) of ascent. The resultant times calculated using the Naismith formula have been tempered by my own timings, depending on the type of terrain to be traversed, the weather conditions expected, and the frequency and length of stops. It is not the intention of this guide to map out an assault course.

All walks are graded with a degree of difficulty classification from 1 to 4.

1   Good path, moderate ascent, no navigational problems.
2   Distinct path, steeper ascents, longer walk.
3   Paths rough in places, ascent 2000ft (610m), exposed in places.
4   Few paths, ascent 2400ft (732m) plus, exposed, compass needed.

Trowupburn farm and valley (Walk 6)

SPECIAL INTERESTS TABLE

Interest	Chapter	Walk
Antiquity	1	1, 3, 6, 10, 11, 12, 15
	2	17, 18, 20, 21
	3	28
	4	40
Drove Roads	1	9, 10, 11, 12, 14, 15, 16
	2	23, 26
	3	28, 29, 32
	4	45
Flora and Fauna	1	1, 2, 3, 7, 9, 15
	2	17, 18, 20, 21
	3	30, 33, 34
	4	37, 38, 39, 40, 41, 46
Geology	1	1, 3, 7, 9
	2	17, 20, 21, 22
	3	33
	4	37, 39, 41, 43, 46
Historical	1	1, 2, 5, 7, 10, 14,15
	2	17, 18, 19, 20, 21, 22, 23, 24, 25, 26
	3	28, 29, 30, 32
	4	41, 42, 43, 45, 46
Literary	2	20, 22
	3	29, 30, 31
	4	10
Lochs, Rivers	1	2, 3, 7
Waterfalls	1	2, 3
	2	17, 18, 20, 22, 23, 26, 27
	3	31
	4	37, 38, 39, 40, 42, 46

Old Industry	1	11, 12, 15, 16
	2	21
Photography	1	1, 3, 7, 9, 11
	2	17, 18, 19, 20, 21, 22, 23, 24, 25, 26, 27
	3	28, 29, 30, 31, 33, 34
	4	37, 38, 39, 40, 41, 42, 45, 46
Religious	2	17, 18, 20, 21
	3	30, 31
	4	42, 45
Scenic Excellence	1	1, 2, 3, 5, 7, 8, 9, 10, 11
	2	17, 18, 19, 20, 21, 22, 25
	3	28, 30, 33, 34, 35, 36
	4	37, 38, 39, 40, 41, 42, 43, 44, 46
Scrambling	1	7, 9
	4	39, 40
Walks – challenging	1	2, 3, 7, 9
	3	33, 34
	4	38, 39, 40, 41, 45
Walks – gentle	2	17, 18, 19, 24
	4	37

CLOTHING AND EQUIPMENT

Five simple words ease the vexed question of what to wear and what to take on a walk: *conditions determine clothing and equipment*. Whether that walk is a leisurely stroll on a balmy summer evening, or a mountain hike on a particularly tempestuous day in February, the answer is always the same. Conditions underfoot and overhead will determine the clothing and footwear needed, and what extra equipment, if any, to take in the sack.

Conditions Underfoot
What to Expect on the Border Hills and the Southern Uplands

The Cheviot Hills, Tweeddale, Ettrick Forest and the Tweedsmuir Hills, at levels below 1500ft (457m), are

23

traversed either by farm tracks or grass-covered paths and invariably provide good dry walking. Above 1500ft (457m) conditions vary a great deal, from narrow dry traces over short and springy grass (as found on Hedgehope and Broad Law), to trenches of gluti-nous peat (the summit plateau of Cheviot). Areas of wet peat do give the observant walker warning signals. Should a summit or ridge exhibit 'legs' of heather running down from the top (similar to a rich brandy sauce flowing over a Christmas pudding), beware, there are peat hags and wet conditions on the apex. Avoid patches of bright-green moss such as sphagnum or featherbed, as they invariably grow over wet-holes. Cotton grass and rushes also signal water underfoot and should be given a wide berth if possible. Bilberry, bents and molinia grass on the other hand signal dry paths, so choose your footwear accordingly.

Lightweight boots or well-soled walking shoes for the lower levels, middleweight leather boots for the higher levels, and leather, rigid-soled boots for scrambling and rock traverses are recommended. Footwear chosen wisely will shorten the journey – take the wrong option and the walk could be a disaster. The question of how many socks to wear is a matter of personal choice, the guideline – be comfortable.

Conditions Overhead
What to expect on the Border Hills and the Southern Uplands

The area, being situated in the eastern half of the country, is not prone to the excess precipitation experienced around Fort William or in the English Lakes. Nor does it suffer from severe cold due to high altitude, as the hills rarely exceed 2500ft (762m), although occasionally, when the air stream is from the northeast, the winds are known locally as 'thin'. Hours of sunshine are also above the national average, but because of the latitude temperatures never become unbear-able. You need clothes to keep you warm and dry in winter, and in summer choose loose-fitting garments made of natural fibres that breathe freely. Also take a hat to protect against the sun's rays, and carry a large, filled waterbottle.

Two physical factors are of prime importance to the hill walker: temper-ature and moisture. If both are in balance and agreeable to the pedes-trian then the walk will be a pleasure. Should that not be so, and the hiker is ill prepared and ill equipped, he or she is unwisely exposing him or herself to the twin risks of hypothermia and dehydration/heat exhaustion. Hypothermia can strike if the tempera-ture of the body core drops below 37°C in continuous cold and wet conditions. Dehydration or heat exhaustion can be induced by exposing the body, and in particular the head, to excess heat, coupled with an inadequate liquid intake.

Wind is a major factor in deciding what to wear and can have a marked effect in both winter and summer on the Border hills. In winter there is always the threat of a chilling northeaster, so the wind chill factor must always be considered. An increase of 10mph in wind speed can reduce the temperature from 18°C to 7°C, or in colder conditions from 10°C to -13°C. Also bear in mind the lapse rate. The higher the climb, the lower the temperature – for every 1000ft (305m) ascended there is a reduction of approximately 3°C.

Experienced and committed walkers are sure to carry their favourite talismans to protect them from the evil eye of the elements. For those not yet into the mystique of what's in the walker's sack (which should be lined with a binliner), let me list the essentials that are needed for high- and low-level walks in the Borders.

High Level

A windproof and waterproof anorak or cagoule, waterproof overtrousers or gaiters, a woolly hat (cotton in the summer), woollen gloves or mitts, and a survival bag. High-energy food (the average high-level walk in this guide will burn up 1500 calories above the normal metabolic rate), with a hot drink in winter and large filled water-bottle in summer. Emergency rations such as dried fruit, chocolate, glucose tablets, Kendal mint cake, or Christmas cake (in season) should be included for all high and long walks.

Low Level

Walking in summer at the lower levels, particularly in sheltered valleys, can induce heat exhaustion or dehydration if the walker is unprotected and exposed for long periods. A lightweight cotton hat

MAPS

The following maps cover the routes in this guide.

OS 1:25 000 Explorer: OL16 – The Cheviot Hills; 338 – Galashiels, Selkirk & Melrose

OS 1:50 000 Landranger, sheet nos.: 67 – Duns, Dunbar & Eyemouth; 72 – Upper Clyde Valley; 73 – Peebles, Galashiels & Selkirk; 74 – Kelso & Coldstream; 78 – Nithsdale & Annandale; 79 – Hawick & Eskdale; 80 – Cheviot Hills & Kielder Water; 81 – Alnwick & Morpeth

OS 1: 25 000 Pathfinder: 460 – Innerleithen; 474 – Jedburgh; 485 – Hawick & area; 486 – Chesters & Hownam

Harvey: 1:40,000 Superwalker – Cheviot Hills; 1:40,000 Walker's Route – St Cuthbert's Way; 1:40,000 Peebles Manor Hills & St Mary's Loch

Forestry Commission – Scotland: Craik Forest Walks & Cycle Trails

with a floppy brim and a full waterbottle will provide all the protection needed. The debate of shorts versus long trousers generates much heat, but suffice to say that some walkers prefer cool, brown, scratched legs, while others prefer protected legs, albeit hot and white.

This guidebook should also be carried at all times.

SAFETY

All the walks in the guide are designed primarily for the walker's pleasure, but

ACTION

1   Prevention is always better than cure, as advocated by two pedestrian giants of the past, Edward Whymper and A Wainwright, who both suggested 'a walk or even a life could be ruined by careless placement of the feet'.

2   Solitude in the hills is to be prized and is much sought after, but from the safety angle solo walks are to be avoided, the ideal number being five walkers of a like mind and similar ability. Such perfection is rarely possible, however, so to reduce the risks observe a few simple guidelines and use that underemployed asset, common sense.

3   Always inform someone of your route and estimated time of return (ETR). If that is not possible, leave your route plan with details, i.e. destination, number in the party, colour of garments and ETR, in a visible position in the car. One school of thought regards this is an invitation to the car thief, but cars can be replaced when lost, whereas human life cannot.

4   Should you have the misfortune to be *immobilised and require help*, and you have access to a mobile phone, dial 999 for the police. On receiving full details of the accident and your position, they will call out the local mountain rescue team and coordinate the rescue operation. Should a mobile phone not be at hand, use the *international rescue call* – either six long blasts on a whistle or flashes with a torch, and repeat at one minute intervals. The reply is three short blasts at minute intervals. Should you be without whistle or torch, *shout*, using the same code. When waiting for help, use the terrain to gain protection from the elements. Shelter from wind and rain or snow, or the sun in summer, and utilise spare clothing and the survival bag (feet pointing to the wind) to maintain body temperature.

5   If a mobile phone is used to call 999, have a six figure map reference ready. Find this as follows: 'eastings' first, i.e. the immediate vertical grid line to the left of your position, then the number of tenths from the

grid line to your position, then 'northings', repeating the procedure using the horizontal grid line below the position (also as instructed on the legend of the OS map). When the mountain rescue team is requested, the victim *must stay put* until help arrives.

6 Should an accident occur when with a companion, write your position, plus all the details in 5, above, on paper, including name, injury and time sustained, general health, age and type of clothing, and dispatch an able-bodied party to the nearest telephone (e.g. farmhouse, or phone box as shown on the OS map).

Two mountain rescue teams cover the Borders: the Cheviot Mountain Rescue (based at Kelso and Yetholm), and the Tweed Valley Mountain Rescue (based at Selkirk). The principal Borders hospital is the Borders General, Huntlyburn, Melrose.

safety in the great outdoors is something we must still be aware of. A careless step into a rabbit scrape or on a loose stone could break a bone or tear a tendon, causing a major problem for the solitary walker. As many of the walks may be completed in total solitude, it is prudent to be familiar with emergency procedures and the equipment needed to minimise discomfort and aid rescue in the unlikely event of an accident occurring.

Equipment

1 First-aid kit, including sterile dressings, lint or zinc tape, antiseptic cream, crepe or elasticated bandages (tubigrip), scissors or a knife, and medication (including salt tablets, painkillers, etc.). The medication must only be for personal use – it is unwise and risky to administer medication to another unless medically qualified.

2 A basic knowledge of first aid should be carried in the head or in the sack.

3 A knife, torch (with a spare bulb and batteries), whistle, spare laces (double up as bindings), emergency food and water, survival bag, compass and map, paper and pen or pencil.

Take Care

Remember that the **grouse shooting season** runs from 12 August to 10 December, so avoid relevant areas.

Adders and **bulls** are also best avoided. The adder (60cm in length, brown with a dark zigzag on the back) is more concerned about avoiding contact with humans. Bulls are somewhat larger and have no such inhibitions.

North Dean to White Law summit in its Autumn glory (Walk 4)

CHAPTER 1

THE CHEVIOT HILLS

Endless ridges straddle the eastern and central border of England and Scotland, in a tangle of green and rounded summits split asunder by steep-sided sinuous valleys. Windswept grasses continually ripple on these upland fells, with the plaintive cries of whaup (curlew) and peewit, together with the bleating of sheep, heard more often than the human voice. The hills and mountains of the Cheviots cannot be likened to the exalted giants of the Western Highlands or the winsome English Lakes, yet these lonely and now peaceful hills have their own appealing romanticism.

The principal summits are clustered in the east, as supplicants to the massif of the Cheviot 2676ft (815m), after whom the range is named, and with the exception of Windy Gyle, Auchope Cairn and the Schil (which straddle the Border Ridge), they all rise in England. Of these, Hedgehope, Cairn Hill, Comb Fell, Bloody Bush Edge and Cushat Law all top 2000ft (610m). At the western extremity of the range the principal hills of Peel Fell and Carter Fell also have a foot on each side of the border. The very nature of the Cheviot terrain makes it possible for the hill walker to traverse the tops without any great loss of height or energy, while still maintaining a steady pace.

Pathways, trails and directional markers are sparse, and in places nonexistent (with the exception of the Pennine Way, the Southern Upland Way and St Cuthbert's Way, some Roman roads and the occasional drove road). Although the majority of walks are over paths and trails that ease the walker's progress, there are isolated locations where 'traffic' is heavy. Before the installation of the slabbed pathway, the summit plateau of Cheviot and sections of the Pennine Way could degenerate into a mire in adverse weather. Exposed rock in the Cheviots is a shy bird, rarely revealing itself in any quantity, making these hills an unhappy hunting ground for the rock climber, and an area with only an occasional pitch for the scrambler (Walks 7 and possibly 9 include scrambles).

The majority of 'walk-ins' are from the Scottish side, where the approaches are not hindered by the serried ranks of conifers in the forests of Kielder and Redesdale. Nor are the Scottish foothills restricted by the activities of a very vigorous MOD, as at Redesdale, where high-powered missiles 'crump' daily into the English side of the range.

Few if any roads, apart from the A68 at Carter Bar, cross the main ridge north to south, nor is there a continuous road that encircles the Cheviots, which results in miles of unpopulated uplands. Apart from occasional isolated hill farms scattered over the area, the only habitation is in a few villages and hamlets on the extremities of the range. Small towns such as Wooler, Kelso and Jedburgh are situated in the surrounding valleys, some 10 miles from the higher ground. This scattered and sparse population, while enhancing the isolation factor so beloved by walkers, can create a problem for the adventurer who lacks transport. Local bus services, or the post bus, can and do assist in such cases.

THE WALKS

In this chapter are 16 walks. Walk 1 starts at Old Yeavering, the extreme eastern limit of the Cheviot range, and ascends the eastern Cheviots, a fine introduction to the outliers of Muckle Cheviot. Walk 2 surmounts Cheviot, the highest mountain in the range, by a well-trodden path that offers to the energetic fine views of the Border hills and the Tweed Valley. Walk 3 climbs Hedgehope Hill, the second highest mountain in Northumbria, includes the finest waterfall in the Cheviots, and traverses moorland and forest with only the birds and animals for company.

A change of start brings Walk 4 to Scotland, where the Halterburn Valley winds through the gentle northern foothills, by the high road and the low road. The Halterburn Horseshoe, a valley and ridge walk of high quality, describes Walk 5 perfectly. Walk 6 follows a reivers' way into England, passing two lonely Border hill farms, several ancient settlements, a burial cairn or two, and several thousand sheep.

Remaining in Scotland, the next five walks have their starts and finishes at the historic farm of Cocklawfoot, deep in the Bowmont Valley. Walk 7 is rich in scenery, wildlife, history, legend and personal reward, though a deal of effort is needed to scramble up the Hen Hole and negotiate the corrie to Auchope Cairn. Walk 8 has a long but pleasant walk-in to the Schil, at 1985ft (605m) the most spectacular non-mountain in the Cheviots. Walk 9 will demand effort and experience from the walker, and involves a little wild walking and perhaps the use of map and compass. The ability to identify Second World War aircraft could also add interest. Walk 10 by comparison is an easier, more sedate mountain route along the historic scenic path to the summit of Windy Gyle – a fine walk on a summer's evening, a gem on a crisp winter's day with a few inches of fresh snow underfoot.

Further west along the Border Ridge, from the tiny hamlet of Hownam, Walk 11 follows the trails of our Iron Age ancestors, the legions of Rome and the cattle drovers. The ascent of Hownam Law brings the walker to the very edge of the northern Cheviots. Secluded Greenhill is the start of Walk 12, a fine ridge and valley walk into the heart of a complex of Iron Age settlements – good paths and tracks add bounce to the step. The black waters of Heatherhope Reservoir start Walk 13, bound for the Street, the Border Ridge and Callaw Cairn, and up to

Scald Hill above Langleeford Hope. (Walk 2)

mysterious Church Hope Hill. Tow Ford on the upper reaches of Kale Water is the start and finish of Walk 14, which ventures into England via Dere Street to visit a Roman encampment at Chew Green. Walk 15 marches north to the edge of the high ground, to return along another section of Dere Street, past the ancient stone circle of Five Stanes and finish at the Roman marching camp of Pennymuir. The Border crossing of Carter Bar starts Walk 16 over Carter Fell to visit old lime kilns and drift mines.

Easter, Newton and Wester Tors

WALK 1 – Early Christianity and Iron Age Forts

Old Yeavering, St Cuthbert's Way, Newton Tors, Yeavering Bell, Yeavering Burn, Yeavering Bell, Old Yeavering

Distance	7 miles (11.3km)
Height Gain	1962ft (598m)
Start/Finish	Old Yeavering, GR 924304
Grade	3
Walking Time	4–4½ hours
Maps	OS 1:25 000 Explorer OL16, The Cheviot Hills
	OS 1:50 000 Landranger sheet 74, Kelso & Coldstream
	Harvey 1:40 000 SuperWalker, Cheviot Hills
Accommodation	Wooler – hotels, bed-and-breakfasts, youth hostel, caravan park
Parking	On the verges at the Old Yeavering T-junction, GR 924304

A fine introduction to the extreme east end of the Cheviot Range via a selection of ascending or descending, rarely on the level, waymarked public footpaths, permitted paths and St Cuthbert's Way. Underfoot ranges from stony roads, dirt-and-grass tracks to narrow peat paths through heather, bracken and hilltop rock.

Compass and map are essential in low visibility or adverse weather conditions.

The Route A country road, the B6351, runs west from the Wooler to Milfield A697 at Akeld for 2¼ miles (3.6km) to **Old Yeavering** junction on the left, bearing a finger post reading 'Yeavering Bell 1 mile, Hethpool 2½ miles'. Limited grass verge parking by the finger post marks the start of the walk.

Walk up the stony cart track, with the domed summit of Yeavering Bell ahead and above, to pass the cottages and a second finger post, then veer right by the farm buildings. At the end of these a stile on the left directs to 'The Hillfort Trail – Yeavering Bell ¾ mile', which will be

Two of the Cheviots' finest grandstands, Wester Tor and Yeavering Bell, are visited en route. These typical Cheviot hills are rich in character, history and far-seeing views.

Old Yeavering 'Ad-Gebrin' or 'Gefrin' it was called in the sixth century, this timber palace built for the kings of Northumbria and enlarged for King Edwin, 616–33. Here also the missionary Paulinus came to Edwin's marriage, and for 35 days afterwards converted Northumbrians to Christianity.

our return route. However, continuing ahead over the burn we take the steadily ascending scenic cart track southwest over several cattle-grids, alongside the tree-lined and bracken-clad gouged course of Yeavering Burn. After about 1 mile (1.6km), as the way levels out and we pass several venerable oaks, a clutch of earth-fast boulders and a conifer stand, we meet the latest of the Borders national trails, **St Cuthbert's Way**, before Torleehouse. (This route enables the walker to tackle the very steep northern flank of Yeavering Bell as a return *descent* and not an initial lung-bursting ascent.)

St Cuthbert's Way A truly Border country middle-distance walk covering 62½ miles (100km) from Melrose in the heart of the Scottish Borders to Lindisfarne – Holy Island – anchored to Northumberland's northern coastline. We meet this popular walk several times within the eastern Cheviots.

At the waymark post on our left we turn left onto a grass, stone-embedded cart track, passing what would appear to be the mounds, ditches, and piles of rocks and stones of a centuries-old farming homestead, as we climb south then east and finally south-southeast to cross the wall by a ladder-stile on the skyline ahead. From this point St Cuthbert's Way demands a few deep breaths as the contours close in and grass gives way to heather and bracken, where feral goats can be seen on the wide and wild expanse of far-seeing ridge and hill. 547yds (500m) from the last ladder-stile look out for an unusual four-way directional marker standing 12 inches above the ground: 'South-south-east Commonburn House, west Easter Tor ¾ mile – Wester Tor 2 miles, east Yeavering Bell ¾ mile'.

At this point, should you consider that the journey to Wester Tor and the return makes the walk too long and/or strenuous, turn left, facing the inviting slopes with visible paths to the intriguing summit of Yeavering Bell. If you wish to explore further, however, and save the best to last, turn right and cross the stone dyke by ladder-stile. Now ascend 492ft (150m) via the permissive path through heather and white grass west and then south and southwest over the southern flanks of Easter Tor with its outcrop of summit rock. This tor is the least interesting of the three, so continue southwest and south-southwest over the more gentle, sloping southern shoulders of **Newton Tors** for 1¼ miles (2km) on a pathway that provides sightings of the formidable bulk of the Cheviot. As the path swings west and then north to the col dividing the flat dome of Wester Tor 1762ft (537m) and cairn-capped Hare Law 1700ft (518m), turn left to join the stone dyke leading west to the summit of Hare Law – a fine grandstand from which to gaze upon the north face of Cheviot and admire the elegant sweep of the College Valley far below. Return via the stone dyke to the jeep track and walk north to the summit of Wester Tor and the cairned rocks on its northeastern shoulder, another superb eyrie from which to appreciate the surrounding hills and the Northumberland coastline.

Newton Tors This attractive hill with its triple peaks – Easter Tor, Wester Tor and Hare Law – is a challenge and a pleasure to behold. A northern outlier of Cheviot and flanking the eastern side of the College Valley, it was formed some 400 million years ago from the larval outpourings of the Cheviot volcanoes. Wester Tor and Hare Law are crowned with distinct and handsome cairns.

The summit of Yeavering Bell

Descend from the outcrop, returning south and northeast on the outward path below Easter Tor, focusing on the twin domes of **Yeavering Bell**, to the four-way directional marker on St Cuthbert's Way. Cross the path east and drop southeast with the waymarked Hill Fort Trail permissive path into the steep-sided bracken-filled gully of Yeavering Burn, then zigzag out to begin an exciting but never strenuous ascent northeast to the col between the twin summit domes. This hill has a presence that befits its status as Northumbria's largest Iron Age hill fort. Stones and rocks are in profusion, the remains of surrounding fortifications and horseshoe dwellings scattered everywhere. Keep to the main path northeast to the col, for it allows clear passage through the defensive wall. The reward is a complete circle of outstanding views and a summit of great interest.

Leave the saddle from between the summit domes through a partial gap in the surrounding wall. Follow the waymarked Hill Fort Trail to descend steeply on a rocky peat path, wet in places at lower levels, that zigzags overall north, descending sharply to the clearly visible buildings of Old Yeavering 853ft (260m) below. This descent requires respect and care in adverse conditions.

Yeavering Bell A shapely conical hill 1184ft (361m) with twin domes on which stood the largest Iron Age hill fort in Northumbria. Prominent elliptical earthworks and ditches, together with the foundations of horseshoe-shaped dwellings with entrances facing southeast, can still be seen.

WALK 2 – The Cheviot

Langleeford, Scald Hill, the Cheviot, Cairn Hill,
Harthope Burn, Harthope Linn, Langleeford

Distance	8½ miles (13.6km)
Height Gain	2028ft (618m)
Start/Finish	Car park east of Langleeford
Grade	4
Walking Time	5½–6 hours (7 hours in adverse conditions)
Maps	OS 1:25 000 Explorer OL16, The Cheviot Hills
	OS 1:50 000 Landranger sheets 74, Kelso & Coldstream, and 80, Cheviot Hills and Kielder Water
	Harvey 1:40 000 SuperWalker, Cheviot Hills
Accommodation	A range, from hotels to youth hostel, in Wooler
Parking	On the grass verges before Langleeford, GR 953225, before the small bridge

No walking guide covering the Borders would be complete without at least one pilgrimage to the summit of Muckle Cheviot, the highest mountain in the Cheviot Hills. This is a circular walk requiring map-reading and compass skills in poor visibility. Good boots and mountain clothing are essential and walking poles do help. Underfoot expect farm lanes, dirt tracks, narrow, rock-strewn and bracken-shrouded peaty paths, paths through naked peat, stone slabs on Cheviot's summit, and grassy paths on the final descent.

Whatever the weather this walk will be a challenge, perhaps best described as beauty and the beast.

The Route At the south end of the main street in Wooler turn right, signposted 'Middleton Hall and Harthope Valley', to travel 5 miles (8km) southwest to Langleeford. Start on the road walking southwest for 200yds (183m) towards **Langleeford** to reach a signpost reading 'Scald Hill 1¾ miles, The Cheviot 3½ miles'. A good path to the right rises rapidly through bracken and acres of bonny blooming heather to the flat and grassy summit of Scald Hill, 1797ft (548m). Leave Scald Hill via a stile to join a conspicuous permissive path alongside the fence running south-south-

Langleeford Surrounded by oak, beech, rowan, hazel, ash and silver birch, Langleeford was first referred to in 1552 in connection with the need for night watches because of marauding reivers from Scotland. In 1791 that most romantic of Borders walkers, Sir Walter Scott, took a holiday at the farmhouse, enjoying the fishing and the walking, and was particularly taken with the pretty milkmaid who brought him goats' milk every morning.

west, going over a wet and peaty saddle, later to rise steeply as a blackened and badly eroded wound in the east side of Cheviot. The final assault of 500ft (152m) is via a choice of distinct pathways – grass, peat and scattered stone – left of the southwest ascending fence. Once the plateau rim is reached the path weaves through a scatter of rocks to the prominent ladder-stile leading to Cheviot's flat and blackened summit. At this point the slabbed pathway over Cheviot's summit to Cairn Hill is met, and on a fine and clear day you will surely consider this to be the finest of walks. In low cloud with squally rain pulsing in on a fractious wind, you may question your sanity. To the uninitiated the summit of the **Cheviot** 2676ft (815m) may be something of a shock – five square miles of featureless and seemingly endless peat hags.

The Cheviot Locally called Cheviot, the Cheviot is the highest mountain in the Cheviot range. The area was fashioned some 400 million years ago by intense volcanic activity, followed by lava flows, a process that was to continue for many millennia. More recently, in 1728, Daniel Defoe ascended Cheviot on horseback and was 'much afraid' he would find the summit a 'knife edged ridge'. His guides, local boys from Wooler, were greatly amused at this, assuring him 'an army could stand upon the top'. The first Ordnance Survey was carried out in the early 1800s by the military, and a trig point placed on Cheviot's summit. No less than two trig points have since disappeared into the peat. The present monolith is mounted on a concrete plinth supported on an 11 foot pile, but many experienced 'Cheviotiers' are under no illusion but that the present trig point is in the process of joining its predecessors.

The route to the Cheviot's trig point follows the prepared path of stone slabs winding west through the peaty wilderness, with the guiding fence always within sight on the walker's left. The summit should be reached within 3 hours of the start, and from its peaty surrounds Cairn Hill 2545ft (776m), a small mound with an accompanying cairn, is clearly visible to the southwest. The walk to Cairn Hill is, for most of the way, along the stone slabs to the right of the fence. Avoid at all costs the left, i.e. south, side of the fence, where two menacing ponds await the unwary. Beyond the slabs to the stone pile of Scotsman's Cairn by Cairn Hill's summit requires care. Leave Cairn Hill and the guiding fence by the stile close to the cairn, descending on a waymarked peat pathway south-southeast for some 500yds (457m), initially alongside a fence on the right. Continue across a wilderness of heather, mat grass and gargantuan peat hags before swinging half-left towards the valley floor, which is met by the bare cleft of red earth that cradles the infant **Harthope Burn**.

Follow the burn east, with the running water on the right. As the burn gathers strength it is crossed several times as the path becomes more obvious, and eventually the walk in the narrow valley between Cheviot and Hedgehope Hill assumes a mantle of tranquillity. Small and stunted silver birch, and later alder and rowan, cling precariously to

Harthope Burn and Harthope Linn The burn rises on the southwest flank of Cheviot and tumbles down the Harthope Valley to Langleeford and beyond. A geological fault caused the steep-sided valley to be formed, and later glaciers from Cheviot scoured and shaped it into the picturesque valley we know today. Several small waterfalls of peat-laden amber water tumble merrily down the upper reaches, the largest and most spectacular being Harthope Linn, with a cascade of 25ft (7.5m), 2 miles (3.2km) upstream from Langleeford.

the steep banks, home to ring ouzels, dippers and many primroses, as the noise of gushing water assails the ears. Beyond a crumbling sheep stell (shelter) **Harthope Linn** (waterfall), with its main cascade plunging through the narrowest of gorges, is compelling, but take care when hunting for that extra special close-up.

From the linn it is but a short 2 miles (3.2km) to Langleeford. The route goes via the renovated farmhouse of Langleeford Hope, along a pleasant farm road and over more stiles, then to the tree-lined, white-walled buildings of Langleeford, the end of the adventure.

Harthope Linn

WALK 3 – Mountains, Crags and a Waterfall

Langleeford, Long Crags, Hedgehope Hill, Langlee Crags, Threestoneburn House, Linhope, Linhope Spout

Distance	10 miles (16.1km)
Height Gain	1898ft (578.5m)
Start/Finish	Upper Harthope Valley, GR 953225 (Linhope Spout)
Grade	3, or 4 in adverse conditions
Walking Time	6 hours
Maps	OS 1:25 000 Explorer OL16, The Cheviot Hills
	OS 1:50 000 Landranger sheets 74, Kelso & Coldstream, 80, Cheviot Hills & Kielder Water and 81, Alnwick & Morpeth
	Harvey 1:40 000 SuperWalker, Cheviot Hills
Accommodation	Wooler, Powburn and Glanton provide food and accommodation
Parking	Off-road parking in Upper Harthope, GR 953225, ½ mile (0.8km) before Langleeford

A challenging, rewarding linear walk of two varied halves. The first an ascending, steep in places, descending adventure on Hedgehope Hill, whose summit provides a splendid far-seeing grandstand and where the surrounding crags are of geological interest, while Linhope Spout supplies a spectacular, at times dramatic, journey's end. Underfoot, waymarked public bridleways, footpaths and permissive paths. On the steep sections of Hedgehope dirt paths are thin and in places slippery. The second half traverses crag-scattered moorland, visits an ancient stone circle, strides through conifer forest rides and pathways leading to the wide Breamish Valley, before the final picturesque mile to Linhope Spout.

The Route Five miles (8km) southwest of Wooler, deep in the Harthope Valley, stands the farm of Langleeford. Start the walk at the road bridge, where a signpost directs

Permissive paths along the route may, unlike designated rights of way, be changed from time to time. In the event of such changes within Northumberland National Park, up-to-date details of alterations will be displayed, together with strategically sited waymarks.

the walker 2½ miles (4km) southwest to the conical summit of **Hedgehope Hill** 2343ft (714m). Harthope Burn is crossed by footbridge, from where a waymarked path leads south over three stiles to the open fell and the distinct outcrops of Housey Crags and Long Crags. Leave Long Crags at its south-west corner via a stile and follow the

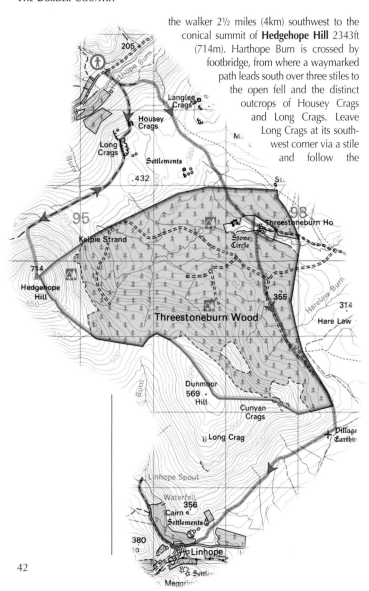

Hedgehope Hill Meaning 'head of the valleys', this mountain is the second-highest peak in the Cheviot range. Because of its distinctive conical shape and its position on the southeast corner of the range, Hedgehope Hill is one of the most distinctive mountains in the Cheviots. From the summit on a crystal clear day, fine views unfold – of the Northumbrian coastal plain, the island of Lindisfarne, the northern Pennines to Cross Fell and perhaps the peaks of the northern Lakes.

distinct path for 1 mile (1.6km) southwest across the wetlands of Kelpie Strand.

A change in the vegetation underfoot clearly signals the imminent ascent of Hedgehope. Rushes, bright-green moss and cotton grass give way to bents, bilberries and mat grass as the faint waymarked path begins to climb steeply, initially south-southwest, then south for a relentless plod to the domed, cairn-and-trig-point-capped summit of Hedgehope Hill. ▶

Three fences meet on Hedgehope's summit, leading the eye over endless heather and tussock with little company save moorland birds and hardy sheep. To the north over the Harthope Valley we see close-ups of Cheviot's riven southern quarter, and on clear days the sandy coastline of Northumberland is visible. Our descent is via our outward route, providing insights into the Harthope Valley, Hawsen Crags and rounded Cold Law beyond. Inspect and enjoy **Long Crags** and **Housey Crags** before descending north beyond the crags to join the bridleway (initially a recent dirt-and-stone track) running southwest to Threestoneburn Wood.

Below and between Housey Crags to the west and the spectacular rock of **Langlee Crags** to the east the pathway splits. Our bridleway forks right, south-southwest, for 1½ stimulating miles (2.4km) to the regimented conifers of Threestoneburn Wood beyond **Tathey Crags**. Before the forest the grass-tracked way passes a metal shed and upright wooden poles, then enters the conifers via a narrow ride. A 15 minute walk reaches a stile and

At the time of writing two recent OS Explorer maps, OL16, The Cheviot Hills, and Harvey SuperWalker, Cheviot Hills, show the permissive path of our ascent forking right at GR 946206, initially on a south-westerly bearing of 240°. Do not take this uncertain *right* fork, as the way is unmarked, not visible and unstable underfoot.

Long Crags, Housey Crags, Langlee Crags, Tathey Crags and Cunyan Crags
Four-hundred million years ago a mass of molten rock welled up beneath the volcanoes of Cheviot and Hedgehope, eventually cooling to form granite. When this molten mass came into contact with volcanic larva, the intense heat changed it chemically into a somewhat different and harder rock. Today we have a circle of this changed rock, 'the metamorphic aureole', around Cheviot and Hedgehope. Natural weathering has worn away the softer rock, leaving the harder rocks exposed as visible outcrops. Later the ice age fashioned the crags by shearing and streamlining the rocks with the directional movement of the ice, in this case north and south.

Long Crags

gate providing access to a clearing surrounding **Threestoneburn Stone Circle**, an enclosure and derelict stone circle north of the burn, some 400yds (366m) west of Threestoneburn House.

Threestoneburn Stone Circle The stones in this circle were arranged elliptically, with 13 shafts, the tallest standing over 5ft (1.5m). Sadly, today only five standing stones remain. It has long puzzled me as to why the burn should be named so. With 13 stones originally in the circle, it would have been logical to name it 'Thirteenstoneburn'. Could it be that 'three' has through time become a mispronunciation of 'thirteen'?

The waymarked route avoids the house by crossing the footbridge to re-enter the forest and continue south through silent shade, via marked pathways and forest tracks, for 1½ miles (2.4km), finally breaking cover at the southern-most tip below the rocks of **Cunyan Crags** above the isolated Breamish Valley. Continue south over open fell to join a westbound bridleway fringing the grassed-over remains of a medieval village (marked on the OS Map).

Linhope Cottages

Swing right onto the distinct bridlepath, with a sheep-fold and tin hut ahead, ignoring all crisscrossed paths and tracks, for a wide and handsome Cheviot hike southwest. Once through the gated stone wall, swing half-left, i.e. south-southwest, between coniferous plantations onto the gated cart track, descending to tiny, picturesque Linhope below the prehistoric village of Greaves Ash.

Continue with the lane, crossing Linhope Burn Bridge, to rise with the waymarked track northwest around Linhope House, then by permissive path to **Linhope Spout**, the Cheviot's most spectacular waterfall.

Linhope Spout The most spectacular of all the Cheviot waterfalls, plunging 56ft (17m) into a deep rock pool 7ft (2m) across and 15ft (4.5m) deep. When Linhope Burn is in full spate the cascade is an awesome sight as it thunders into the pool below and hurries on between overhanging birches.

WALK 4 – A Gentle Introduction to Cheviot's Foothills

Halterburn Valley, Pennine Way, Border Fence, White Law, Old Halterburnhead, Halterburn Valley

Distance	5 miles (8km)
Height Gain	984ft (300m)
Start/Finish	Halterburn Valley, GR 840277, or Kirk Yetholm (add 2 miles)
Grade	2
Walking Time	2½ hours
Maps	OS 1:25 000 Explorer OL16, The Cheviot Hills
	OS 1:50 000 Landranger sheet 74, Kelso & Coldstream
	Harvey 1:40 000 SuperWalker, Cheviot Hills
Accommodation	Yetholm – hotel, bed-and-breakfasts, youth hostel, caravan park
Parking	Limited parking between road and Halter Burn, GR 840277

A gentle introduction to the foothills of the Cheviots, this circular walk includes sections of the waymarked Pennine Way (with fine views of the high Cheviots, including the Cheviot, en route), coupled with a picturesque return in the Halterburn Valley. Good paths and an easy ascent of 984ft (300m) make this 2½ hour journey a pleasure.

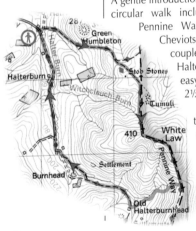

The Route At the northern end of the Halterburn Valley a cattle-grid signals the starting point (limited parking on the verges of the farm track on the left). From the start make for the stream (Halter Burn), easily forded in summer, or take the wooden bridge in winter. With a stone dyke on the left for 200

The Border fence The first written evidence of the actual position of the eastern border was in 1173, when reference was made to the Tweed as the border. In 1222 a joint boundary commission met to define the border, but the task proved too much, so only a small section was agreed upon. Further work between 1542 and 1604 achieved little. The border as we know it today seems to have been born between 1604 and 1648, after the Union of the Crowns in 1603. Today's border fence remains an extremely useful navigational aid, and many have good reason to be grateful for its presence on these bleak and lonely hills (see Walks 5 and 14).

yards, follow the track and then the pathway east contouring the lower southern slopes of coned Green Humbleton as far as the sheep pens and Pennine Way marker post. Ascend east-southeast with the grassy track, passing a finger post indicating the relative routes of the Pennine Way and St Cuthbert's Way, to the mound ahead and beyond that the **Border fence**. Before the gated border line, just over the mound turn right for 40 yards or so to inspect the **Stob Stones** and the extensive rippling hills beyond. Return to the gate, which marks the boundary between Scotland and England with a drystone dyke and wire-and-post fence, but do not pass through.

The Stob Stones To the west of these two prehistoric earth-fast boulders, in the hazy distance of the Tweed Valley, stand the three distinctive peaks of the Eildon Hills at Melrose, aligned precisely by the leading edge of the larger of the two Stob Stones.

Follow instead the directional Pennine Way finger post south, with wall and fence on the left, via a sharply descending and then ascending path, wet and boggy in places, leading to the col below the summit of **White Law** 1407ft (417m). This testing section of ½ mile (0.8km), parallel to the wall, rises to the visible T-junction of stone dykes and stile on the col between White Law and Whitelaw Nick. Once over the stile turn left,

White Law The name, one can only surmise, originates from the vegetation that covers the upper slopes. Much of the grass on White Law is mat grass (Nardus stricta), an unusual species that in June bears an unbranched spike and in late summer bleaches almost white, giving rise to the local description 'white lands', hence the name White Law (hill).

ascending for 150yds (137m) to the summit of White Law, the highest point of the walk and a fine vantage point.

A few yards beyond the apex of White Law the border fence (now a wire-and-post fence) turns right, i.e. south, and descends sharply to the saddle 300ft (91.5m) below. Here a small gate in the fence marks the point where the route leaves the **Pennine Way** by turning right, i.e. west, onto a descending grassy path, and then a track through the bracken-clad hillside of Steer Rig, to cross the shallow burn to the ruin of Old Halterburnhead in the valley below.

The Pennine Way Tom Stephenson, late of the Ramblers' Association, was the founding father of this long-distance walkway, 270 miles (434km) from Edale to Kirk Yetholm. It is immortalised in the writings of A Wainwright in his *Pennine Way Companion*, where he described the traverse of the Cheviot range from Byrness to Kirk Yetholm as, 'the longest and loneliest of all'.

Leave the sad ruins of Old Halterburnhead to the squabbling rooks and take the farm track north along the valley floor towards the working farm of Burnhead. Two hundred yards (183m) before the steading a Pennine Way finger post directs us right, by footbridge, wicket gate and wallside path, east of the farm, before rejoining the road in the **Halterburn Valley**. It is a pleasant stroll to the starting cattle-grid, allowing the walker time to pause and 'smell the roses'.

The Halterburn Valley This 2½ mile (4km) stretch of the valley is perhaps more familiar to Pennine Wayfarers than resident Borderers. Forlorn reminders of former days still remain in the crumbling and decaying ruins of Old Halterburnhead, inhabited by itinerant sheep and noisy rooks. The walk alongside the burn is a delight, where from spring to late summer plants in bloom please the eye and brighten the day, primroses in particular, and musk on the banks of the burn.

Old Halterburnhead

Kirk Yetholm This village, so close to the English border, was at one time the rallying point for the Scottish Border Gypsies, providing a convenient springboard from which to nip over into England in times of strife – a far cry from 1540, when Gypsy King John Faa signed a treaty with James V of Scotland in which he was described as, 'Our lovit Johnne Faa, Lord and Earl of little Egypt'. The last king, Charles Blyth Faa (whose coronation coach was drawn by six donkeys), died in 1802, and was succeeded by a Gypsy queen.

49

WALK 5 – Up and Down the Cheviot Hills

Halterburn Valley (cattle-grid), Pennine Way, Old Halterburnhead, the Curr, Black Hag, White Law, White Swire, Halter Burn Valley

Distance	8 miles (12.9km)
Height Gain	1821ft (555m)
Start/Finish	Halterburn Valley, GR 840277, approximately 1 mile south-southeast from Kirk Yetholm
Grade	2; 3 in winter conditions or poor visibility
Walking Time	4–4½ hours
Maps	OS 1:25 000 Explorer OL16, The Cheviot Hills
	OS 1:50 000 Landranger sheet 74, Kelso & Coldstream
	Harvey 1:40 000 SuperWalker, Cheviot Hills
Accommodation	Kirk Yetholm and Town Yetholm – hotel, bed-and-breakfasts, caravan park, and youth hostel in Kirk Yetholm
Parking	Below cattle-grid between road and Halter Burn

In addition to a rich mix of upland and hill flora and fauna, one of the principal highlights of this walk is the view that meets the eye with every turn as height is gained. Few walks can match the constantly changing horizons; none can surpass them.

A walk that typifies the Cheviot Hills, with frequent ascents and descents, following as it does both the 'high way' and the 'low way' alternatives of the Pennine Way. The pathways, a mix of dirt or peat, stone and occasionally grass, are mainly sound and firm in summer, though wet spongy sections are met in winter.

Choose a fine, clear day, it matters not what time of year, as all seasons have their highlights.

The Route Start from the off-road parking below the cattle-grid, heading south along the narrow road across the valley floor towards the few buildings of Halterburn. On our left the busy Halter Burn, although this is crossed several times as we progress into the valley, and above it the steep slopes of Green Humbleton, met at the end of our journey. Cross a cattle-grid and pass a stable and store before the steading of Burnhead. The Pennine Way leaves the farm lane left, as per the finger post, onto a narrow dirt-and-grass wallside path that bypasses the farm, and with stiles and a bridge rejoins the Pennine Way farm

Kirk Yetholm Together with its twin, Town Yetholm, Kirk Yetholm was home to the royal line of Faa Gypsies – several houses around the village bear names such as Gypsy Row and Gypsy Palace. Knowledgeable travellers of yesteryear gave Kirk Yetholm a wide birth, for the sight of a stranger aroused the cry, 'Oot aik sticks and bull pups.' Nor was there any love lost between the two Yetholms, and even today 'Yetholm cleeks' still adorn the walls in Town Yetholm, very useful when it came to repelling intruders from that other place.

track running southeast. From this point, as we meet the silent, sad stones of what was Old Halterburnhead, surrounded by the evidence of ancient settlements and homesteads, the solitude of this curving, narrowing valley kicks in.

Above on our left is the high ridge that carries our return pathway from Black Hag via Steer Rig to White Law, one of the best viewpoints in the eastern Cheviots. Heading south and rising more steeply towards the nondescript lump that is the **Curr** 1849ft (564m), we meet and pass through a drystone wall that runs down from Latchly Hill en route to ascending Steerrig Knowe. Although our path, flanked by bracken, heather and white grass, tends to zizag and contour around the hill's shoulders as it climbs by Birky Knowe, the direction is south to the col ahead, between the rounded summits of the Curr and **Black Hag** (not the most charismatic of summits). Once through the gate, however, it is a seat 'in the gods' from which to enjoy the **unique display of the Cheviot Hills**. Continue east then southeast with the slightly descending grass track to the triple finger post ahead, passing on the left the rocky outcrop of Corbie (crow) Craig below the well-named

The Curr Flat topped and sombre, it stands at the head of the Halterburn and Bowmont valleys, its position rather than its form being the lure. The northern prospect from the Curr is particularly pleasing as the wide and graceful sweep of the Tweed Valley meets the eye.

1801ft (549m) summit of Black Hag. It's a track that can be seen spearing south to the rock-crowned summit of that 'nearly mountain' the Schil 1985ft (605m); we go only as far as the triple Pennine Way finger post.

Black Hag Appropriately named, 'black' refers to the heather cover, while 'hag' applies to the bunkers of peat. From its summit attractive views can be seen to the south, freestanding Schil crowned by its rocky tor and circlet of outcrops, and beyond the dour north face of Cheviot and the Border Ridge extending westwards for 9 miles (14.5km) to Lamb Hill 1677ft (511m).

White Law north of Steer Rig

Views of the Cheviots and beyond West and below the Schil there is Sourhope Burn Valley, its floor and flanks peppered with the remains of ancient settlements, homesteads, cultivation terraces, forts and cairns. The burn runs southwest towards Cocklawfoot and the Border Ridge from the Cheviot, then west to beyond Windy Gyle, Beefstand Hill and Lamb Hill (Walks 7–10). These names reflect that this was and still is a prime site for cattle and sheep farming. (There is of course a famous breed of sheep known as Cheviot.)

One finger points to the Schil, 'Pennine Way', the second finger points the way we have just walked and says 'Low Level Alternative Route', and the third finger 'Pennine Way', which is our pathway (also the Scottish–English border line) on a bearing of 345° over the flattened summit of Black Hag. The fence ahead is crossed by ladder-stile and marks a gradually descending fenceside walk north along Steer Rig that provides not only sightings of White Law, our next ascent, but also east over the V that is Trowup Burn Valley to the Northumberland coastline, and ahead to the Tweed Valley and the Lammermuir Hills beyond. Surrounded by a carpet of wind-bent white grass our twin track drops to the col above Old Halterburnhead. This is a place to rest and enjoy before the short sharp 262ft (80m) ascent north to the grandstand summit of White Law, with fine views over the College Valley to Newton Tors and Yeavering Bell (Walk 1), in addition to the Tweed Valley and beyond.

From the summit of White Law descend northwest alongside the fence to the stepped stile on the col below Whitelaw Nick, with its one-time fort. Cross the stile and with care descend north, alongside a stone wall, to the ancient border line crossing of **White Swire**. From here follow the winding, descending, now wide, dry and grassy track northwest (unless you wish to make a short detour west from White Swire to the Stob Stones – see Walk 4). A few yards beyond a prominent earthwork on the left of the path we are joined by St Cuthbert's Way

Old Halterburnhead below Bught Knowe

from the right, and with the joint long-distance paths continue descending, above Shielknowe Burn and below domed Green Humbleton, to cross Halter Burn, by bridge in winter, by ford in summer, to our starting point.

White Swire The first recorded mention of White Swyre ('swyre' is the old spelling) was in the Royal Command of 1222, when Henry III of England ordered the Bishop of Durham and the Sheriff of Northumberland, 'to travel to White Swyre, and there settle the marches (boundary) between England and Scotland, restoring them to their status in the time of King John and his predecessors'.

WALK 6 – A Border Foray over White Swire

Halterburn Valley, Border Fence, Wideopen Head, Trowupburn, Elsdonburn, Eccles Cairn, Halterburn Valley

Distance	8 miles (12.9km)
Height Gain	1070ft (326m)
Start/Finish	Halterburn Valley, GR 840277
Grade	2
Walking Time	4 hours
Maps	OS 1:25 000 Explorer OL16, The Cheviot Hills
	OS 1:50 000 Landranger sheet 74, Kelso & Coldstream
	Harvey 1:40 000 Walker's Route, St Cuthbert's Way
Accommodation	Kirk Yetholm and Town Yetholm – hotels, bed-and-breakfasts, caravan and camping site, youth hostel at Kirk Yetholm
Parking	Halterburn Valley, GR 840277, between road and Halter Burn

The ascents on this route are never severe along the way and the paths and tracks are distinct and generally firm underfoot. It is, however, recommended that walking boots be worn as low-lying sections can be squelchy after heavy rain.

The Route Cross Halter Burn by ford or wooden bridge and follow the Pennine Way east-southeast, skirting the southern flank of Green Humbleton, as far as the sheep pens and a waymark post. The grassy path winds as it ascends (note the hidden **Stob Stones** to the right), but basically maintains the same bearing until a gate in the border fence – **White Swire** – and another Pennine Way sign is reached. Here we leave the Pennine Way.

A stimulating, waymarked walk offering fine views of the hills above the College Valley and of the eastern Cheviots, both seen at their best on a clear day.

The Stob Stones Prehistoric standing stones. See Walk 4.

White Swire A border crossing frequently used by Border reivers in the 16th century. Freedom fighters or terrorists, they owed allegiance to none save their own kith and kin. Riding families with the feared names of Armstrong, Elliot, Scott and Kerr, Hall, Foster, Charlton and Robson rode these border crossings, especially when the moon was low in the autumn sky and the cattle fat and ready for the taking.

A grassy track runs southeast and then east, contouring above the Tongue and below White Law, to reach a stone dyke complete with waymarked gate. Our path holds the same bearing past Wideopen Head (a graphic description), offering fine views of the glaciated valley of Trowup Burn. Round Madam Law and descend rapidly right of the sheep pens to the valley floor at **Trowupburn**. From Trowupburn (a typical Border hill farm) the road winds north, then north-northeast along-side Hetha Burn, skirting a coniferous plantation (favoured by the colourful chaffinch), then past ancient earthworks to reach the bridge across Elsdon Burn 1 mile (1.6km) from Trowupburn farm. Here the route follows St Cuthbert's Way. ◄

The eastern banks of Elsdon Burn provide a pleasant place for a mid-walk break, and during the summer months motorists also find it an attractive picnic spot.

Five-hundred yards westwards the road brings us to Elsdonburn farm, 'Border Ridge 1½ miles'. Rise left and right through the steading with the gated

Trowupburn Also spelt 'Trolhopeburn' or 'Troughburn', in the days of the English King John the lands around this farm were given to Melrose Abbey by Robert Muschampe. A charter also granted the monastery's servants leave to use mastiffs for shepherding, but in doing so the dogs had to be controlled by the blowing of horns.

Trowupburn farm and valley

track that runs southwest above the gully of Elsdon Burn. Beyond the second gate, fork right to cross Shank's Pike before crossing the pasture of **Scaldhill Shank**, a bearing of 251° magnetic, to the two-step stile on the waymarked perimeter of Scaldhill plantation. Initially the narrow coniferous way runs through a pitch-black tunnel, before emerging by stile onto the fell. (*This coniferous route is not shown on the older OS 1:50 000 Landranger sheet 74 map.*)

Scaldhill Shank By Scaldhill Shank, between the two present-day plantations, lies this large, saucer-shaped enclosure. Because it is sited on lower ground it probably dates from Roman-British times, when the need for fortified settlements on high ground had diminished.

Eccles Cairn The burial place of a prehistoric chieftain – unfortunately the stones have been removed to build the drystone dykes we see today. To the west and below is Green Humbleton, whose summit is encircled by the ditches and ramparts of a prehistoric encampment.

Eccles Cairn to Cheviot

Ahead the grassy flanks of Eccles Cairn, its summit barely visible, rise beyond the damp surrounds of Tuppies Sike (stream). Cross grassland and sike (bearing 257° magnetic) aided by waymarks to **Eccles Cairn**, a humped vantage point just off the public path and providing breathtaking views of the Border country. Leave this grandstand via a marked trod southwest to the border line, following St Cuthbert's Way west into Scotland through the gated wall, to join the Pennine Way. Descend into Halterburn Valley on the outward route.

WALK 7 – The Lure of the Hen Hole

Cocklawfoot, Auchope Rig, Red Cribbs, College Burn, the Hen Hole, Auchope Cairn, Auchope Rig, Cocklawfoot

Distance	8 miles (12.9km)
Height Gain	2414ft (736m)
Start/Finish	Cocklawfoot, GR 853186, 8 miles (12.9km) south from Town Yetholm
Grade	4
Walking Time	6 hours
Maps	OS 1:25 000 Explorer OL16, The Cheviot Hills
	OS 1:50 000 Landranger sheets 74, Kelso & Coldstream, and 80, Cheviot Hills & Kielder Water
	Harvey 1:40 000 SuperWalker, Cheviot Hills
Accommodation	Inns, bed-and-breakfasts in Kirk Yetholm and Town Yetholm, and a youth hostel in Kirk Yetholm
Parking	Cocklawfoot, before the farm buildings, a bridge and a ford

An ever-changing scenic adventure for experienced mountain walkers, carrying a high degree of difficulty and the highest ascent within this guide. Moderate to strenuous, with short sections of rock scrambling in the Hen Hole, the paths vary from wide grassy tracks to rough thin trods over open fell. Boots, map and compass essential. In winter snow the Hen Hole can be hazardous.

This trek carries a very high rating of views and interest. Leave your route details, etc., on display in your car.

The Route Leave Town Yetholm on the B6401 road for Morebattle. One mile (1.6km) south branch left (signposted 'Cocklawfoot 7 miles') onto an unclassified road, winding along the beautiful strath of Bowmont Water to end at the lonely farm of Cocklawfoot.

Walk east through the farmyard for approximately 300yds (274m), with the Cheviot Burn tinkling on the left. At the first fork turn left, i.e. north, to ford the burn and reach an infant coniferous plantation on the left. Pass through the second gate on the left, ascending a

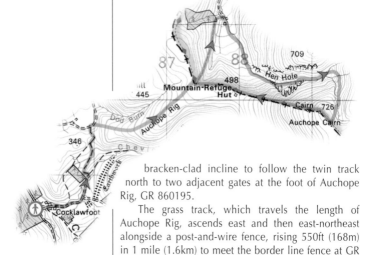

Auchope Rig and the Hen Hole

bracken-clad incline to follow the twin track north to two adjacent gates at the foot of Auchope Rig, GR 860195.

The grass track, which travels the length of Auchope Rig, ascends east and then east-northeast alongside a post-and-wire fence, rising 550ft (168m) in 1 mile (1.6km) to meet the border line fence at GR 874201. This ridge walk affords ever-increasing visual delights, with Mallie Side's ancient earthworks visible

to the south across the Cheviot Valley. Beyond, the Border Ridge, with Score Head, King's Seat and Cocklawgate, runs into England before rising slowly and majestically westwards to Russell's Cairn and Windy Gyle 2031ft (619m) (Walk 10), the third highest mountain straddling the border line. The distinctive Schil, at 1985ft (605m) just 15 feet short of mountain status, stands to the north.

When the border fence is reached the destination for the day is revealed. A dark and savage cleavage known as the Hen Hole lies to the southeast, wedged between the rocky crags of the Cheviot 2676ft (816m) and Auchope Cairn 2382ft (726m). A double gate in the right-angled fence allows passage on a thin path,

Red Cribbs This old drove road, running from the Bowmont Valley to the College Valley, was described by a warden of the eastern marches in 1597 as, 'Cribbheade – a passage and hyeway for the theefe'.

through tussock grass, to continue north-northeast descending into the College Valley alongside the naked red earth of **Red Cribbs**. The path is at first faint and indistinct, but when the head of Red Cribbs is reached the narrow track on the left of the gully becomes more definite and descends sharply into the charming alpine **College Valley**. Follow this narrow track to the valley floor, aiming between the lower corner of a coniferous plantation, a tin shed (sheep feed store) and a sheep stell (shelter). Underfoot it is inclined to be wet and boggy – note the predominance of rushes, and perhaps catch sight of a **heron**.

College Valley This most picturesque of Cheviot valleys does not get its name from any ancient seat of learning, but from the Anglo-Saxon 'col' or 'cool', and 'leche', meaning a bog or stream flowing through flat damp ground.

Herons The largest bird in the Borders, the grey and graceful heron fishes the burns for small trout, standing motionless on spindly legs waiting patiently to pounce. Along the burns, usually above 1000ft (305m), ring ousels can also be seen. Known as mountain blackbirds, the male is black with a distinctive crescent of white across the chest. These shy and seldom-seen birds return to breed among the heather and rocks close to the mountain burns. More surprises await as we clamber deep into the Hen Hole. The cliffs and crags towering above are home to carrion crows, ravens and several breeding pairs of peregrine falcons, and until 1936 this narrow gorge was the last home in England of the golden eagle.

Once the burn and its adjoining track are reached, turn sharp right, i.e. south, and then southeast, gradually climbing to the entrance of the **Hen Hole**, not a public right of way but marked on the Harvey map as an 'Intermittent path', rising with the College Burn to the adjacent 700m contour line east from the stony summit of Auchope Cairn. Once the Hen Hole is entered the path, in places faint, ascends with the burn, crossing it several times. In wet or icy conditions vegetation and dampness on the rocks can be hazardous. The way passes three differing waterfalls, first the Three Sisters, followed by two more tumbling cascades, as the narrow path rises relentlessly below towering Raven Craig to the first of the corries on the west shoulder of Cheviot. Here the College Burn runs from the south as the way enters a higher but smaller corrie on the southwest shoulder of Cheviot. The trace has now all but disappeared, but with the College Burn now on the left and the summit of Auchope Cairn above, no navigation problems can arise. Once the flat floor of the corrie is reached the burn turns left, and now is the time to take a deep breath and ascend briskly due west for a short distance through the peat hags to meet the wooden walkway leading right to Auchope Cairn's summit.

In the company of the cairns, including a shelter cairn, enjoy the breathtaking views in all directions – the Tweed Valley, the North Sea and the Northumbrian coast, and the mountains of Tweedsmuir faint and far beyond the triple-coned sentinels of the Eildons.

Descend from Auchope Cairn northwest on the well-worn Pennine Way, with the border fence on the left, to the saddle before and below the mountain refuge hut. Continue west with the fence, leaving the Pennine Way as it veers right, and return to the gated right angle in the fence at the top of Auchope Rig, GR 874201. Pass through the gate and follow the farm track by the fence, southwest, descending Auchope Rig for ¾ mile (1.2km)

The Hen Hole This ravine was known in centuries past as 'the Hell Hole of Cheviot'. From this lonely and lovely place, sculptured by the ice age, is said to come music of such sweetness that men, and women too, are lured into the Hen Hole, never to return. Legend also recounts that the notorious free-booter Black Adam lived in a cave in these crags (the right-hand edge of the buttress on the Cheviot side is today a rock climbers' route known as Black Adam's Corner), and the cave could only be reached by a leap of seven paces. This wild and evil reiver received his just desserts when, after raiding a wedding party at Wooperton, with the bridegroom absent collecting the minister, he tore the jewels from the guests then ravished and stabbed the bride-to-be. The returning husband-to-be, Wight (meaning strong and stocky) Fletcher, vowed revenge and gave chase through storm and dark-ness, relentlessly pursuing Black Adam to his lair in the Hen Hole. Finally and dramatically, outside Black Adam's cave, after being locked in mortal combat, the pair crashed down the crags to the College Burn and their deaths.

> Slowly right owre then they fell,
> For Fletcher his hold did keep;
> A minute and their twa bodies
> Went crashing doun the steep.
>
> Loud and lang Black Adam shrieked,
> But naething Fletcher said;
> And there was neither twig nor branch
> Upon their rocky bed.
>
> *Anon*

The Three Sisters waterfall, the Hen Hole

to reach the two gates at Auchope Rig foot, with views northwest to the sheep centre of Sourhope. The gates in turn lead south through the pasture to the corner of the small replanted coniferous plantation passed on the outward journey. Cocklawfoot lies ⅓ mile (0.53km) to the southwest, our journey's end.

WALK 8 – The Schil, Guardian of the College Valley

Cocklawfoot, Auchope Rig Foot, Schilgreen, Pennine Way, the Schil, Auchope Rig, Cocklawfoot

Distance	7½ miles (12.1km)
Height Gain	1263ft (385m)
Start/Finish	Cocklawfoot, GR 853186
Grade	2; in poor visibility and winter's precipitation can rise to 3
Walking Time	4½ hours
Maps	OS 1:25 000 Explorer OL16, The Cheviot Hills
	OS 1:50 000 Landranger sheets 74, Kelso & Coldstream, and 80, Cheviot Hills & Kielder Water
	Harvey 1:40 000 SuperWalker, Cheviot Hills
Accommodation	Inns and bed-and-breakfasts in Kirk Yetholm, Town Yetholm and Morebattle, and a youth hostel in Kirk Yetholm
Parking	Cocklawfoot, on grass verge before the ford

Apart from the final ascent to the rock-strewn, domed summit of the Schil, which is demanding as opposed to steep, the walk is a rambler's delight. This is isolated upland Cheviot walking on tracks and paths that are distinct and sound, with the exception of some unpaved sections of the Pennine Way ascending and descending to and from the Schil's summit. The walk is never exhausting but always exhilarating, due in no small measure to the close-ups of the massif of the Cheviot and the dark incisive cleft of the Hen Hole in its southwestern flanks.

A stimulating walk through upland country, giving wonderful views of the Cheviot landscapes.

The Route The isolated Cheviot farm of **Cocklawfoot** stands by Kelsocleugh Burn on the Scots side of the Border Ridge and marks the start of the walk. Walk east past the farmsteading, no doubt to the noisy accompaniment of the Border collies. Swing left at the first fork and cross the burn before reaching a small planting of conifers. Pass through the second gate on the left, ascending north, initially on a

Cocklawfoot Reputed to be Hexpathgate of centuries past, this was a regular border crossing for the lawmakers and the lawbreakers. Later this route was adopted as a local drove road to move cattle from the fertile Tweed Valley to the hungry markets of industrial Tyneside.

broad twin track, up and over a bracken- and rush-clad pasture. The variable grass track leads to a T-junction with two fences and two gates to negotiate at the foot of Auchope Rig. Continue to walk north for 50yds (46m), descending to the wide and well-kept farm track at GR 860197. Turn right and follow the track north.

Any road or track that unveils the route for a distance of 2½ miles (4km) through hills such as these must rank as unique. Take full advantage of the opportunity to gaze around and drink your fill of Cheviot landscapes. Directly ahead the dark mass of Black Hag, to its left the uninspiring mound of the Curr (Walk 5), and to the north-northeast **the Schil** 1985ft (605m), crowned with a most handsome andesite (volcanic rock) coronet. On the left side of the track are the remains of an ancient homestead and later there is evidence of an Iron Age settlement. On the right Alderhope Burn dances in from Birnie Brae, having gouged a deep gully into the fellside, home to countless **sheep**, moorland birds and heaths and heathers.

After a rectangular coniferous plantation is passed on the left, the track forks before Schilgreen, the last building in the Rowhope Valley. Carry on north, i.e. right, at the fork, ascending steadily for 1½ miles (2.4km)

The Schil Standing guard at the head of the College Valley, the Schil is a fitting sentinel for the most picturesque valley in the Cheviot range. Although not of mountain status, this mountainous hill has a charisma all of its own that draws the walker, and once on its rocky peak uninterrupted views from the North Sea to the Ettrick Forest can be enjoyed.

to the Pennine Way path and the border fence. At the border fence cross the stile and turn sharp right, i.e. south-southeast, ascending with the fence to the summit of the Schil. Once on the summit, do cross the fence and scramble up the crown of rocks: 360° of best Border landscape, including the north face of the Cheviot, will take your breath away. ▶

Back to the fence, descend southeast on the Pennine Way, utilising the fence and sections of the slabbed pathway on the right as an invaluable guide for the 1¼ miles (2km) to the gate at GR 874202.

The walking is good in dry conditions, perhaps not so good after periods of high precipitation. As the gate is approached the peat is forgotten, for ahead the gully of Red Cribbs and the spectacular gash in Cheviot's flank, the Hen Hole (Walk 7), command attention.

Underfoot conditions bear witness to the fact that thousands of Pennine Wayfarers' boots have passed this way.

Sheep One mile (1.6km) to the west of GR 859200 stands the farm of Sourhope, an experimental centre of the Scottish Hill Farming Organisation. Cheviot sheep, known previously as the Long Breed, abound on these hills. Today the breed is more compact in build, and classed as native or indigenous, other native breeds being the Border Leicester and the Scottish Blackface. Cheviot ewes when mated with a Border Leicester tup (ram) will produce a lamb known as a Scots Half-Bred. These hardy breeds, living on exposed uplands, are 'hefted' onto the land, in other words if the farm is sold the sheep remain. Each family of sheep, having lived for generations on this or that particular 'heft', knows where to take shelter and where the first and best grazing lies. They have also developed immunity to the diseases carried on their particular hillside, for every year a proportion of the ewe lambs are hefted, or kept by, to carry on the family.

The northern rocky summit of the Schil

At the right angle in the border fence, GR 874202, two gates take you through to the grassy track on Auchope Rig. A fine gradual descent southwest rambles alongside another fence for 1 mile (1.6km), offering the walker an elevated display of the 5 miles (8km) of Border Ridge from Cairn Hill to Windy Gyle (Walk 10). At the foot of Auchope Rig the two gates we left four pleasant hours ago come into view. Pass through, go south to the plantation and join the farm road to Cocklawfoot. The Border collies will give the same vociferous greeting as they gave on departure!

WALK 9 – To the Changing Summit of Cheviot

Cocklawfoot, Auchope Cairn, Cairn Hill, the Cheviot, Hen Hole Corrie, Auchope Cairn, Auchope Rig, Cocklawfoot

Distance	10¾ miles (17.3km)
Height Gain	2017ft (615m)
Start/Finish	Cocklawfoot, GR 853186, 8 miles (12.9km) south from Town Yetholm
Grade	3 or 4, depending on overhead and underfoot conditions
Walking Time	7 hours
Maps	OS 1:25 000 Explorer OL16, The Cheviot Hills
	OS 1:50 000 Landranger sheets 74, Kelso & Coldstream, and 80, Cheviot Hills & Kielder Water
	Harvey 1:40 000 SuperWalker, Cheviot Hills
Accommodation	Inns and bed-and-breakfasts in Kirk Yetholm and Town Yetholm and a youth hostel in Kirk Yetholm
Parking	Cocklawfoot Farm, before the farm buildings, bridge and ford

This classic Cheviot journey ventures to the highest point of the Cheviot Hills, rounding Muckle Cheviot's southern summit perimeter to enjoy far-reaching vistas along the way to the gradually sinking trig point.

Choose a day that is dry and clear, and have the correct equipment, including map and compass, to suit the conditions underfoot and overhead. Winter walkers should please ensure that adequate clothing is worn and emergency rations are carried. The final foray on the summit plateau provides not only additional, extensive views, but also seldom-seen insights into the upper reaches of the narrow, mysterious, rock-clad Hen Hole.

The Route From Town Yetholm by car, take the B6401 road for Morebattle, branching left at the 'Cocklawfoot' signpost onto an unclassified road, then through the valley of Bowmont Water to the lonely farm of Cocklawfoot.

A continuous ascending journey over farm tracks, grassy paths, naked peat, wooden walkways and stone-slabbed pathways rewards the hill walker with extensive views and much interest.

This, one of the most serious of walks in the guide, begins at Cocklawfoot. Walk east past the farmsteading to the first fork and take the left track to cross the Cheviot Burn ford.

Continue past a small replanted plantation (on the left) and pass through the five-bar metal gate, left, to rise sharply with the bracken-clad track, and then swing right to follow the track and subsequent single paths north to two adjacent field gates at the foot of Auchope Rig, GR 860195. The ascending track runs east and east-northeast along Auchope Rig, with a post-and-wire fence, rising 550ft (168m) in 1 mile (1.6km) to the border fence at GR 874201. This ridge walk offers a basket of classic Cheviot views.

Ahead at the gated junction of two fences we meet the border line, with Auchope Cairn to the east and Cheviot east-northeast filling the screen, but kept apart by the ominous rocky defile of the Hen Hole. Pass through turning right, i.e. east, onto a rough, fenceside path through tussock grass and peat leading to the **mountain refuge hut** below Auchope Cairn. In addition to the border line fence on our right we also have the waymarked **Pennine Way** as our guide east to the summit of Auchope Cairn. Once past the refuge hut descend a

Mountain refuge hut The present wooden hut was constructed several years ago by a combined team of Gurkhas and an RAF mountain rescue team, replacing the longstanding but well-worn railway wagon. Many weary Pennine Wayfarers had reason to be thankful for the old hut, as was recorded by the affectionate graffiti on its walls.

little before what can be, in adverse conditions, 'a bit of a plod', following the well-worn peaty path as it hugs the border fence to the stony, cairn-scattered summit and grandstand of Auchope Cairn.

Continue east-southeast for ½ mile (0.8km) from Auchope Cairn, aided by the wooden walkway of the Pennine Way. (Incidentally, at the lowest point of the walkway, GR 893196, just beyond the point where it swings southeast, you can see to the north, i.e. left, over the wilderness of heather and peat hags, the rim of the steep-sided corrie above the upper reaches of the Hen Hole and the western, cairned rocky outcrop overlooking the Hen Hole. This is our goal when we return from the summit of Cheviot.) Ahead, at a junction of ways, we meet fences, stiles and a signpost: 'Pennine Way' to the right, 'The Cheviot 1½ miles' to the left.

The Pennine Way Many thousands of complaining feet have pounded this section of the Pennine Way, damaging the binding vegetation on the upper surface of the peat. The result is erosion. In order to prevent further erosion, the Northumberland National Park Authority has laid sections of stone-slabbed or duckboard walkways along the worst affected parts. Centuries ago bridges were floated on bales of wool, hay or straw, and today sections of walkway are floated on bales of heather in an effort to stabilise and sustain the way.

Not so many years ago the way to Cairn Hill and Cheviot's summit from this point was a serious, glutinous experience involving plodding through peaty bunkers, marked by rotting marker posts, out of which **skeletons of aircraft** from the Second World War occasionally rose from the mire. Today, thanks to the Northumberland National Park, a partial walkway of large flagstones has taken the misery, and some of the excitement, out of the

Crashed aircraft No less than nine aircraft from various air forces have come to grief on the summit of Cheviot. When the peat dries out, the mangled metal skeletons rise phoenix-like to the surface, only to sink again with the first rain. Bits of the metallic skeleton of a Lancaster Bomber can be seen on drier days north of the western approaches to Cairn Hill. The outer remains of a Flying Fortress are clearly visible by Braydon Crag during a dry period. Wing struts, tail fins, undercarriages, and even engine pistons remain, although the bowels have long since been cannibalised. An attempt was made to extract one of the crashed aircraft from its peaty grave for monetary gain, using a tractor and winch. Unfortunately, before the mission was completed a storm broke and the attempt was abandoned for the day, with the rescue equipment *in situ* until more favourable conditions prevailed. When the bounty hunters returned there was no sign of their equipment. Tractor and all had joined the aircraft in the peaty grave, and remain there to this day.

final push east to Cairn Hill and Scotsman's Cairn, then northeast to **Cheviot's trig point** 2676ft (815m). After a suitable time admiring the vistas that extend in all directions, near and far, or if the weather is foul, wondering what on earth you are doing here, return via Cairn Hill to the wooden walkway northwest from the Pennine Way junction towards rock-capped Auchope Cairn, but only as far as GR 893196 (see bracketed text above).

Cheviot's trig point The summit plateau of the Cheviot consists mainly of acres of mucilaginous peat, formed because rainwater cannot soak into or permeate the non-porous granite saucer of Cheviot's summit. This permanent pond prevents the heather and moss from decomposing completely, and eventually the partially rotted vegetation forms a cap of black, glutinous peat. Granite also encourages the formation of acid soil, which in turn stimulates the growth of heather and ling, a cycle that does little for the walker. The area on and around Cheviot was known centuries ago as the Forest of Cheviot, within which the laws applying to wild game were enforced. All dogs, except those used for the chase, had to have one foot shortened in order to slow them down. In 1168 fines totalling 22s 10d were imposed on local dog owners by Ralph, son of Main, for not shortening the feet of their dogs.

To Cairn Hill by a slabbed way

Leave the walkway right at GR 893196 to traverse heather and hag northeast for approximately 200yds (183m) to descend into the gully of College Burn (indicated on OS 1:25 000 Explorer OL16, The Cheviot Hills, at GR 894197) at an angled point where the burn, having risen below the summits of Cheviot and Cairn Hill, swings right, i.e. north, before running left, i.e. west, into and through the Hen Hole. Cross the burn and ascend north to above the gully, and later the corrie, onto a thin trod to contour at approximately 2300ft (710m) above sea level around the corrie rim of the **Hen Hole**. Later veer left, i.e. to loop west to the outcrop rocks and conspicuous cairn – unnamed on all my maps, we shall call it 'the Hen Hole cairn'. (This trod is shown on the Harvey map as an 'Intermittent path'.) The outcrop provides a fine vantage point from which to savour the dark and mysterious gorge of the Hen Hole far below. *Do take care and steer clear of the summit rim of the Hen Hole corrie.* Return on the outward trod to the wooden walkway, then northwest to reach the cairn-sprinkled summit of Auchope Cairn, from where fresh vistas delight the walker.

The Hen Hole This wild, rock-bound gorge, one of the most impressive of its kind in the Cheviots, offers its crags and buttresses to rock climbers: Cannon Hole Direct 120ft (36.5m) (severe), Black Adam's Corner 120ft (36.5m) (difficult), Zigzag (difficult), College Groves (severe) and Long John (severe).

The westerly descent on the Pennine Way from Auchope Cairn passes the mountain refuge hut. Continue west with the Pennine Way for 300yds (274m), branching onto the pathway close to the left-hand fence leading to a gated right angle in the fence at GR 874201. Pass through and follow a wide farm track alongside the fence, southwest along Auchope Rig for ¾ mile (1.2km), to reach two more gates at Auchope Rig foot. Pass through the gates to walk south to the corner of the small coniferous plantation, descending to the southwest to Cocklawfoot.

Although no public rights of way, except the Pennine Way path to Cheviot's summit and the permissive path descending northeast to Scald Hill and then east to the Harthope Valley, cross over the summit plateau, faint trods have, over time, been followed by careful and considerate walkers. In recent years it has been suggested, possibly due to changes of ownership, that the flat-topped plateau of Cheviot might at some time be converted from its total wilderness into a grouse moor. Such a change of land use would naturally impose seasonal restrictions on the traverse of the summit during the nesting and shooting seasons. Notices will no doubt be displayed if and when this should come about, and it behoves all who wish to walk this way to respect those who live on or earn a living from this land.

Cairned outcrop above the Hen Hole corrie

WALK 10 – By Clennell Street to Windy Gyle

Cocklawfoot, Clennell Street, Outer Cock Law, Border Gate, Windy Gyle, Windy Rig, Kelsocleuch Rig, Cocklawfoot

Distance	7 miles (11.3km)
Height Gain	1276ft (435m)
Start/Finish	Cocklawfoot, GR 853186
Grade	2 in good weather, 3 in winter conditions
Walking Time	4 hours
Maps	OS 1:25 000 Explorer OL16, The Cheviot Hills
	OS 1:50 000 Landranger sheet 80, Cheviot Hills & Kielder Water
Accommodation	Hotels and bed-and-breakfasts at Kirk Yetholm and Town Yetholm, youth hostel at Kirk Yetholm
Parking	Cocklawfoot, on grass verge before the ford

A delightful walk across the fell ways of the past – along a drovers' way to the border gate on the national boundary, and thence to Windy Gyle 2031ft (619m), one of the prime viewing sites in the Cheviots.

Seven miles over easy, grassy pathways (slabs on the Pennine Way) make this hike a pleasant challenge.

The ascents are never severe and navigation presents no problems on this high-interest and far-seeing circuit. Walking boots are recommended.

The Route The old drove road called **Clennell Street** that crosses Kelsocleuch Burn at Cocklawfoot is

Clennell Street This street is not Roman, but an old drove road referred to in medieval charters as 'magnum viam de Yarnspath'. It runs from Yetholm and Cocklawfoot over the Border Ridge to north of Alwinton in Upper Coquetdale. Stobies 1770 map of Roxburghshire shows a road from Cocklawfoot crossing the border at Cocklawgate and leading to Upper Coquetdale, but neither this map nor the first edition of the Ordnance Survey map of 1863 marks Clennell Street as a drove road.

The border gate Known also as Cocklawgate, in medieval times as Hexpathgate, this border crossing was a meeting place of the wardens of the middle marches. Wardens from both sides of the border met occasionally during the 15th and 16th centuries. Six were appointed to administer law and order, three from each country, and with few exceptions the appointments were made on the principle that the most active poacher makes the best gamekeeper.

the starting point of the walk. Cross the bridge to the farmyard, pass through a gate then turn sharp right to a second gate shaded by a venerable sycamore tree. Initially the farm track climbs steeply south-southeast to a small coniferous plantation overlooking a prehistoric fort and earthworks on the immediate skyline, the first of many encountered on this walk. Go through the gate on the path slicing through the trees and continue to climb and wind over the ridge of Cock Law. After a section of motorcycle ruts in the track another gate is met north of Outer Cock Law, and from here the path rises sharply left as it circles this sturdy northern buttress of the Border Ridge and the northern corrie of Windy Gyle. Note the cultivation terraces to the right. Above Outer Cock Law the track levels out as the border fence is reached at the **border gate**, with an attendant Pennine Way signpost and stile.

One-and-a-quarter miles (2km) to the southwest, i.e. right, the prominent summit of Windy Gyle can be seen, and with the border fence, the Pennine Way and a slabbed pathway as guides, the route is

easy and distinct. A large and well-formed cairn, **Lord Russell's Cairn**, stands some distance north of the boundary fence as the final ascent is made to the large reconstructed shelter cairn and tumulus that cap the grandstand summit of **Windy Gyle**. A ½ mile (0.8km) descent northwest from Windy Gyle, down the well-trodden Pennine Way, to the col of Windy Rig (aptly named), meets a small and infrequently used gate leading north onto a faint path high above Kelsocleuch Burn.

Outer Cock Law and its earthworks

As the path descends to Windy Rig it becomes more distinct – take care to use the right fork to Kelsocleuch Rig when the path splits. Ahead a coniferous plantation can be seen apparently blocking the track. As the trees

Lord Russell's Cairn This cairn stands below the summit of Windy Gyle to the east, several yards north of the border fence. Somewhere between the cairn and Cocklawgate, during a wardens meeting in the summer of 1585 (a year of Border 'decaie' – decay or breakdown), Lord Russell was shot and mortally wounded. He was accompanying his father-in-law, John Forster, the English warden, when, according to Forster, there was some, 'lyttle pyckery between the rascalles of Scotlande and Englande'. Suddenly a shot rang out and Russell fell. Scant consolation for the slain lord that he remains one of the few Borderers who has a local landmark named after him.

Windy Gyle The third highest mountain that straddles the border, Windy Gyle carries a large collection of broken rocks and is topped by a tumulus. The site is thought to be the burial place of Iron Age chieftains. As a viewing platform it has few rivals, when the air is clear, offering 360° views of the Northumbrian coast, the northern Pennines, the English Lakes, the Cheviots, Tweeddale and the Southern Uplands.

Take care through the forest ride as the way underfoot is strewn with felled branches overgrown with grass.

are reached it becomes obvious that the route continues through a gate and into a wide forest ride. ◄

On emerging from the trees turn sharp left to continue on a track between a stone dyke and the conifers. At the corner of the plantation by a small burn to Kelsocleuch, turn right and descend with the burn as far as the farm road. Turn left to return north to Cocklawfoot.

The border gate

WALK 11 – A Walk into the Sixth Century BC

Hownam, the Street, Hownam Burn, Kersmoor Head, Hownam Law, Hownam Rings, Hownam

Distance	7 miles (11.3km)
Height Gain	925ft (282m)
Start/Finish	Hownam village, 12 miles (19.3km) south of Kelso
Grade	2 in good weather, 3 in winter conditions
Walking Time	4–5 hours
Maps	OS 1:50 000 Landranger sheets 74, Kelso & Coldstream, and 80, Cheviot Hills & Kielder Water
	Harvey 1:40 000 SuperWalker, Cheviot Hills
Accommodation	Hotels and bed-and-breakfasts at Morebattle, Kirk Yetholm and Town Yetholm, and a youth hostel at Kirk Yetholm
Parking	In the village, limited to verge side (please show consideration)

A walk over the foothills of the northern Cheviots along ancient ways that ascend to the distinctive, loaf-like summit of Hownam Law.

An historic walk with many views and items of interest from ancient times along the way.

Pathways are good and clear, although without waymarks, and care is needed when descending through the summit rocks of Hownam Law's southwest corner. Walking boots are recommended.

The Route The remote village of **Hownam** is the start and the finish of this exploration into Borders history.

Hownam Pronounced 'hoo-nam', this quiet village in the valley of Kale Water was, in the 17th century, a favourite haunt of the Covenanters (those who sought to preserve presbyterianism in Scotland). No doubt the secluded fells that surround Hownam would be ideal for prayer meetings, far away from the prying eyes of the dragoons of John Graham of Claverhouse, scourge of the Covenanters. The village church has six old gravestones built into the south and east walls, an economy not infrequently met with on the north side of the border.

From the Street to abandoned Seefew Cottage and Belford

Commence the walk where a side road, GR 778192, rises east from the village. At the lone house with off-white walls, swing right with the **Street**, as our initial route is known, to ascend with the farm track to a stunted plantation on the skyline. Continue ascending as the track turns east until a junction is reached by a gate in the stone dyke. Pass through the gate to leave the Street and follow the grassy track east, i.e. straight ahead, descending for 500yds (457m) towards abandoned Seefew Cottage. Before the cottage a faint grassy track enters from the left, i.e. north (this path is clearer 100yds (91m) ahead). We are now on the gated track to Hownam Burn and Kersmoor Head.

The Street An old drove road starting in Hownam, the Street crosses the border at Mozie Law and runs south down to Coquetdale in Northumberland. The grassy journey along its ridges provides views of high quality on both sides of the Border.

The track crosses Hownam Burn before ascending for 350yds (320m) to meet a path on the right. Follow this narrow trace north by contouring the hill on the left as far as the gate, and pass through to cut diagonally across the small rough pasture to another small gate in the far corner. When the pasture has been crossed, ford the burn ahead to turn right and climb northeast for 1 mile (1.6km) on the path to Kersmoor Head 1106ft (337m), bounded by conifers.

The flattened peak of Hownam Law now towers above to the north, with two or three paths offering a selection of steep ascents. Take the one that looks the most comfortable, and enjoy the ¾ mile (1.2km) climb to the summit of **Hownam Law** 1473ft (449m) – satisfaction and visual pleasure will be the rewards.

The descent from the southwest corner of the horizontal summit is steep, and care is needed until the corner of a stone dyke is reached. From the right angle to Hownam Burn, 1 mile (1.6km) below, it is a steady walk alongside the stone dyke (keep the wall on your right, which for the final few hundred yards changes into a fence). Several gates have to be negotiated, as have two right angles in the dyke. Remember to walk only south or west, and keep the now empty farm of South Cote well to the left.

Hownam Law A fine distinctive hill whose position on the northern extremities of the Cheviots, and its loaf-like summit, make it an outstanding example of Cheviot architecture. It is generally agreed to be the best seat in the house when it comes to viewing the Cheviots from the Scots side. The flat top of the law is ringed in places with a massive 10ft (3m) thick wall that once protected its Iron Age fort. Traces of the horseshoe houses within the fort can be seen in the saucer depressions.

At Hownam Burn cross by the two marker posts and make for a gate 150yds (137m) to the south. From there a pronounced farm track is met a further 100yds (91m) south, where a left turn brings the walker to a fenced field. Skirt the field to a fork in the track and take the right fork to the hilltop at **Hownam Rings** 1017ft (310m), GR 790194.

Hownam Rings This hill fort straddles the ridge several hundred yards north of the Street. The site was excavated in 1948 and revealed a whole series of settlements, thus paving the way to an understanding of prehistoric building methods. Radiocarbon tests now show the early constructions to be sixth century BC, giving a total occupation span of 700–800 years.

Leave the Rings on the south side of the hill. Eighty-five yards (78m) away a selection of upright stones, the **Shearers**, GR 791192, stand straight and mysterious, inviting inspection. The path continues south for 150yds (137m) to a gate that adjoins the Street, which is followed west as it descends the last mile to Hownam village.

The Shearers A line of 28 stones running east to west, at present 11 of the Shearers are at ground level, the remainder standing up to 3ft (0.9m) above ground. They are now thought to be grounders of an ancient field dyke of the late Roman period, not ancient standing stones, as was first thought.

WALK 12 – By the 'Clattering Path' to Iron Age Forts

Greenhill, the Street, Blackbrough Hill, Mid Hill, Heatherhope Reservoir, Greenhill

Distance	7 miles (11.3km)
Height Gain	915ft (279m)
Start/Finish	Greenhill, 1¼ miles (2km) south from Hownam, GR 788177
Grade	2; 3 in poor visibility or in winter
Walking Time	4 hours
Maps	Combined OS 1:25 000 Explorer OL16, Cheviot Hills, and Pathfinder 486, Hownam OS 1:50 000 Landranger sheet 80, Cheviot Hills & Kielder Water
Accommodation	Inn and bed-and-breakfasts in Morebattle
Parking	Limited parking on the grass verge north of the Y-junction at Greenhill

An intriguing walk into the heart of the Cheviots, the first half swings along an old drove road, calling at two of the largest Iron Age forts in the area. The descent into the steep-sided and secluded side-valley above Heatherhope Reservoir provides Border solitude at its best, and prepares the walker for the peaceful return along a stony farm road past Heatherhope Reservoir to Greenhill.

Hill walking boots are recommended.

The Route A single-track road winds 1¼ miles (2km) south from Hownam (take the left fork from Hownam) to Greenhill, standing at the junction of two typical, hidden Cheviot valleys, Capehope and Heatherhope.

With Heatherhope Burn on the left, take the farm track east for 400yds (366m). At the bridge leave the farm road on a narrow pathway that ascends left, i.e. north-east, into the side-valley of Headshaw. The path, north of Headshaw Burn, varies from distinct to faint as it climbs for ¾ mile (1.2km) to the **Street**. The Street is the grassy rutted track that is met at the walled col forming the top

This is a ridge and valley walk on narrow trods through tussock and heather, and along farm tracks (occasionally rutted) with many ascents and descents, the steepest being the descent through Muckle Sund Hope.

The Street This ancient trail ascends at length over steep-sided hills from Hownam to cross the border at Plea Knowe, between Windy Gyle and Mozie Law, continuing on over Black Braes to end its journey at the confluence of the Coquet and Rowhope Burn. It served as a drove road for local traffic, and also had military connections. On General Roy's military map of 1755 it has the impressive name, 'Clattering Path'.

South on the Street

of the T. Turn right at the junction, i.e. southeast, and ascend steadily on this ridge road, in company with visiting curlews, trilling larks and a variety of soaring birds of prey, for 1½ miles (2.4km). The way twists in places while keeping to an overall bearing of southeast. When a five-bar gate in a wire-and-post fence impedes progress, pass through the gate and immediately turn right to follow a thin trace through the heather, parallel to a wire-and-post fence.

Blackbrough Hill A truly magnificent site for the large Iron Age fort that straddles its summit. With natural defences on three sides, in the form of steep rock- and scree-clad slopes, it is surrounded by an elliptical rampart 10–15ft (3–4.5m) high, and is 300yds (274m) in circumference. Minor ramparts and ditches surround the main wall, with offset main gateways. Hut circles can be seen (with difficulty) scattered inside the fort.

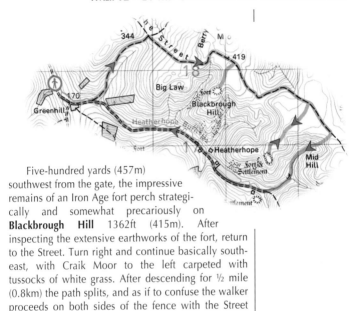

Five-hundred yards (457m)
southwest from the gate, the impressive
remains of an Iron Age fort perch strategically and somewhat precariously on
Blackbrough Hill 1362ft (415m). After
inspecting the extensive earthworks of the fort, return
to the Street. Turn right and continue basically southeast, with Craik Moor to the left carpeted with
tussocks of white grass. After descending for ½ mile
(0.8km) the path splits, and as if to confuse the walker
proceeds on both sides of the fence with the Street
swinging left and continuing along the eastern side of
the fence. We keep to the track on the right side, a
steep ascent through heather that passes through
several ancient earthworks, and when it reaches flatter
ground swings right from the fence, i.e. southwest. It
then contours for ½ mile to the summit of
Greenbrough Hill, above Heatherhope Reservoir,
where further remains of an Iron Age fort and settlement above Sundhope Kipp are evident.

Greenbrough Hill and fort Matching Blackbrough as a site, this fort is not
as large or as impressive, though its population may have equalled
Blackbrough. Several settlements can be found on adjacent hillocks with
evidence of hut circles. Both sites were obviously important members of the
network of forts that stretched across the Cheviots from Hownam Law to
Coquetdale around 500 BC.

Blackbrough Hill fort

Leave the fort and contour northeast along the edge of the summit ridge – but not too close, as the exposure in places is extreme – until the fence guiding the Street is in sight. Swing right along the fence towards Mid Hill, keeping the fence on the left. Below on the right, i.e. southwest, a steep-sided gully known as Muckle Sund Hope cuts a dramatic slash between Sundhope Kipp and Mid Hill. At the head of this gully, GR 822171, a five-bar half-gate in the fence indicates a faint trace leading down the burnside. Descend southwest, bearing 240°, on this trace to the valley below, steeply at first, then more gently as the path improves, for ¾ mile (1.2km) to Heatherhope Burn.

Surrounded by sheep shelters and occasional railway wagon fodder stores, the road winds in a leisurely fashion northwest past the black waters of **Heatherhope Reservoir**, then for a further 1¾ miles (2.8km) through this forgotten, picturesque valley to Greenhill.

Heatherhope Reservoir A small and now redundant reservoir which in its heyday supplied water to the good folk of Kelso. Alongside the road to Greenhill and Hownam, spaced at regular intervals, stand cast-iron inspection valves marked KWC – Kelso Water Company. Even now in certain quarters you can still hear, 'The waters nay as guid as Heatherhope.'

WALK 13 – A Redundant Reservoir to Celtic Hilltop Forts

Heatherhope Reservoir, the Street, Mozie Law, Beefstand Hill, Callaw Cairn, Church Hope Hill, Heatherhope Reservoir

Distance	8 miles (12.9km)
Height Gain	1171ft (357m)
Start/Finish	Heatherhope Reservoir, GR 808167, 2½ miles (4km) south-southeast from Hownam
Grade	3
Walking Time	4½–5 hours
Maps	OS 1:25 000 Explorer OL 16, The Cheviot Hills
	OS 1:50 000 Landranger sheet 80, Cheviot Hills & Kielder Water
Accommodation	Inn and bed-and-breakfasts in Morebattle
Parking	Alongside the road below the reservoir dam

Two-and-a-half miles (4km) from the Cheviot village of Hownam slumbers the dark and silent reservoir of Heatherhope, the start and the finish of this 8 mile (12.9km) walk.

Tracks and paths are always distinct, while the ascents, although testing, are never exhausting. The section along the Pennine Way is mainly on a slabbed path. Winter walks over this route are most enjoyable, when the air is clear and overnight snow scrunches underfoot. Wildlife abounds, particularly birds of prey and some feral goats. Extensive views covering 360° are of great interest. ▶

The Route A narrow road runs southeast from Hownam to Greenhill, then forks left as the road surface changes from tarmac to stony hardcore, signposted 'Private Road', and narrows to single track leading to Heatherhope Reservoir.

Walk southeast alongside the reservoir to pass a small feed store (old railway wagon). To the left an

Enclosed by rippling ridges, domed hills and scree-scattered gullies, home to several visible Iron Age forts and encampments, this walk is an adventure of discovery.

At the time of writing the estate had recently changed ownership, and I understand that plans are afoot to convert sections →

87

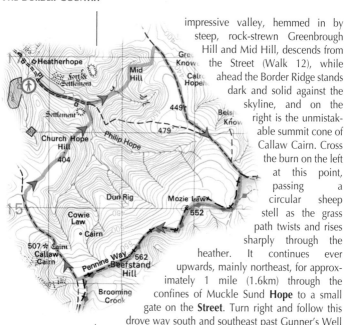

impressive valley, hemmed in by steep, rock-strewn Greenbrough Hill and Mid Hill, descends from the Street (Walk 12), while ahead the Border Ridge stands dark and solid against the skyline, and on the right is the unmistakable summit cone of Callaw Cairn. Cross the burn on the left at this point, passing a circular sheep stell as the grass path twists and rises sharply through the heather. It continues ever upwards, mainly northeast, for approximately 1 mile (1.6km) through the confines of Muckle Sund **Hope** to a small gate on the **Street**. Turn right and follow this drove way south and southeast past Gunner's Well for its final mile in Scotland, taking care to turn right at the first five-bar gate. The path soon joins the Pennine Way at the shoulder of Plea Knowe, just east of and below Mozie Law (a boulder seat and finger post are firmly embedded in the ground at this point).

Turn right, i.e. west, at the finger post, following the Pennine Way alongside the Border fence, over the undulating heather-capped summits of Mozie Law 1811ft (552m) and Beefstand Hill 1841ft (561m), on the oft-tramped, now slabbed, pathway of the Pennine Way.

← of the area to grouse moor. Should this occur, walkers are advised to avoid the area during the spring nesting season and autumn shoots.

Hope A word often found on Scottish Borders maps with a meaning that has little in common with the English dictionary. In this case the word 'hope' means 'the upper end of a narrow mountain valley'. It can also mean 'a hollow', or 'a mound'.

The Street A list of border crossings compiled in 1597 included many east of Hawick, though the major drove roads crossed into England west of Hawick. Such crossings as Carter Bar (Walk 16), Dere Street (Walk 15), the Street (Walks 11, 12, 13), Cocklawfoot and Clennell Street (Walk 10), and Red Cribbs (Walk 7) are all mentioned. It is more than likely that these crossings were used for local traffic, for the customs post at Kelso did little to encourage the mass movement of Highland cattle east of Hawick. The routes to the west were more private, so to speak, and thus claimed the bulk of the Highland trade as it flowed south from Falkirk. So great was the demand for Scottish cattle that early in the 19th century numbers in excess of 100,000 annually crossed the Border hills, and that was only the recorded ones!

Beyond the western flank of Beefstand Hill we leave the Pennine Way at the rickety gateway by the triple fence junction ½ mile (0.8km) from Beefstand summit. From the gate it is barely ½ mile (0.8km) north, on a fenceside grass pathway through heather, to the prominent cairn crowning **Callaw Cairn** 1663ft (507m). Immediately below Callaw Cairn, to the west, lies the stony gorge of Callaw Hope, and all around the flowing curves of the grass- and heather-clad hills that descend so gracefully to the Tweed and Coquet.

Blackbrough Hill north from Beefstand Hill

Callaw Cairn This distinctive hill, as the name suggests, carries a well-constructed and prominent cairn that is visible for many miles and provides a fine vantage point from which to enjoy far-ranging views of the eastern Cheviots. The origins of the cairn appear to be lost, though it is likely to be the burial place of chieftains from one or more of the many fortified Iron Age settlements and forts in the vicinity. Whitestone Hill running northwest from Callaw Cairn is the site of several large and well-defined fortified Iron Age hilltop settlements. This section of the Cheviots was heavily populated by the Celtic Selgovia and Votadini tribes, and judging by the defensive pattern (offset rings of earthworks) of the fortified settlements they did not live in peaceful times.

Heatherhope from Callow Cairn

From Callaw Cairn's eastern flanks continue initially north with the wide track over the Callaw Moor pathway – in places wet underfoot. When the path enters a heather-clad plateau swing right, i.e. northeast, with the track for a further ½ mile (0.8km) to the pimply cairn on grassy Church Hope Hill 1325ft (405m). From here a wide and obvious track, steep in places, leads to the valley floor, joining the road to the reservoir by the old railway wagon.

WALK 14 – In the Footsteps of Agricola's Legions

Tow Ford, Woden Law, Blackhall Hill, Brownhart Law, Chew Green, Nether Hindhope, Tow Ford

Distance	10½ miles (16.9km)
Height Gain	1250ft (381m)
Start/Finish	Tow Ford, GR 761132
Grade	2; 3 in winter conditions
Walking Time	6–6½ hours
Maps	OS 1:25 000 Pathfinder 486, Chesters & Hownam, and 498, Carter Bar
	OS 1:50 000 Landranger sheet 80, Cheviot Hills & Kielder Water
Accommodation	Inns, bed-and-breakfast and refreshment in Jedburgh and Morebattle
Parking	On grass verge at T-junction east of Towford

An informative, stimulating and historic walk exploring the windy fells in the footsteps of the Roman legions – marching along Dere Street past a Roman 'artillery range' on Woden Law, to the extensive encampment at Chew Green.

The Route Tow Ford stands in the upper reaches of Kale Water, 4 miles (6.5km) south of the village of Hownam and ⅔ mile (1km) south of the Roman camps of Pennymuir (Walk 15). The T-junction by a cattle-grid just east of Tow Ford marks the starting point for the walk. **Dere Street** is signposted and ascends east-southeast to the col between Langside Law and Woden Law.

A circular journey on good paths where the ascents are appeased by the historical and visual interest met along the way.

Dere Street A medieval name for the umbilical cord of Roman military might, the lifeline connecting Corbridge on Hadrian's Wall, to Chew Green, to the headquarters in Scotland at Trimontium (Melrose), and thence to Cramond on the Firth of Forth and beyond to Perthshire. Built around 80 AD under the command of Agricola, it has since been utilised as a drove road, and today the higher stretches are a delight to the hill walker, easing the journey and stimulating the mind.

Woden Law Named after a Norse god, this strategically situated hill was home to Celtic tribes during the Iron Age. Dispossessed by the Romans, they later reoccupied the site when the Roman Empire collapsed. Double ramparts and an intervening ditch initially surrounded the summit, but these partially disappeared when the Romans used the native fort for siege practice and military exercises. The precision-built earthworks on the northeast corner, consisting of two banks between three ditches 40ft (12.2m) to 98ft (29.9m) from the original defences, are obviously Roman. In this system Roman siege machines were placed on flattened platforms on the outer bank, just beyond the range of the inner defences.

The steady incline of Dere Street – with fine views northeast of the domed Cheviot Hills – past several earthworks is indication enough, if indeed any be needed, of the skills of the Roman military surveyors and engineers.

On reaching the col with its stone-built shed, turn right with the farm track, i.e. south and southeast (the path to the summit of **Woden Law** 1388ft (423m), with ample evidence of Iron Age and Roman occupation, is 30yds (27m) to the right), rising gently for 1¼ miles (2km) towards the craggy, rock-strewn summit of Blackhall Hill 1572ft (479m). ◄

Before the gate on Hunthall Hill the track branches into three. Take the right-hand path through the gate – waymarked 'Chew Green' – to the east and southeast. Dere Street now contours above the head of Hindhope Valley and sweeps majestically below the rocky outcrops

Ascending Dere Street from Tow Ford

and scree of Blackhall Hill to the flat ridge of Gaisty Law. (This path, though perfectly safe, may cause vertigo sufferers some discomfort; as an alternative, use the ascent to Blackhall Hill.) Using the marker post on the mound of Black Halls, ½ mile (0.8km) ahead to the

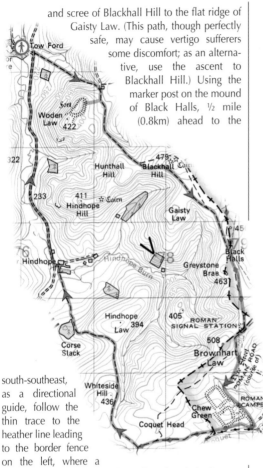

south-southeast, as a directional guide, follow the thin trace to the heather line leading to the border fence on the left, where a much broader track is joined. Head south with the fence to the next gate, where the signpost and well-trampled path suggest the route has joined a section of the Pennine Way.

The many directional indicators between this gate and Coquet Head remove any possible navigational problems, informing us that Chew Green is 1 mile

(1.6km) to the south. Pass the eastern flank of Brownhart Law 1663ft (507m) – a Roman signal station – ignore the signpost 'Permissive Path, Pennine Way' that points to the right, and continue to the massive complex of the Roman encampment at **Chew Green** on the eastern flat lands of Coquet Head. Leave the encampment at its southwest corner and follow the waymarked Pennine Way west for 1 mile (1.6km) across Coquet Head – the damp source of the River Coquet, clothed with bobbing cotton grass – to the point at an angled fence where the Pennine Way swings left, i.e. south (the former signpost 'Nether Hindhope 3 miles' is no longer there).

Chew Green Site of an extensive Roman camp (name unfortunately unknown) built under the command of Agricola. Standing on a broad strip of open moorland near the damp source of the Coquet, it would be an eminently suitable site that was also easily defensible. The distinctive earthworks signify a large marching camp, a convoy post and a labour camp. Dere Street runs alongside the camp and connects it with Brownhart Law, a signal station ½ mile (0.8km) to the north. Chew Green later became a meeting place for the wardens of the middle marches, a place to settle disputes in the violent 15th and 16th centuries.

From the right-angled fence leave the Pennine Way and follow the fenceside path (this route is marked on OS map sheet 80 as a 'Path') northwest to pass through a gate onto open fell. Beyond the gate a grass track leads north through upland windswept pastures, passing Whiteside Hill on the left with the infant Hindhope Burn far below on the right. Below to the northwest a plantation of conifers at Corse Slack, west of Hindhope Law, can be seen, with a farm track descending alongside. Take this route to pass by the steading and farmhouse of tree-sheltered **Nether Hindhope** onto the tarmacked valley road, and on the way glance up to the right to the corrie of Hindhope crowned by flat-topped Hindhope Hill and stony Blackhall Hill (our earlier route along Dere Street).

Nether Hindhope Three crossings of the border ran south from this ancient farm to Chew Green, and in 1542 Sir Robert Bowes noted that reivers' raids caused 'brode waies or rakes' (broad ways or paths).

On the narrow metalled road it is a pleasant 2 mile (3.2km) walk north to Tow Ford alongside meandering Kale Water, now flowing sedately round its oxbows, its banks heavy with musk in late spring and early summer, and watched over by the heights of Hindhope Hill and Woden Law – hills that are home to several species of soaring birds of prey.

Hidden Nether Hindhope overlooked by Hindhope Hill

WALK 15 – The Iron Age and the Romans Inspired this Walk

Pennymuir, Dere Street, Chatto Craig, Upper Chatto, Whitton Edge, Dere Street, Five Stanes, Pennymuir

Distance	10 miles (16.1km)
Height Gain	772ft (235m)
Start/Finish	Pennymuir, GR 755144, 3¾ miles (6km) south of Hownam
Grade	2 or 3
Walking Time	5 hours
Maps	OS 1:25 000 Pathfinder 486, Chesters & Hownam
	OS 1:50 000 Landranger sheet 80, Cheviot Hills & Kielder Water
Accommodation	Hotels, bed-and-breakfasts, caravan parks and fish and chips available in Jedburgh
Parking	Alongside a corrugated iron hut on the grass verges by the cattle-grid

There is much to see and experience on this walk through time, and it is not difficult for the mind to drift through the centuries to the times of the Roman legions and our Iron Age ancestors.

It is said that if you listen carefully you can hear the tramp of the 'square-bashing' legions.

A bright and breezy hike over the fells that rise west of the once-waterlogged Kale Water Valley. Pathways and tracks are generally good underfoot, with the exception of sections of rutted, motorbike-churned Dere Street, and the ascents are never breathless.

I would recommend a spring, summer or autumn day with good visibility, as the views of the Cheviots, Teviotdale and the Tweed Valley are extensive and rewarding. Walking boots are needed for winter walking or in adverse weather conditions.

The Route The walk starts at **Pennymuir** on the minor Hownam to Carter Bar road. Pennymuir today consists of a black-and-red corrugated-iron hut (village hall), a cattle-grid and a stile. Centuries ago it housed two legions in the adjacent encampment and was a much grander affair. ◀

Pennymuir In the first and second centuries AD a Roman marching encampment stood a few hundred yards south and east of Pennymuir. The best-preserved example of its type in Scotland, the remains of the four angular encampments that made up the complex can still be traced today. Covering an area of 40 acres, at any one time the camp could house two legions, i.e. 6000 men, in tented accommodation.

Cross the stile at the east corner of the village hall and ascend with waymarked (a Roman helmet) Dere Street north-northwest alongside a fence and a small plantation. Approximately 1 mile (1.6km) along **Dere Street** five large stones (not the Five Stanes) can be seen on the west side of the drystone dyke. Further north on the skyline at Trestle Cairn a wire-and-post fence comes in from the east, i.e. right. Cross the stile by the gate and turn right, following the fence east, descending gradually for 200yds (183m) to a gate. Just beyond this a lone, large and prominent **standing stone** can be seen on a small knowe at GR 758161. Closer inspection reveals that its leading edge points directly northeast to **Chatto Craig**, topped by its Iron Age fort.

Dere Street This road was in use before the Roman occupation of Britain, but honed and refined by the skills of Roman military engineers and surveyors to produce the road we now know as Dere Street. Later it was greatly favoured by drovers, who walked their cattle from the Scottish Highlands and islands, via Falkirk, eventually threading through the Borders on roads such as Dere Street.

From the solitary stone walk northeast, and follow the distinct bridleway for 1¼ miles (2km) of picturesque and entertaining walking, past Chatto Craig 1024ft (312m) to the farm of Upper Chatto. Pass through the farmsteading with its white farmhouse – adorned with sculptures fashioned from old agricultural machinery – to descend with the tarmac road as

Chatto Craig and Cunzierton Hill These conspicuous hills carry the circular remains of native forts, or camps, and cairns, as opposed to the Roman quadrangles seen at Pennymuir and on Woden Law (Walk 14).

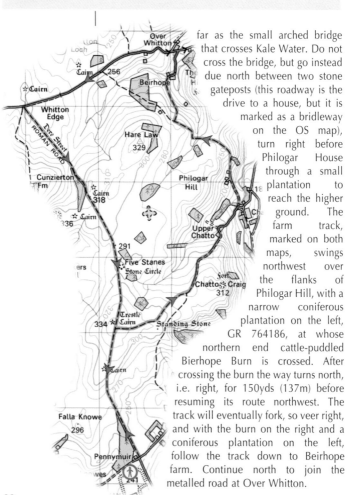

far as the small arched bridge that crosses Kale Water. Do not cross the bridge, but go instead due north between two stone gateposts (this roadway is the drive to a house, but it is marked as a bridleway on the OS map), turn right before Philogar House through a small plantation to reach the higher ground. The farm track, marked on both maps, swings northwest over the flanks of Philogar Hill, with a narrow coniferous plantation on the left, GR 764186, at whose northern end cattle-puddled Bierhope Burn is crossed. After crossing the burn the way turns north, i.e. right, for 150yds (137m) before resuming its route northwest. The track will eventually fork, so veer right, and with the burn on the right and a coniferous plantation on the left, follow the track down to Beirhope farm. Continue north to join the metalled road at Over Whitton.

Ascend west (left) for ¾ mile (1.2km) to the summit of Whitton Edge, noting several prominent **standing stones** and the black waters of Whitton Loch lying to the north. The grass verges on this stretch of road are wide and pleasant underfoot. At the hogsback leave the metalled road left, a few yards past the cattle-grid, and with the finger post 'Dere Street' turn southeast to join the straight and grassy track of Dere Street. ▶

In keeping with its Roman pedigree, Dere Street runs in a straight line to the standing stone on the ridge ahead (only deviating to contour any hill in its path) and is a delight to walk. On the windswept fells, southeast of the distinctive dome of **Cunzierton Hill** and 1½ miles

Standing stone pointing to Chatto Craig

It is very evident that Dere Street was a drove road of some importance, as signified by the two stone dykes lining the route, reminiscent of the green roads found in the Yorkshire Dales.

Standing stones and stone circles The many stones that stand lonely and sightless on these fells are thought to date from the period 2000–1000 BC, and in all probability they marked the burial places of chieftains from the settlements at lower levels such as Chatto Craig. Stone circles marked communal burial sites, the remains being interred in burial urns, and hence known as 'beaker burials'. Five Stanes stone circle is the most complete circle on the walk, and a central point in the alignment with other similar remains.

Five Stanes stone circle, Dere Street

Dere Street, south from Whitton Edge

(2.4km) from Whitton Edge, stands the **stone circle of Five Stanes**, a few yards east of Dere Street. From the circle of Five Stanes pass **Trestle Cairn** via slowly descending Dere Street, with fine vistas to the south and east of the rolling, rounded Cheviots, constantly dappled by the shadows of scudding clouds racing over the waving tussocks and the black and purple heather. It is 2 miles (3.2km) back to Pennymuir.

WALK 16 – Border Line and Miners' Road over Carter Fell

Carter Bar, Catcleuch Shin, Carter Fell, source of Bateinghope Burn, Buzzard Crag, Carter Pike, Carter Bar

Distance	6¼ miles (10.1km)
Height Gain	561ft (171m)
Start/Finish	Carter Bar, GR 698068, on the A68(T) border crossing
Grade	2; 3 in winter or after heavy rain
Walking Time	4 hours
Maps	OS 1:25 000 Explorer OL16, The Cheviot Hills
	OS 1:50 000 Landranger sheet 80, Cheviot Hills & Kielder Water
Accommodation	Hostel, caravan, campsite and refreshments south at Byrness on the A 68(T)
Parking	The border crossing at Carter Bar on the A68(T) (refreshments available)

Carter Bar is the beginning and the end of this walk, which runs alongside the border line yet remains in Northumberland for its entirety. The walk traverses Carter Fell, which can be very wet underfoot, passing evidence of old limestone quarries and kilns en route within the area of **Whitelawmoor**, and is visually pleasing and rich, not only in solitude but also moorland flora and fauna. Although graded 2 in dry conditions, walking boots are essential in wet or winter conditions. Fence lines and

The central ridge of the Cheviot range allows but one road to cross its lonely acres – the medieval border crossing of Redeswire, now known as Carter Bar 1371ft (418m).

Whitelawmoor This has been a national nature reserve since 1999, and covering 1500 hectares it ranks high in the pecking order of blanket bog habitats. It contains sphagnum moss, cloudberry and cotton grass (Scotsman's heids), and also found are red grouse, merlins, peregrine falcons, buzzards, hen harriers and the striking emperor moth. Foxes are often seen and frogs often heard.

Carter Bar This border crossing was known in medieval times as Redeswire, a name first mentioned in the epic poem 'The Brus' by John Barber in 1376. Later, in 1575, as witness to the skirmish of Redeswire, it was immortalised in the Border ballad 'Raid of the Redeswire'. This site is revered every year by the good folk of Jedburgh during Common Riding week.

> The seventh of July, the suith to say,
> At the Redeswire the tryst was set;
> Our Wardens they affixed the day,
> And, as they promised, so they met,
> Alas! that day I'll ne'er forget!
>
> *Anon*

quarry tracks assist navigation. By Buzzard Crag, met along the miners' road, our return route, are two sets of lime kilns that burned limestone from a nearby quarry. This route is best enjoyed when the dry days of summer or winter's frosts dry and harden the peat hags.

The Route Combine this border crossing on the A68(T) with the views in all directions, and it is small wonder that dozens of touring buses and cars pause awhile to give their occupants a chance to behold the Border country.

From Carter Bar walk west through the wicket gate at the corner of the coniferous plantation towards the steep but short incline of Catcleuch Shin 1785ft (544m). The path marches with the fence along the south side of a section of the Border Forest Park. At the summit of Catcleuch Shin the heathery hogsback, or summit ridge, of **Carter Fell** can be

Carter Fell A dour and sombre place when the wind blows free and blustery rain lashes the face, this fell drapes the border. Yet it was on the summit and the exposed slopes to the south that men laboured to win coal, and poor-quality coal at that, from its reluctant slopes. Five drift mines bored between the inhospitable cleughs and hags, and several crumbled lime kilns with spoil heaps littering the summit, can still be seen today.

seen stretching endlessly to the southwest. The faint track runs alongside the border fence (our guide for the 2½ mile (4km) felltop crossing), first southwest to the highest point of Carter Fell 1899ft (579m) – marked with a trig point – then after 1½ miles (2.4km) to a mound scattered with cairns, shafts and old industrial workings, below which to the north a small tarn nestles. Also at this deer-fenced corner (which marks the boundary of Kielder Forest Park) stands a huge 6½ft (2m) ladder-stile.

At this point swing left and walk approximately southeast (a bearing of 152°), with the forest boundary fence on the right, for 250yds (229m) to an area of bare earth and stones (although after heavy rain a quagmire) marking the source of Bateinghope Burn. Turn left again to walk approximately east over the heather-free area across the open fell. Ahead and below, the distinct cleugh and infant burn of Bateinghope slice through the heather-clad peat, east and then northeast. Descend on thin sheep paths with the cleugh and burn for ¾ mile (1.2km) until the remains of spoil heaps and crumbled stone buildings are met on either side of the small burn, where there is also a little waterfall.

By the waterfall and ruined stone building, with the spoil heaps on the south side of the burn, an old mine track is met and followed northeast as it leaves the burnside, on an initial bearing of 40°. The gradually ascending rush-ridden track passes by the naked rock outcrops of Buzzard Crags. This twin track,

Spoil heaps by Bateinghope Burn

rounding the rocky summit outcrop of Carter Pike by stile or wooden gate, is all that remains of what was once a well-constructed mine road to and from the main road at Carter Bar. For 2½ miles (4km) this old road contours and slowly descends to Carter Bar, and in doing so continually delights the eye with unfolding vistas, in particular flat-capped Lumsdon Law, **Redesdale**, **Catcleugh Reservoir**, the entire Cheviot range and north over the Tweed Valley to the Lammermuirs.

Redesdale A valley of space and wildness whose sons acknowledged no law and feared no one, except their neighbours, and whose main interests were those of protection racketeer and reiver. Long after the country had settled down under the rule of the Tudors, Redesdale continued its lawless ways. Today, to the east of the A68(T) in upper Redesdale, 70 square miles (181 sq km) of open fell is now a vast military training ground. Enormous tracts of ground are closed to walkers, with the peace and solitude that is indigenous to these hills shattered by the crump and crash of cannon.

Catcleugh Reservoir A shimmering mass when seen from Carter Fell, tastefully surrounded by a variety of trees, this reservoir draws its water from the isolated fells that feed the head of the Rede. Created in 1905 by Newcastle and Gateshead Waterworks, it supplies Newcastle and district with Borders water.

Black Cleugh to Catcleugh Reservoir

North over Teviotdale from Rubers Law (Walk 25)

CHAPTER 2

TWEEDDALE AND TEVIOTDALE

This open Y-shaped basin of 1870 square miles (4843 sq km) contains the valleys through which the twisting rivers Tweed and Teviot tumble to the North Sea. Ringed on three sides by solid rounded hills and rolling moors, it presents an attractive and yet dependable picture. At Kelso, where the two rivers meet, the valley widens and the graceful sweep of Tweeddale captures and holds the gaze – agriculturally bountiful and visually compelling, it invites exploration. To the north the long low moorlands of the Lammermuir and Moorcroft Hills protect Tweeddale from winter's icy blasts, while its western flank is sheltered by the massifs of Manor and Moffat, and to the south it is supported by the ever-faithful bastion of the Cheviots. The twin dales of Tweed and Teviot are, for such latitudes, green and pleasant lands.

The infant Tweed, some say, rises at Tweed's Well on Tweedshaws, 9 miles (14.5km) north of the market town of Moffat. Others are of the opinion that it sprins from the loins of nearby Hart Fell 2651ft (808m), and back up their theory with the old couplet:

Annan, Tweed, and Clyde
Rise a' oot o' ae hillside.

Whatever spring is the true source, the Tweed flows for 98 glorious miles (158km) north to Peebles then east to Kelso, finally turning northeast to end its journey at Berwick-upon-Tweed. Its main tributary, the Teviot, trickles to life at Teviotstone on the northern flank of White Hope Edge, 15 miles (24km) south-west of the mill town of Hawick, through whose marches it flows into ever-widening Teviotdale to join the silvery Tweed at the Junction Pool, the famous salmon pool at Kelso. Both are supported and fed by:

The Ettrick and the Slitrig
The Leader and the Feeder
The Fala and the Gala
The Ale and the Kale
The Yod and the Jed
The Blackadder and the Whiteadder.

Both rivers have been at the hub of Border life for centuries, from when the four great Border abbeys and their accompanying communities grew and prospered on their banks, through the bloody days of the fighting families, when the reivers built their pele towers and strongholds on both banks of Tweed and Teviot. Then, as peace slowly returned, agriculture and the woollen industry developed, resulting in the emergence of the Border towns of today. Peebles, Innerleithen, Walkerburn, Galashiels, Melrose, St Boswells, Coldstream and Berwick-upon-Tweed all grace the banks of the Tweed, while Hawick and Jedburgh stand astride or close by the Teviot. Only Kelso adjoins both.

Bus services connect all the towns and villages in Tweeddale and Teviotdale, and timetables are freely available at bus stations, council offices and tourist information centres throughout the region.

Accommodation, ranging from hotels and inns, bed-and-breakfasts (in town and country), youth hostels, caravan and campsites, is available throughout Tweeddale and Teviotdale, as is food and refreshment. Full details are available from tourist information centres (a list of these can be found in Appendix 3, Useful Information), together with information about abbeys, stately homes, pele towers, museums of all types, Border festivals and a comprehensive list of outdoor activities.

Incidentally, contrary to popular belief, the River Tweed did not give its name to the world-famous Tweed cloth and woollen garments, so beloved by country gentlemen and so disliked by small boys. The name 'Tweed', as used when referring to the high-quality cloth, came from the mispronunciation of the word 'tweel', a name used in the Borders in the early 1800s to describe a local cloth. The mispronunciation, it is said, originated in London!

THE WALKS

Each walk in this chapter is like a piece in a jigsaw – each has a separate identity, but if all are completed the whole will provide a full and rewarding picture of Tweeddale and Teviotdale.

Walk 17 is, to a certain extent, the rogue of the chapter, yet the cliffs of St Abbs Head and the life on and around them are too good to miss. This coastal and cliff walk is of the highest order. By way of contrast, Walk 18 starts at the Junction Pool where the Tweed and Teviot meet in the shadow of Kelso Abbey, and meanders along the riverbank of the Teviot via the ruins of Roxburgh Castle to discover, eventually, the village of Roxburgh. High above both rivers, offering wonderful views, stands Smailholm Tower, the best preserved of all the Border strongholds and the highlight of Walk 19. Walk 20 has views of the Tweed and Tweeddale that are beyond compare, as it passes by the impressive ruins of Dryburgh Abbey, a statue of a national hero and a plethora of wildlife. The triple peaks of the Eildon Hills, symbols of the Borderland, are the pinnacle of Walk 21,

Mertoun Bridge over the River Tweed (Walk 20)

which also includes Melrose and its ancient abbey. Walk 22 ascends the far-seeing ridges of Broomy Law and Three Brethren before descending to the banks of the picturesque Tweed, while Walk 23 leaves the wide and fertile lower valley of the Tweed and explores its upper reaches by means of the Minchmoor drove road and a wooded valley walk to the historic village of Traquair.

Transferring the interest to Teviot, Walk 24 is a gentle stroll to the 1815 Waterloo Monument on Peniel Heugh, a ridge that divides Tweeddale and Teviotdale and offers views of both. Walk 25 to Rubers Law is short in length but one to be savoured, with the glorious sweep of Teviotdale far below. The chapter ends as it began, with two walks that perhaps geographically do not belong, for they explore Liddesdale, a dale in its own right whose waters flow into the Solway Firth on the west coast. Walk 26 is fractionally over the edge of Teviotdale, but it is inexorably linked by family and blood with many of the walks in this chapter, and includes a sight of dark and dour Hermitage Castle, whose walls have witnessed murder most foul. The circular journey takes in bracing fells, a stretch of historic railway line and a druidical circle that witnessed the following:

They placed him in a cauldron red,
And melted him, lead, and bones, and all.

Walk 27 is a circular ascent of Crib Law in Craik Forest and earns its right to be included in Chapter 2 by its proximity to Borthwick Water, a reivers' river that joins the Teviot west of Hawick.

WALK 17 – Sea View Figure-of-Eight

St Abbs, Bell Hill, St Abb's Head, Pettico Wick,
Mire Loch, St Abbs, Coldingham Bay, St Abbs

Distance	5½ miles (8.8km)
Height Gain	308 feet (94m)
Start/Finish	St Abbs, GR 919673
Grade	2
Walking Time	3½ hours
Maps	OS 1:50 000 Landranger sheet 67, Duns, Dunbar and Eyemouth
Accommodation	St Abbs – hotels, bed-and-breakfasts, and Coldingham Youth Hostel above Coldingham Bay
Parking	Parking in the harbour basin and along the roadway overlooking the harbour

Although this walk carries a grade 2 degree of difficulty, **do take care on the exposed cliff edges, as there are no protective fences.**

A delightful and easy four-seasons figure-of-eight stroll, always within sight or sound of the restless North Sea. Never exhausting, it provides striking views of and from the coastline cliffs, plus a walk alongside a unique freshwater loch. Cliffs, loch, grassland and St Abbs Head nature reserve are all enhanced by a unique flora and fauna. Underfoot a variety of paths, tracks, country lanes, steps and stiles, pebble bays and tarmac surfaces provide yellow-arrow-head-signposted passage for this unusual and stimulating walk from and to the fishing and 'diving' harbour of St Abbs.

The Route The walk starts in the village of **St Abbs**. From the harbour climb the steps to the road alongside the church, where 100yds (91m) west a pathway turns

St Abbs 'St Aebbe', whose 17th-century settlement was built on Kirk Hill, gave the name to the present fishing village and the rocky promontory of St Abb's Head. The remains of a monastic settlement, 70yds (64m) by 25yds (23m), can be seen close by the present lighthouse, while to the north on the cliff edge the smaller foundations of a nunnery are just visible.

sharp right, i.e. north, with an accompanying signpost and noticeboard giving directions and details of the trails around St Abbs Head nature reserve.

Pass through two gateways to the open cliffs, then turn sharp left and follow the cliff path as it ascends along the cliff edge above Starney Bay before descending to sea level. Along this section there are seats providing fine views of St Abbs, the North Sea and the surrounding stacks and cliffs. At sea level a stile is met, leading onto a wide grass pathway. Twenty-five yards (23m) past the stile turn sharp right to leave the wide pathway and ascend the paths over the grandstands of Bell Hill, White Heugh and then Kirk Hill. From Kirk Hill the path continues northwards, giving the first sighting of St Abb's Head, with the triple buildings of **St Abb's Head Lighthouse** standing pristine white against the sky and the sea.

Bell Hill and gull-washed cliffs above Starney Bay

St Abb's Head Lighthouse Commissioned in 1872, unfortunately it is not open to the public. A radio beacon operates from the lighthouse and constant contact is maintained with the lighthouses of Bass Rock, Bell Rock, the Isle of May, and Fidra in the Firth of Forth. It is also a meteorological station producing weather reports every three hours. A small doubt as to the reliability of today's sophisticated equipment is raised by the presence of a working sundial in the lighthouse garden!

At the wall around the lighthouse, turn left and climb the small hillock on whose summit stands a directional disc, with distant views of the Cheviot Hills and striking views of the seacliffs to the north, and an information board. Descend from the north side, passing the remains of a monastery to join a metalled road. This road can be used for descent as it zigzags west to Pettico Wick. For those anxious to see more of the cliffs that are home to thousands of screeching **seabirds**, walk north. *A westerly descent to Pettico Wick can be made down a very steep grassy gully, but only experienced mountain or hill walkers should attempt this descent.* Otherwise it is prudent to return to the road.

Seabirds The dramatic cliffs and stacks of St Abb's Head are home to the largest colony of cliff-nesting seabirds on the southeast coast of Scotland. Kittiwakes and guillemots are the most numerous, followed by razorbills, shags, herring gulls, fulmers and puffins. Far below, in the foaming sea and on the rocks, live the common limpet, mussels, acorn barnacles, shore crabs and seaweed.

Once the road has reached its lowest level, turn south to **Mire Loch**. Cross a waymarked stile, pass beds of 2 metre high reeds, and take the path on the west side of the loch, carpeted with primrose, violets and clumps of gorse in spring and summer, and lined with a few stunted pines and alders bent double by the winter's wind (nesting sites for herons). The path around the southern end of the loch and the western flanks of Kirk Hill has a **fenced-off area** close by

Mire Loch A narrow freshwater loch some 400yds (366m) long, it provides food and shelter for migrant birds in spring and autumn. Hundreds of gulls, fulmers and kittiwakes bathe in its waters each afternoon, after which they flutter to the east bank to preen and gossip. Swans, heron, tufted duck and coot all have a place on the loch, with goldcrest on the banks.

Mire Loch to distant Cheviot

Fenced-off area Covering the knowes (small hills) above the cliffs, sheep's fescue, red rockrose, sea pink and mouse-ear chickweed grow in great profusion, with 10 species of butterfly found feeding on them. The rare northern brown argus caterpillar feeds entirely on the rockrose, hence the area fenced off by Scottish Natural Heritage to prevent grazing animals eating the plant.

marked with notices erected by Scottish Natural Heritage. Two hundred yards (183m) south of the fenced area the outward path is rejoined at the stile and followed to St Abbs.

At the crossroads on the main street in St Abbs, high above the harbour, turn right into Creel Road and Creel Path. This pleasant, southwest agricultural walk is waymarked to Coldingham Bay, and after it passes behind three hotels above the bay we leave the Creel Path. Emerge from behind St Vedas Hotel at the road end to Coldingham Youth Hostel, and descend east into the rock-and-sand-strewn inlet ringed with a crescent of brightly painted bathing huts that is **Coldingham Bay**.

At the northern end of the sands, marked 'Coastal Path to St Abbs', a stepped way ascends to a clifftop pathway returning northeast to St Abbs.

Coldingham Bay Should the weather and, what is more unlikely, the North Sea, be warm, **take great care if you feel like a swim – there is a strong undertow on this beach. Safe bathing is clearly indicated by green flags on the beach, unsafe bathing by red flags.**

WALK 18 – Two Castles and a Keep

Kelso, Roxburgh Castle, Roxburgh, West Bank of the Teviot, Rail Bed to Roxburgh, Kelso

Distance	10½ miles (16.9km)
Height Gain	138ft (42m)
Start/Finish	The Junction Pool of Tweed and Teviot, Kelso, GR 724335
Grade	2
Walking Time	5 hours
Maps	OS 1:50 000 Landranger sheet 74, Kelso & Coldstream
Accommodation	Kelso – hotels, inns, bed-and-breakfasts, caravan parks; a variety of meals available
Parking	The Junction Pool of Tweed and Teviot overlooking Kelso; also in Kelso

Enchanting as this there-and-back waymarked riverside walk is in all seasons, it is particularly so in the freshness of spring or in the blaze of colour that is autumn. It meanders along the west bank of the River Teviot before looping along the old Jedburgh to Kelso railway track, then returns to Roxburgh and Kelso. Ascent is negligible and the paths are distinct, although narrow, along the riverbank. Graded 2, due to its length, it provides fine views of two Kelso castles and peaceful lower Teviotdale. **This walk is not recommended when the Teviot is in flood.**

The route utilises a section of riverside path that for centuries has connected the medieval Border abbeys of Kelso and Jedburgh.

Kelso Bridge The bridge was designed in 1800 by the Scots engineer John Rennie as the prototype for his larger creation, Waterloo Bridge across the Thames (now demolished, but its lamps live on along the parapets of Kelso Bridge). This pleasing bridge has five arches with paired columns and a classical tollhouse. Grooves in the parapet are said to have been made by travellers reluctant to pay the toll, so they rubbed their coins down before paying the tax – nothing changes! (See also Chapter 5, Kelso Town Trail.)

The Route From the west end of **Kelso Bridge** follow the road northwest by the banks of the Tweed to the old corn mill overlooking the Junction Pool of Tweed and Teviot. Here the road swings left alongside the Teviot for several hundred yards before crossing a picturesque stone bridge, circa 1795. A few yards beyond the cottage a finger post, right of the road, directs the walker left through the narrowest of gaps in the wall leading onto a riverside path, right. The route is waymarked with A centrally superimposed on W (Borders Abbeys Way). As the river swings west, leave the path to ascend the mound to the right to carefully inspect the last few remains of **Roxburgh Castle**. From the old to the relatively new, **Floors Castle**, colourfully embattled, overlooks the Tweed to the north.

Roxburgh Castle and Floors Castle A few 'caste doune' walls are all that remain of Roxburgh Castle today. Built on the grassy ridge between the Tweed and the Teviot, it was thought to be impregnable. Once a royal residence, it guarded the royal burgh of Roxburgh (a different site from the present village). Continually under siege, and frequently changing hands in the Middle Ages, it fell to the English, who held it for nearly 100 years until 1460. James II of Scotland, while laying siege to the castle, was killed by a 'misframit gun' that exploded during inspection, 'mair curieous nor becam him or the majestie of ane King'. His queen, undeterred by his untimely demise, captured the castle, and as if to wipe the memory of this troublesome place from her mind, ordered it to be torn down and made completely untenable – and so it remains.

Floors Castle has no such history, but remains desirably tenable. The seat of the Dukes of Roxburghe, it was designed in 1718 and completed in 1721, then extended by W H Playfair between 1841 and 1849 to become the present imposing building.

Return to the riverbank, with care, and follow the waymarked riverside pathway south for 2 miles (3.2km) to the farm of Roxburgh Mill – the path narrows at times and several stiles (waymarked) have to be negotiated. As the village of **Roxburgh** draws nearer, the distinct but

Roxburgh The church was built in 1752 and has since been restored. In the churchyard Andrew Gemmels rests in peace. He died in 1793 at the age of 106 and was the original of Walter Scott's Edie Ochiltree in *The Antiquary*. The 1847 viaduct, designed by J Millar, personifies Victorian solidarity.

now redundant viaduct can be seen rising high above the Teviot. Before Roxburgh Mill the riverside pathway joins a narrow lane that passes the farm and leads to the village. Once past the farm and a few new village houses, take the left turn to a furniture workshop, then left again to return to the riverside directly beneath the west end of the high bridge where a small footbridge is strapped to the huge uprights. (Note in the pasture on the right the crumbling remains of 'Wallace's 16th-century keep' (tower).)

Pass through a wicket gate beneath the 16-pillared viaduct and continue south, initially on a wide track, hugging the west side of the riverbank, for approximately 1 mile (1.6km).

The pathway narrows and snakes with the sweeps of the tree-clad banks of the Teviot. Never difficult

On the east bank of the Teviot are the undulating fairways and manicured greens of Roxburgh Golf Club, and later derelict Sunlaws Mill below several caves, the one called Horse Cave having had the honour of stabling, in 1745, the horses of Jacobite Bonnie Prince Charlie.

The remains of Wallace's Keep

117

underfoot, and with well-placed waymarks and wooden walkways, this stretch is a riverside delight. As the looping Teviot, with a long, narrow central island, comes in from the left, and the riverside trees and scrub thin, we leave the river, right, to ascend with a moss-covered 'stane-dyke' to the rail bed of the old Kelso–Jedburgh Line – a suitable spot for the mid-walk break.

Turn right, i.e. north, noting to the right on the skyline the bulky summit of Hownam Law (Walk 11), and follow the tracks of the old steam trains to Roxburgh. This is a pleasing, easy stretch providing fine views over fertile Teviotdale that comes to a sudden end as we leave the rail bed, descending to join the village road through a wicket gate leading half-right onto the road northeast through the charming village of Roxburgh.

Continue to Roxburgh Mill farm and return to Kelso along the west bank of the Teviot on the outward path, noting Heiton Mill on the east bank and the profusion of birdlife along the way. The views of Kelso are particularly pleasing when the route leaves the riverbank and approaches the end of the walk.

The restless Teviot by Heiton Mill

WALK 19 – A Walter Scott Connection

Smailholm, Westfield, Smailholm Tower, Mein's Plantation, Smailholm

Distance	3½ miles (5.6km)
Height Gain	216 ft (66m)
Start/Finish	Smailholm village
Grade	1
Walking Time	2½ hours
Maps	OS 1:50 000 Landranger sheet 74, Kelso & Coldstream
Accommodation	Kelso and St Boswells – a varied selection plus refreshments
Parking	Limited parking in Smailholm on verge of a side road signposted 'Smailholm Tower'

A ramble from and to the hamlet of Smailholm along quiet country lanes and farm tracks, to the best-preserved of all Borders strongholds, the prominent 15th-century pele tower known today as Smailholm Tower. Choose a fine day as the views are extensive, and of interest not only to the historian and the photographer but to all who appreciate the great outdoors, particularly those south over the Tweed Valley to the Cheviot range.

Smailholm village and Sandyknowe farm are of particular interest for their connection with Scott.

The Route The small village of **Smailholm**, GR 648364, straddles the B6397 northwest of Kelso, an ideal starting point for the walk. Leave the village on a minor road to the west-southwest and follow its twists and turns for 1¼ miles (2km) to a single-storey cottage called Westfield. As Westfield cottage is approached the **Brotherstones** can be seen 1 mile (1.6km) to the west on higher ground.

Smailholm Smailholm is old Northumbrian 'smael ham', meaning small village. A solid church nestles on the south side of the hamlet.

The Brotherstones Standing stones dated 2000BC, the Brotherstones are set as a pair 42½ft (13m) apart on Brotherstone Hill. The larger stone to the southeast stands 8¼ft (2.5m) high, its brother reaching 5¼ft (1.6m). Both are supported by packed rocks at the base, and taper at the top. Lower down the shoulder of Brotherstone Hill is a much bulkier stone, 6½ft (2m) high and known as the Cowstone. The Cowstone is aligned exactly with the two Brotherstones and Hareheugh Craigs, strengthening the theory that the Brotherstones and the Cowstone have clearly defined astronomical functions connected with the summer and winter solstices.

At Westfield take the farm road to the left, i.e. southeast, rising gently for ¾ mile (1.2km) to gaunt and austere **Smailholm Tower**. Perched at 680ft (207m) above sea level on the rocky outcrops, it commands extensive views of the Tweed Valley, lower Teviotdale and the eastern and central Cheviots. **Sandyknowe** farm lies a few hundred yards to the east of the old pele tower and is easily reached on the farm road. Please ensure the gates are left as you found them. Pass through the steading and follow the narrow road northeast to Mein's Plantation, a small mixed wood on both sides of the road.

At a sharp right-angle junction in the road turn northwest, i.e. left, follow the twisting lane for 1½ miles (2.4km) to return to the village of Smailholm.

Sandyknowe Today a thriving, well-managed Borders farm, from 1776–9 young Walter Scott spent many happy months with his paternal grandfather at Sandyknowe, and it was here that the seeds were sown in that most romantic of young minds. The close-by village of Smailholm is in the third canto of 'Marmion', and also the ballad 'The Eve of St John'.

Smailholm Tower A fine example of a Border pele tower. First constructed in the 15th century, it was a Pringle stronghold, with the first recorded assault in 1546 by Sir John Ellerker, who laid siege to 'Smallum towre'. Defensive rather than offensive, the simple rectangular tower of whinstone walls 6½ft (2m) thick, and red sandstone cornerstones, stands 56½ft (17m) high. It is five storeys in all, with small windows and only a stout door on the ground floor. Surrounding the tower stands a substantial enclosing wall with a narrow gate at the west end. To the northwest stood outbuildings, built in 1650 by Scott of Harden, a direct ancestor of Sir Walter Scott. Today the tower houses the ghosts of the past in a fine display of Borders dress, both military and domestic. (Open April–September, Monday–Saturday 9.30am–6.00pm, Sunday 2.30pm–6.00pm. Winter – weekends only.)

Smailholm Tower above Sandyknowe

WALK 20 – Dryburgh Abbey and the Winding Tweed

Scott's View, Bemersyde, Wallace's Statue, Dryburgh Abbey, St Boswells, River Tweed, Mertoun Bridge

Distance	4¾ miles (7.6km)
Height Gain	98ft (30m)
Start/Finish	Scott's View, GR 594342/Mertoun Bridge, GR 609320
Grade	1
Walking Time	3 hours
Maps	OS 1:50 000 Landranger sheet 74, Kelso & Coldstream Harvey 1:40 000 Walker's Route, St Cuthbert's Way
Accommodation	Kelso and St Boswells provide varied accommodation and food
Parking	On the fringes of the viewing layby at Scott's View, GR 594342

Rich in scenic beauty and medieval history, and bursting with wildlife, this journey provides easy walking on good paths, the exception being the final stretch of riverside path south from the golf course to Mertoun Bridge, which is liable to flood after exceptionally heavy rains.

A wistful linear stroll from Sir Walter Scott's favoured viewpoint, by winding country lane and tree-lined dirt track, to the colossus of Scotland's national hero, William Wallace, then to Dryburgh where stands the most haunting of all Borders abbeys. From here a footbridge leads onto the banks of one of the Tweed's great windings – the Dryburgh Crescent.

The Route Start the walk at **Scott's View**, taking the road south (note the standing stone in the field on the right) to the village of Bemersyde where well-tended cottages protect the entrance to **Bemersyde House**.

Five hundred yards (457m) south of Bemersyde our route turns right, at a parking space, into a small signposted copse, and leads west for 450yds (411m), at which point walkers will be stopped dead in their tracks by a statue in red sandstone of **William Wallace**, gazing west to the triple peaks of the Eildon Hills. Turn sharp left, just beyond the colossus, onto a beech- and conifer-lined pathway descending south to the village of Dryburgh. Below the tiny

Scott's View Scott's View stands at 748ft (228m) above sea level on the western flank of Bemersyde Hill, and is where Sir Walter Scott, the Borders' most outstanding romantic, paused many times to drink his fill of the scenery. Far below, a picturesque horseshoe of the Tweed encloses the site of the Celtic monastery of Old Melrose, and beyond, the triple peaks of the Eildon Hills (Walk 21) spear the skyline. Lockhart, Sir Walter's son-in-law and biographer, recounts the oft-repeated tale of when Scott was taken to his final resting place in the confines of Dryburgh Abbey. The horses drawing the hearse paused at this very spot, as indeed they had done many times in the past. This time Scott was to have his final view of his beloved Borders.

Bemersyde House Bemersyde House has been the hereditary seat of the Haig family for over 800 years. Indeed, the Borders' own Nostradamus, Thomas of Ercildoune (Earlston), known locally as Thomas the Rhymer, prophesied, 'Betide, Betide, whate'er Betide, There shall aye be a Haig in Bemersyde.' Only the keep of the mansion is of great antiquity. A tower from the 16th century remains, with the bulk of the house mainly 18th century.

William Wallace statue and engraved urn Thirty-two feet (9.8m) high and mounted on a plinth of local red sandstone, the inscription at his feet proclaims: 'William Wallace – Great Patriot Hero ill Requited Chief'. Erected in 1814 by the Earl of Buchan (an eccentric member of the house of Scott), history relates that Sir Walter was not best pleased by his kinsman's tribute to Wallace.

village, on a horseshoe of the Tweed, stand the sorely mutilated remains of **Dryburgh Abbey**. To the west of the abbey an hotel, to the north a stud farm, and in the summer months an invasion of motorised travellers.

Leave the village, left, at the post office corner, descending past a turreted stone **gateway and iron gates** to the riverside and the **footbridge** over the silvery Tweed, overlooked by the 'Muses of Nature' housed within a columned rotunda. Once over the

Dryburgh Abbey Dryburgh Abbey was completed in 1140 for and by the White Friars during the reign of David I. It was finally sacked and brought to its knees in 1545 by the infamous Earl of Hertford, during Henry VIII's 'rough wooing' of the Borders. Dryburgh fell, along with the abbeys of Kelso, Jedburgh and Melrose. What little remained was ravaged in later years by the followers of John Knox, an act which prompted the Border prayer:

> From all the knockdown race of Knox's
> Good Lord deliver us.

Within the shattered walls Sir Walter and son-in-law Lockhart lie at rest, close to the Tweed and always within reach of that sound said by Lockhart of Scott to be, 'of all others most delicious to his ear'. Only the Scotts of Abbotsford, the Haigs of Bemersyde, and the Erskines, Earls of Buchan, have the right of burial within the abbey. (Open to the public all year round.)

Gateway and iron gates A Latin inscription states, 'HOC POMARIUM SUA MANUSATUM PARENTUBUS SUIS OPTIMIS SAC', translated as, 'An apple orchard planted by my own hand in memory of my excellent parents', by David Stuart Erskine, Earl of Buchan. The gate bears the Erskine coat-of-arms.

Footbridge A former chain bridge, financed by David Stuart Erskine, Earl of Buchan, for £7201 and erected by T & T Smith of Melrose in 1817, which had but a short life, collapsing into the Tweed during the violent storms of January 1818.

Tweed turn sharp left onto a waymarked path (the waymark is the Celtic cross of St Cuthbert's Way), then after 100yds (91m) fork right onto a waymarked, undulating tree-lined riverside path running with the Dryburgh Crescent for ¾ mile (1.2km). After crossing a small wooden bridge, swing right, away from the river, and ascend steep-sided Hawthorndene to temporarily leave St Cuthbert's Way onto a public footpath, left, and rise for 35 paces to a wall/waymarked wooden steps. Beyond the steps the path leads between gardens and trees to Braeheads and **Mrs Buller's** (strategically placed) **seat**. Pass the seat and continue southeast, initially on the pathway, to a tarmac lane that rejoins St Cuthbert's Way above the clubhouse of St Boswells Golf Club. Continue with the lane, enjoying the Eildon Hills over the left shoulder, and at the junction ahead turn left with the waymark to descend past the clubhouse to a waymark on the right directing walkers: 'Onto the golf course – keep close to the fence – look out for flying golf balls.'

Mrs Buller's seat This seat offers explosive views of the triple peaks of Trimontium – the Eildon Hills – home to prehistoric man and Roman, and from where Sir Walter Scott, 'could identify 43 places famous in battle and verse'.

Continue as directed northeast, with the golf course and the Tweed beyond always on the walkers left, for ²/₃ mile (1km). Eventually leave the golf course before rejoining the **riverbank** as it swings southeast into yet

Riverbank A stretch of the Tweed rich in birdlife and flowering plants. Said Lockhart, in his *Life of Scott*, 'The sound of all others most delicious to his ear, the gentle ripple of the Tweed over its pebbles.'

Mertoun Bridge Carries the St Boswells to Kelso road. Built 1839–41 by William Smith of Melrose, engineer, and designer James Slight of Edinburgh, it is a construction of five arches with piers of local stone. Originally the arches were of wood.

another dramatic loop. The riverside path, narrow in places and wet when the river is in flood, runs southeast with a fence and the River Tweed to the five arches of **Mertoun Bridge**.

William Wallace's statue

WALK 21 – Three Peaks (Trimontium) above Melrose

Melrose Abbey, Priorwood Gardens, Eildon Hills, Melrose

Distance	4¾ miles (7.6km)
Height Gain	1696ft (517m)
Start/Finish	Melrose Abbey; Melrose
Grade	3, on account of steep ascents and descents
Walking Time	3 hours
Maps	OS 1:25 000 Explorer 338, Galashiels, Selkirk & Melrose
	OS 1:50 000 Landranger sheet 73, Peebles, Galashiels & Selkirk
Accommodation	Melrose – hotels, bed-and-breakfasts, youth hostel, caravan site
Parking	Free car park between Melrose Youth Hostel and the abbey

The triple peaks of the Eildon Hills stand in solitary splendour in the centre of the enclave that is the Borders. Low in height yet so prominent, they unconsciously throw out a challenge to the walker.

The pathways are good, although one or two short, steep sections can be very slippery when wet or frozen. The three peaks can be traversed, when dry, in walking shoes or lightweight boots. Choose a dry day with good visibility.

The Route Prominent Cistercian **Melrose Abbey** provides an ideal starting point for the walk, seen from the free car park between Melrose Youth Hostel and the abbey. ▶

Priorwood Gardens A section of this garden is devoted to various species of apple trees, spanning nearly 2000 years of apple growing.

This journey is a delightful mix of an ancient abbey and pleasing Border town, with the steep cones of the Eildon Hills providing the challenge, the views, and the isolation.

Should you wish, visit the abbey and nearby **Priorwood Gardens** after the ascent of the Eildon Hills.

Melrose Abbey In the front rank of Scottish monastic buildings, Melrose Abbey was founded and endowed in 1136 by King David I, in succession to the Celtic monastery at Old Melrose. The first Cistercian settlement to be established in Scotland, it lay in the path of the English invaders and was repeatedly devastated. Robert Bruce bequeathed not only money to restore the building, but also his heart. After 1385 the abbey was rebuilt under the direction of the French master mason Jean Moreau, only to be finally plundered in 1544–5 by the Earl of Hertford. An appealing selection of humorous figures adorns the exterior walls: a mason with his mallet, a cook with his ladle, a fat monk, and high on a gargoyle a pig playing the bagpipes!

Melrose Abbey

Walk southwest from the car park into the triangular market place with its weathered market cross. From the opposite corner Lilliesleaf Road, south, passes under the Melrose bypass road bridge, and after 200yds (193m) signs on the left- and right-hand walls signal 'St Cuthbert's Way Eildon Walk'. Turn sharp left down a narrow stepped vennel (alley) and over a small footbridge to rise left and right on a waymarked, wooden-stepped (133 of them) way ascending south-southeast.

The waymarked ascent, now a grass-and-earth fenceside pathway, makes for the northern (or left) Eildon Hill directly above. Several gates allow direct waymarked passage, finally emerging onto the grass-and-gorse-clad lower slopes of the Eildons, before winding waymarked St Cuthbert's (Trimontium) Way leading south to the saddle connecting the two highest Eildons. Once on this central ridge a choice of tracks and paths (some waymarked) greet the walker and allow easy passage southwest to the start of the upper reaches of Eildon Mid Hill, the coned, cairned and highest of the three hills, and then via a choice of two visible dirt-and-stone trods to the unseen summit.

I have found the right fork provides a slightly easier ascent and rewards the walker with fine views to the north and west. Although the summit of this central **Eildon** is only 1386ft (422m) above sea level, the exhilaration it provides totally exonerates the hill for its lack of height. ▶

Leave the summit and descend steeply in a south-westerly direction along a path through the heather that is narrow and in places unstable underfoot (use Cauldshiels Loch below as a marker). Once the flatter ground is reached, a distinct path curves east and then

A directional disc by the trig point on the central Eildon, though worn and faded in places, points out the items of interest on the distant horizons.

The Eildon Hills Heather clad in a landscape where the hills are mainly grass covered, the Eildons (pronounced 'eeldons') are volcanic in origin. Not one area of the Borders escapes the gaze of the Eildon climber, nor is there a summit in the Borders from which the Eildons cannot be seen. Sir Walter Scott, who frequently walked his guests on the Eildons' flanks, claimed he could 'point out 43 places famous in war and verse'.

Below the northern summit the ramparts of a large hill fort can be seen. Enclosing an area of 40 acres (16 hectares), this Iron Age settlement was the headquarters of the Selgovia tribe. It has long been a mystery as to how so many hundreds existed on the hilltop without a recognised water supply – surely it wasn't carried up the hill every day?

129

south, i.e. right, at the cross tracks ascending steadily to the heather-covered top of the lowest Eildon – Eildon Wester Hill, 1216ft (371m). Even from this modest height the views across the Tweed Valley to the Cheviots beyond are most rewarding.

Return north and northeast towards the central ridge on the distinct heathery path of ascent, then via a wide dirt track through a pleasing mix of deciduous and coniferous trees. On the ridge top at a crossroads of paths (complete with Trimontium waymarks) go straight across, right, via an ascending northeast track to the final grass-and-heather-clad North Eildon summit 1326ft (404m). ◀

North Eildon has a tidy summit cairn and surrounding Iron Age encampment.

Descend east-northeast via the left of two summit paths, in places very steep, which in wet conditions can become extremely unstable. Continue with the waymarked way, from grass to gorse, and as trees are approached swing onto the left, i.e. roughly westbound, pathway contouring west on the lower slopes of the North Eildon to rejoin the outward stepped path of St Cuthbert's Way. Turn right and descend with the fence-side track, and eventually the 133 steps, into Melrose.

Eildon Mid Hill

WALK 22 – Three Brethren and Border Mischief

Peel, Broomy Law, Three Brethren, Yair and Yair Bridge, the Banks of the Tweed to Peel

Distance	7½ miles (12.1km)
Height Gain	1123ft (342m)
Start/Finish	Peel village, GR 436349, below the A707 Selkirk road
Grade	2 in dry conditions; 3 in winter
Walking Time	5 hours
Maps	OS 1:25 000 Explorer 338, Galashiels, Selkirk & Melrose
	OS 1:50 000 Landranger sheet 73, Peebles, Galashiels & Selkirk
Accommodation	Clovenfords and Selkirk – a selection of hotels, inns and bed-and-breakfasts
Parking	Forest Enterprise car park, 250yds (229m) west from Ashiestiel Bridge

This route reveals the central Border landscape and peers into the valleys of the Tweed and Ettrick, particularly from the site of Three Brethren. The final leg follows the line of the Tweed for a gentle stroll by riverside and oak-lined track. Said the Fairy Queen to Thomas the Rhymer,

A delightful walk of ever-changing vistas in the central Border country.

> Gin ye wad meet wi' me again,
> Gang to the bonny banks a' Fairnilee.

The Route Peel is reached via the A707 Innerleithen to Selkirk road, crossing the Tweed to Peel and Ashiestiel over a single-arched stone bridge. Walk west along the quiet, tree-lined road, with its recently built private houses on the site of Peel Hospital, for ½ mile (0.8km) to the signpost 'Williamhope'. Turn immediately left at the signpost and rise with the narrow winding road, south, for 1½ miles (2.4km). Note statuesque Peel House on the left overlooking hurrying Glenkinnon Burn, flanked by a fine

Peel Peel is the site of a hospital built during the Second World War, later to act as a general hospital serving the Borders region until the 1980s. The mansion of Peel House can be seen through the trees, and a little distance west stands Ashiestiel on the banks of the Tweed, home of Sir Walter Scott before Abbotsford: 'Here were spent the seven happiest years of his life.'

collection of deciduous trees, before passing Shirra's Knowe (Sir Walter Scott connections). At the southwestern corner of the coniferous plantation on Craig Hill, before Capper Cleuch on the right, leave the road to turn left and pass through a five-bar gate 30yds (27.5m) from the road.

A somewhat overgrown grassy track through the declining deciduous trees crosses a feeder of Glenkinnon Burn – relatively dry in summer – to begin our ascent on a fell track for the first 914yds (1km) on a bearing of 203° to the ridge below flat-domed Broomy Law. At the first rise a five-bar metal gate allows passage onto the open fell, where an overgrown grassy track climbs steadily south through rushes, bracken and heather. As height is gained a large stone, **William's Cross**, can be seen to the right, and ahead two sad and lonely trees signal a large **cairn** on the skyline. This cairn is not only of great interest, but also acts as a marker. Continue south past the square cairn to breast the ridge and meet the

William's Cross and cairn The 'cross' is in reality a great stone positioned south of Glenkinnon Burn, and reputed to be the spot where Sir William Hope Douglas, knight of Liddesdale, was put to the sword by a kinsman in 1353. Half a mile (0.8km) to the south and 350ft (107m) above the 'cross' stands a square cairn, 7ft (2m) high and topped with a single stone on its edge. A plaque disputes the position of William's Cross: 'By Tradition, This is where Sir W Hope Douglas was slain', Glendinning, 1913. Sir William Hope Douglas was also known as 'the Flower of Chivalry', a title he ill deserved, for in 1342 he dragged Sir Alexander Ramsay, the Sheriff of Teviotdale, from the sheriff's court in Hawick, incarcerating him in Hermitage Castle. Sir Alexander starved to death in 17 days.

Southern Upland Way on an old drove road below the heather-clad summit of Broomy Law.

Turn left, i.e. east, and follow the clear grass path of the Southern Upland Way (waymarked with a thistle) high above the

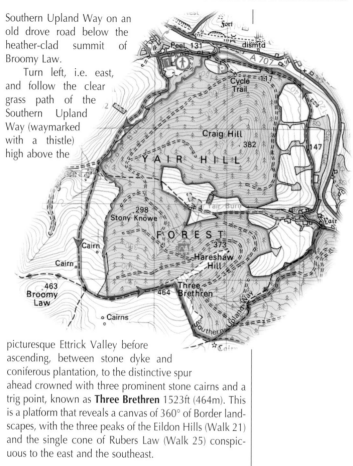

picturesque Ettrick Valley before ascending, between stone dyke and coniferous plantation, to the distinctive spur ahead crowned with three prominent stone cairns and a trig point, known as **Three Brethren** 1523ft (464m). This is a platform that reveals a canvas of 360° of Border landscapes, with the three peaks of the Eildon Hills (Walk 21) and the single cone of Rubers Law (Walk 25) conspicuous to the east and the southeast.

Three Brethren A fine vantage point capped by three very fine conical cairns, built to mark the limits of the estates of Yair, Philiphaugh and the burgh of Selkirk. From this distinctive top the rolling hills of the Borders flow gently to distant horizons.

The restored 'Three Brethren'

Descend south-southeast on a stone-and-dirt track, with a cleared, brashed forest on the left and a fence on the right, leading to a col by Little Crib that is the focal point of four pathways, with a five-bar gate and stiles. Our descending pathway – as directed by the thistle symbol and yellow arrowhead – swings left, i.e. north-east, to cross a waymarked major forest road, finally spilling onto a 'turning circle' of forest roads. Cross the bare earth circle to a waymarked pathway that runs northeast by Friar's Croft, with Shorthope Burn on the right, initially on a grassy, bracken-lined, tree-cleared pathway. Later pass through a stand of silver birch, flanked by conifers, and swing northeast with the well-drained shady path through a pleasing mix of broadleaves and a minimum of conifers, emerging onto a tarmac road leading east-southeast with the Southern Upland Way to **Yair Bridge**, straddling the picturesque waters of the Tweed. ◀

Just beyond Yair Bridge is a roadside car park and picnic area for Forest Enterprise's Lindinny Wood, with details of an alternative walk to the Southern Upland Way and Three Brethren.

Do not cross the bridge, but return west on the lane, marked 'Private Road', past the entrance to **Yair House**. Continue west with the ascending narrow tarmac, past the point where we emerged onto the lane that led to Yair

Yair Bridge and Yair House Built in 1762 to replace a ford near the mouth of Caddon Water, Yair Bridge has been repaired many times but never widened. A narrow structure with no footpath, its three arches remain exactly as they were in 1762. Yair House stands on the south bank of the Tweed surrounded by elegant deciduous trees. Built in 1788, it took its name from the hill and the Forest of Yair to the west. On the opposite river-bank is the haunting ruin of Fairnilee, where Alison Rutherford wrote her matchless version of 'The Flowers of the Forest', the old lament for Flodden. The room where she wrote the lyric is preserved to this day.

Bridge, to pass extensive farm buildings on the left. Ignore the farm lane on the left and continue northwest for a short distance to a T-junction. Turn right, rising slightly to pass beneath a small ornamental arched footbridge, to walk northeast and east on a farm track flanked with venerable broadleaves. Ahead on the left stand two solitary conifers that mark the final leg to Peel. The 2 mile (3.2km) walk over a wide farm track, stony in places, travels with the line of the river north, turning west beyond Woodpark Plantation through the conifers on the lower slopes of Caddon Shank. Return via a single line of fine oak and a five-bar metal gate, plus sightings of single-arched Ashiestiel Bridge, to our starting point, Peel.

Yair Bridge over the River Tweed

WALK 23 – The Cheese Well and the Bear Gates of Traquair

*Traquair, Minch Moor, Bold Rig, West Bold,
Haugh Head, Traquair*

Distance	10 miles (16.1km)
Height Gain	1288ft (393m)
Start/Finish	Traquair village
Grade	2; 3 in adverse conditions
Walking Time	5½–6 hours
Maps	OS 1:25 000 Pathfinder 460, Innerleithen
	OS 1:50 000 Landranger sheet 73, Peebles, Galashiels & Selkirk
Accommodation	Refreshments and varied accommodation available in Innerleithen and Walkerburn
Parking	Traquair village hall car park

This route along the historic Minchmoor Road rewards with spectacular views from Minch Moor summit.

A fine bracing walk over one of the oldest routes through the Borders, historic Minchmoor Road, now a section of the waymarked Southern Upland Way. Passing Minch Moor 1860ft (570m) and the Cheese Well 1564ft (477m) – home to the little people – along the way, we later descend on forest roads through Elibank and Traquair Forest to the Tweed Valley and the oldest fortified mansion house in Scotland, Traquair House. Although the paths and roads are particularly good underfoot, walking boots are recommended.

The Route Traquair lies on the B709 1½ miles (2.4km) south of Innerleithen. At the Traquair war memorial turn south, i.e. left, onto a secondary road leading to the village hall and the school. Start the walk from the village hall, turning south to follow the road to the school. At the fork a Southern Upland Way waymark (a thistle) indicates straight ahead for Minch Moor. Ascend steadily southeast, squeezing between the first of many plantations flanked by two stone dykes, indicating that this was an old drove road of some standing. Before

Traquair and Traquair House The name Traquair means 'hamlet of the Quair'. The village, dating back to Roman times, was once larger than Peebles or Innerleithen. A royal hunting lodge was built on the site of Traquair House, the last monarch to hunt from there being Mary Queen of Scots in 1566. The Bear Gates are perhaps the most publicised feature of the house, supposedly closed after 'the '45' by an earl of Traquair loyal to the Stuart cause, never to be reopened until a Catholic Stuart sat on the British throne. This romantic myth is, however, no more than a myth. The gates were closed by the seventh earl who, after the death of his dear countess, decreed that they should not be reopened until a worthy successor was found.

conifer-clad Dumbetha Knowe the 'road' swings left, i.e. ascending east on gated (use the wicket gates) **Minchmoor Road** to pass Minchmoor Bothy (six bunks) by a major forest road cross-roads. Continue rising east with the

plentiful waymarks through a replanted plantation before reaching an open area of heather moor below the summit dome of Minch Moor.

Minchmoor Road This moorland route has been traversed for centuries by a variety of pedestrians. Monks from Kelso Abbey walked this way to their lands at Lesmahagow, Lanarkshire, in the early 1200s. In 1296 Edward I and his English army used the route to Peebles, and in 1645 Montrose's broken and battered troops staggered over its windy fells after the Battle of Philiphaugh. In more recent times it has been the route used by drovers on the way south to England, via Hawick, with their black Highland cattle.

Contour east and east-southeast to cross a small burn at GR 357336, where 10yds (9m) to the right lies the **Cheese Well**, surrounded by heather and two marker stones. Several hundred yards east of the Cheese Well turn right at the finger post onto a path ascending through heather for ¼ mile (0.4km) to the cairn and trig point marking the flat summit of Minch Moor. On a clear day spectacular views reward the climb to the top of Minch Moor – of the Moorfoots, the Manor and Moffat Hills and Yarrow Valley. Return to Minchmoor Road (Southern Upland Way), turning right onto the broad track between regimented ranks of the conifers. Three-quarters of a mile (1.2km) of gentle descent on the 'thistle' path arrives at a wide forest road by a clearing. At this junction leave the Southern Upland Way by turning left, i.e. north.

The Cheese Well It has long been the custom in the Borders to keep in with a well's fairies, or 'little people', by leaving a morsel of cheese to ensure a safe and successful journey, hence the name Cheese Well. Two flat lichen-encrusted stones by the spring, the diamond-shaped one bearing the thistle, and each with the inscription 'Cheese Well', bear witness to this custom.

Descend with the forest road for 1½ miles (2.4km). First northwest, then north along the open flank of Bold Rig to Shiel Craig to a T-junction, turning sharply onto the road from the right leading southwest and south then northeast and north to the valley floor and Minchmoor Burn. Three-hundred yards along the burnside the road

forks – take the left-hand road alongside the silver birch by Bold Burn, for 1¼ very pleasant miles (2km), to reach an engineering works and eight wooden Forestry Commission houses at the T-junction of Glenbenna and an unclassified road.

The Southern Upland Way from Traquair to Minch Moor

At the junction turn left, to follow the quiet and narrow road past West Bold farm towards Innerleithen. Note the fine old trees on the left, and the notice stating 'Plora Wood is managed by the Woodland Trust', with an invitation to enjoy a ramble through it. To the right the silvery Tweed hurries along the valley floor, with **Walkerburn** across the river and the pyramid of Cairn Hill providing a distinctive backdrop. When **Innerleithen**

Walkerburn and Innerleithen Woollen towns both, Innerleithen's first mill dates back to 1790, opened by Alexander Brodie, and Walkerburn's was opened in 1854 by Henry Ballantyne. Innerleithen proudly displays a plaque stating that Robert Burns visited on 14 May 1787, perhaps to sample the waters of the oldest spa in Scotland. A printing works dating back to 1840 is open to the public. Walkerburn houses the Scottish Museum of Textiles.

The Cheese Well,
Minch Moor

hoves into view at the junction of the Tweed with Leithen Water, below Cadon Bank wood, pause to look west over the white tollhouse to the conifers of Cardrona Forest cloaking the heights of Wallace's Hill. And when the B709 from Innerleithen is met, pause to look north over the Tweed, Innerleithen and craggy Pirn Craig to conical Lee Pen, before following the road south-south-west to Traquair and the village hall. If time allows, I would strongly advise a visit to the Bear Gates of Traquair House, ½ mile (0.8km) north of the village, and signposted.

WALK 24 – Venerable Beech and Waterloo Monument

Harestanes Countryside Visitor Complex, Woodside, Peniel Heugh, Waterloo Monument, Woodside, Harestanes

Distance	4 miles (6.4km)
Height Gain	561ft (171m)
Start/Finish	Harestanes Visitor Complex, GR 641245, 1mile (1.6km) east of Ancrum via the B6400
Grade	1
Walking Time	2½ hours
Maps	OS 1:25 000 Pathfinder 474, Jedburgh
	OS 1:50 000 Landranger sheet 74, Kelso & Coldstream
Accommodation	Nearby Ancrum for food and accommodation
Parking	Harestanes Visitor Complex

High above the River Teviot, several miles north of Jedburgh, a distinctive monument thrusts skywards from the rocky outcrops of Peniel Heugh, offering a complete circle of Border country views, particularly of Teviotdale, the Cheviots, the Eildons and Tweeddale. This short, there-and-back ramble, in which ascents are never too steep or too sustained, allows the walker to complete the waymarked route in light walking footwear.

The Route Start from Scottish Borders Harestanes Visitor Complex (closed in the winter, but not the car park) barely ²/₃ mile (1km) east from the A68(T). Leave the car park north, as directed by a 'Walks' finger post, via a footpath, parallel with the roadway and adjacent timber yard, that displays at its start a notice giving the colour codes of the walks available. Our route to Peniel Heugh is waymarked with green arrowheads.

Take the path north, passing beneath a venerable pine – an example of the many fine specimens encountered en route – to

141

the road junction and swing right, i.e. east, via a stone-and-dirt path shared initially with long-distance St Cuthbert's Way, as it threads between avenues of stately beech, oak and conifer. Traffic on the adjacent B6400 can barely be heard and rarely seen as we cross a foot-bridge, pass an old pergola and an occasional seat, accompanied by birdsong and the ever-present, firmly anchored giant trees. Emerge onto an estate road leading south to Monteviot House and Gardens.

Waymarks direct left, i.e. north, between two sets of heraldic ornamental stone gateposts and over the B6400 to walk north on the tarmac drive, flanked by oak and rhododendron, for 274yds (250m) to the tidy estate house and kennels of Woodside. As the house is reached, branch right at the Y-junction, as indicated, onto a rising, curving cart track between a coniferous plantation on the left and a cultivated field on the right. The flat summit of Carter Fell (Walk 16) is clearly visible, straddling the Border Ridge directly south over the walker's right shoulder, before meeting and crossing a north/south tarmac road half-right and then left to pass through a five-bar gate into a coniferous and deciduous woodland. ◄

Note the restriction notice forbidding vehicles and asking walkers and horse riders to stick to the designated paths, plus keep dogs on a lead.

The waymarked cart track climbs northeast through yet more established trees – beech and oak predominate – making the way shaded and cool, yet never claustro-phobic, and allowing fine views behind into the delights of Teviotdale, with coned Rubers Law above Denholm particularly prominent. Keep with the waymarks that direct north-northeast at each fork as height is gained and **views** extend. Ahead the sky gleams through the now predominating conifers, revealing also the grass-and-rock-capped summit rim of our destination – Peniel Heugh. Another left fork takes us ever nearer, and the final fork reveals our first close-up of the towering monu-ment. Continue left, and after a dip in the track swing half-right with a narrowing pathway leading to a wicket gate, then via a pathway between a stone dyke and wire fence and a second gate to the summit of Peniel Heugh and its crowning glory, the extraordinary **Waterloo Monument**.

Views from Peniel Heugh From east to south the horizon is filled with the rounded summits and ridges of the Cheviot Hills, including at the eastern end the summit of Muckle Cheviot (Walks 2 and 9, magnetic bearing 79°) plus Hownam Law (Walk 11, bearing 105°) and at its western end Peel Fell 1975ft (602m), (bearing 170°). West and southwestern views run through to the Ettrick Forest and delightful Teviotdale, with triangular Rubers Law (Walk 25, bearing 200°) above Denholm prominent, while to the northwest we have the three peaks of the Eildon Hills (Walk 21, bearing 301°) as the centre point. West runs Tweeddale to the Tweedsmuir Hills and Peebles, and northeast the rather flat Lammermuir Hills provide the northern bastion of the fertile and green valley of the Tweed.

The summit of Peniel Heugh 777ft (237m) is ringed on its south and west flanks by fine tall trees, though from its rocky top the views are fortunately not obstructed. The remains of two nearby Iron Age hill forts and the visible earthworks and embankments of an ancient encampment or fort (thought to be Roman, it overlooks Dere Street, Walks 14 and 15) can be seen 527yds (500m) to the east. Far beyond the Beaumont Valley into the Cheviot Hills is also visible. After a complete external inspection of the monument (it is unsafe to enter), pause before leaving to enjoy the wide sweeps of Tweed and Teviot, surrounded by the Border hills. Leave the rocky outcrops on the summit to rejoin the now descending path, our route of

Waterloo Monument This spectacular 150ft (48m) round tower of local quarried whinstone, topped with a wooden pagoda, was raised in 1815 by the Marquess of Lothian and his tenants to celebrate the Duke of Wellington's victory over Napoleon Bonaparte at Waterloo. A stout metal door prevents entry to the tower, as the structure is unsafe at higher levels. Wall plaques relate in detail the dimensions of the tower, together with the name of the stonemason from the village of Maxton. The seat of the Marquesses of Lothian, Monteviot House, lies to the south, surrounded by an impressive collection of trees that speaks volumes for the estate's skills in forest management.

The Waterloo Monument, Peniel Heugh

ascent, and return with the arrowheads on the reverse side of the marker posts towards Harestanes. After entering the woodland walk north of Monteviot House, continue to the T-junction finger post and swing left, i.e. south, alongside a burn to meet the driveway running west from Monteviot House to beyond Harestanes. For the final yards walk with the roadside footpath to return to the complex and well-earned refreshment.

WALK 25 – An Iron Age Fort, Roman Signal Station and Covenanter's Pulpit

Denholm, Rubers Law, Denholm Dean, Denholm

Distance	5 miles (8km)
Height Gain	1096ft (334m)
Start/Finish	Denholm, east of Hawick on the A698
Grade	2
Walking Time	3 hours
Map	OS 1:25 000 Pathfinder 485 Hawick & Area
	OS 1:50 000 Landranger sheet 80, Cheviot Hills & Kielder Water
Accommodation	Denholm – inns and bed-and-breakfasts and meals
Parking	Denholm Green – avoid restricting access for others

Although short in stature, a mere 1392ft (424m), solitary, coned Rubers Law is fine of form, and thanks to its central position overlooking the Teviot Valley, an outstanding Border hill.

Starting and finishing in the picturesque village of Denholm, the way is via country lanes, woodland, and pasture paths alongside gated and stiled stone walls and wire fences, and is never too severe until the summit of heather trods and rocky outcrops is met. Half the descent is via the ascent route, while the remainder is circular, with the final stage through a section of picturesque, arboreal Denholm Dean. The dean not only provides a pleasing addition to the ascent of Rubers Law, but also, independently, a fine short woodland and burnside walk of 2¼ miles (3.6km).

The Route Start the ascent of Rubers Law from the green in the centre of **Denholm**, on which stands the prominent monument to **Dr John Leyden**, and with the main street walk east passing the Fox and Hounds to swing right with the main road – a road that is soon abandoned as it veers east. Our route begins its steady, straight ascent east via a house-lined tarmac

Rubers Law is a 'weel-ken't' central landmark that provides 360° views of the Border country, and whose summit can be seen from the majority of walks included in this guide.

Denholm Denholm derives from the Old English 'denum', meaning 'at the valley'. This charming village stands at the confluence of Dean Burn and the River Teviot. Teviotdale was renowned for its fairies, or 'little people', and witches, with the last Denholm 'witch' buried at nearby Spital (just beyond Denholmhill Wood) in the early 1600s. In the 1700s flax, for weaving into linen cloth, was grown on the common land, and in the mid-1800s Denholm was a thriving, busy community supporting five inns and a lady spirit dealer.

lane – the Loaning – and then by a stony track waymarked 'Scottish Public Right of Way Society to Bedrule' to a T-junction ahead. Here, with the yellow waymark, we swing left with the grass-and-weed-lined track northeast and later east via the grassed-over and scrub-lined track to meet the coniferous plantation, now visible above us to the right. Views are now opening up, in particular to the north to the domed bulk of the two Minto Hills, and northeast, where the prominent tower of the Waterloo Monument on Peniel Heugh (Walk 24) can be seen.

As we approach the northeast corner of the conifers of Denholmhill Wood and pass through a swing gate, the way narrows to a single-stone-laid path that rises southeast, on the perimeter of the established conifers, to the horizon ahead. Two-thirds of the way along this perimeter path, marked by a single hawthorn bush alongside a wild rose on the left, and on the right a wide grass track leading southwest through the mature, well-spaced conifers, we turn right to pass through the conifers on a pleasant, narrowing but distinct path for approximately 875yds (800m). This trod swings left and right as the coned summit of Rubers Law comes into view to the south through the

Dr John Leyden On the village green stands the 1861 memorial to one of Denham's most famous citizens. The son of a shepherd, and a great friend of Sir Walter Scott, Dr John Leyden was a poet, a collector of ballads, a linguist, a surgeon, a professor in Bengal and a judge in Calcutta. He died at the age of 36 in Java. Another Leyden of Denholm was William, a well-known landlord, athlete and pedestrian who in the 1860s walked to Innerleithen, took part in the annual games, and returned the same day – a round trip of 50 miles (80km).

Monument to Dr John Leyden

trees, before emerging, from beneath the coniferous umbrella, at a T-junction X (an important point on the descent route – see top of p.149) of Gled'swing Strip and Rubers Law Covert. Continue SW to the boundary fence and exit the woods X by a gate, then go left by a small stile into a field lined on its left by a wiremesh fence and a stonewall.

Our way is now an overall 'gradually steepening' 1 mile (1.6km) south-southeast to the small hillock of Black Dod, with wall and fence on our immediate left, via what appears to be a wallside pathway. Do keep to this grass track, and if you walk with a dog please keep the lead on as these pastures are grazing grounds for cattle and sheep. As we ascend not only does Rubers Law get ever closer, but also the canvas of Teviotdale is filled by ever-expanding views of the Border country. A field pond to the right is passed as we leave the conifer strips behind, and the contour lines narrow when Black Dod is reached. From the last of the recent plantations bear half-right to rise steeply with one of the several paths leading to a broken drystone wall on the immediate horizon.

Once reached, walk with the aged wall to its corner ahead and follow the narrow track to a small but pictur-esque copse of aged, gnarled and contorted Caledonian pine clustered below the heather line of the northern, rumpled rock summit of **Rubers Law**, a hill that has the history of centuries imprinted on its craggy profile: 'Dark Rubers Law, that lifts his head sublime, Rugged and hoary with the wrecks of time'. From this point a

---

Rubers Law Rubers Law is a dark and distinct hill that stands alone. Short in height but strong in character, it is topped with the relics of previous ages – an Iron Age fort and Roman signal station. It also has 'the gift of Cheviot' – the power to draw rain clouds to its summit.

When Ruberslaw puts on his cap
And the Dunion on her hood,
Then a' the wives o'Teviotdale
Ken there will be a flood.

selection of narrow trods through heather quicken the step and ease the final ascent. However, the ascent should be approached with care, for many of the rocky mini summits have on one side immediate and unexpected steep drops. Surrounding the one bearing the white trig point, I counted at least a dozen of these smaller summits with more than one exposed flank. Note especially the rocky gully known as **Peden's Pulpit** on Rubers Law's southwest corner. Descent is via the route of ascent as far as the T-junction X of the coniferous strips.

Peden's Pulpit The heights of Rubers Law also provided a haven in the 17th century for persecuted Covenanters – on its rocky summit, a pulpit, Peden's Pulpit, from which Alexander (Sandy) Peden of Hawick preached the gospel of the Scottish National Covenant of 1638. Hard times produced hard men, described by the pen of Sir Walter Scott as 'hard and dour men, who prove their doctrine orthodox, by apostolic blows and knocks'.

Re-entry to the T-junction woodlands of Gled'swing Strip and the west end of Denholmhill Wood is via the small stile and gate, on the right on our outward journey, then 10 paces east to join the path left through conifers, soon to meet a stone wall ahead. Before the wall our path swings right for a short distance to meet and pass through the wall, via a wooden gate, into a pasture. Swing left and with the pathway descend northwest, with Denholm, tree-clad Denholm Dean and the Eildon Hills now in full view. Gorse, hawthorn, wild roses and ash close in on our descending path that leads onto a wide cart track that swings left below a humming electricity station by the twisting road that descends north into Denholm. Pass by the station and through a large metal gate opposite the pleasing property called Little Rulwood.

Turn right and walk north down the twisting country road for 100 yards or so where, just before a solitary house on the left, a wide gap in the hedge on the left allows access via a grassy pathway into the descending

Denholm Dene

delights of the public path through Denholm Dean, listed in 1898 as a 'holiday beauty spot'. Take the first pathway on the right, which drops sharply and is stepped in places, to meet Dean Burn and cross by wooden footbridge. There are several more footbridges to be crossed over the burn as it winds north through dense and pleasing woods, accompanied by constant birdsong and tinkling water. Emerge over a wooden bridge by outcrops of red sandstone into the west end of Denholm by a public convenience, a post office, a bakery, the Text House and a pub.

WALK 26 – A Druids' Stone Circle, Castles Most Sombre and a Rail Bed

Ninestane Rig, Stone Circle, Old Railway (south via Bell Hill and Bught Knowe), Arnton Fell, Blackwood Hill, Ninestane Rig

Distance	10¼ miles (16.5km)
Height Gain	1135ft (346m)
Start/Finish	GR 510979 on the B6399, 1½ miles (2.5km) north of Hermitage
Grade	4
Walking Time	Allow 6 hours
Maps	OS 1:50 000 Landranger sheet 79, Hawick & Eskdale
Accommodation	Facilities available in Newcastleton
Parking	On the grass verge of the B6399 by a stone animal shelter, GR 510979

Underfoot the route fluctuates between forest paths and a dismantled railway track, now in the throes of having a short section of single track restored by rail enthusiasts. However, this does not prevent the walker from enjoying this section before the serious tramp over Arnton Fell and Blackwood Hill. Stout footwear, suitable clothing to match the weather, map and compass are recommended. The steep climb to Arnton Fell gives this adventurous walk its grading. *Avoid the summer months when sections of the walk lie beneath a rank blanket of overgrown bracken, tussock grass and rushes.*

The Route Access to Liddesdale is not easy, as befits **the Debateable Land**. Two roads wind in from the north, the B6357 from Jedburgh and the B6399 from Hawick. A narrow unclassified road from the A7(T) Langholm to Hawick road also winds eastwards along Hermitage Water for nine miles. Start the walk by the side of the B6399 road, 1½ miles (2.4km) north of Hermitage, GR 510979.

A fascinating walk that on a fine day unfolds the wild and isolated valley of Liddesdale.

The Debateable Land In the 15th century the lands from Liddesdale to the River Sark were disputed by Scotland and England, and with neither side able to claim ownership, the rule of law was nonexistent, a situation quickly appreciated by the boisterous Borderers. To make matters worse, in the 1500s the adventurous Armstrong family produced a baby boom, spilling over into the Debateable Land from upper Liddesdale and creating a powder keg situation. Both England and Scotland were then forced to take action, which they did as soon as they had concluded their own war of the 1540s. In keeping with the times, it was proclaimed that anyone in the Debateable Land was free to plunder, burn and kill without fear of prosecution, a fact quickly grasped by the Scottish warden Lord Maxwell, who in 1551 promptly ravaged the entire area, destroying buildings and a goodly proportion of the inhabitants. Forced into action in 1552, England and Scotland, with the French ambassador called in to see fair play, split the Debateable Land down the middle.

The start – the B6399 by Hermitage Water

Walk south by the roadside for approximately 200 yards (183m) towards a small bridge – on the left is a Border Forest Park noticeboard. Between the noticeboard and the bridge a signpost (when not hidden amid bracken) to Ninestane Rig points southeast alongside the forest boundary fence. Ascend with the forest fence for ¾ mile (1.2km) to a stile leading into the trees. It is

waymarked 'Ninestane Rig' and directs the walker onto the rig and to the stone circle. A thin trod, overgrown in summer, travels with the forest ride north-northeast for ¼ mile (400m) to an overgrown clearing in which the **stone circle** stands. From the stone circle the path continues north-northeast on a forest ride for 1½ easy but rather monotonous miles (2.4km) before descending east to the southern end of a railway cutting, south of the now defunct Whitrope Tunnel. This cutting is one of many on the dismantled track of the old **Liddesdale Line Railway**.

Stone circle A druidical circle of standing stones on Nine Stanes Rig (the old spelling) is reputed to be the place where the detested wizard Lord Soulis was rolled in lead and boiled alive.

> At the Skelf-hill, the cauldron still
> The men of Liddesdale can show;
> And on the spot, where they boiled the pot,
> The spreat and the deer-hair ne'er shall grow.
>
> *Leyden*

Two standing stones in the circle were used to suspend the fiery cauldron, and even today the vegetation (spreat rush and deer-hair upland grass) within is somewhat sparse!

Liddesdale Line Railway From Canonbie in Cumbria to Hawick in Roxburghshire, this rail bed twisted and turned through Liddesdale to join the Bellingham to Hawick branchline at Riccarton Junction, before diving underground at Whitrope Tunnel. Today the stripped track is there for the benefit of walkers as it winds its picturesque way to Newcastleton, 22 miles (35km) from Hawick.

Once on the rail bed turn sharp right, i.e. south, for a 4 mile (6.4km) hike of high calibre. Never claustro-phobic, surrounded by timber, the old rail track reveals nostalgic memorabilia from the steam age among the

The view from Arnton Fell exposes Liddesdale in its entirety, with **Hermitage Castle** far below to the west on the banks of Hermitage Water.

isolated remains of Riccarton Junction. Just past the junction the track forks – take the right fork, i.e. south, then southwest for 3 miles (4.8km) to the boundary fence at the southern extremity of the forest. Turn sharp right at the first gate, crossing the track to ascend Arnton Fell ¾ mile (1.2km) north-northwest. The ascent alongside the trees is a steep plod of 672ft (205m), and near the crest of the fell the trees end, leaving the wall as the sole navigational aid to the summit cairn. ◀

Hermitage Castle This overpowering, charismatic castle, greatest of all Border fortresses, dates from the 12th century and has in its day been home to men whose cruelty and iniquity knew no bounds. Landlords such as Soulis, Black Douglas, Bothwell and Armstrong have all left their stamp on its character. In the 1820s an outside wall was split asunder as if by the hand of retribution. Many famous visitors have come and gone, certainly the most romantic of whom was Mary Queen of Scots. In 1566 Mary rode from Jedburgh to Hermitage Castle in six hours to spend a few hours with the sorely wounded Earl of Bothwell (the result of an altercation with Little Jock Elliot of Park). The queen returned to Jedburgh the same day and was rewarded for her concern and efforts with 10 days on her sick bed, close to death.

Hermitage Castle

From the summit cairn the way goes north, along the west side of a guiding wall and the rejoined conifers, for 1½ miles (2.4km) to Bell Hill. As the forest turns sharp left, i.e. west, the path descends steeply to Roughley Burn.

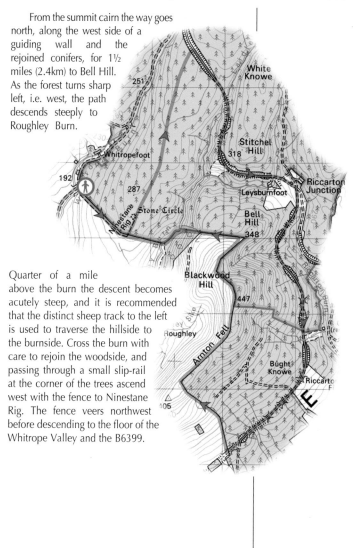

Quarter of a mile above the burn the descent becomes acutely steep, and it is recommended that the distinct sheep track to the left is used to traverse the hillside to the burnside. Cross the burn with care to rejoin the woodside, and passing through a small slip-rail at the corner of the trees ascend west with the fence to Ninestane Rig. The fence veers northwest before descending to the floor of the Whitrope Valley and the B6399.

WALK 27 – 'Bundle and Go' – a Reivers' Cry

Craik Village, Aithouse Burn, Wolfcleuch Waterfall, Crib Law Summit, Hog Knowes, Dirthope Burn Source, Aithouse Burn, Craik Village

Distance	8 miles (13km)
Height Gain	787ft (240m)
Start/Finish	Car parks and picnic area at GR 348080, southwest from Craik village
Grade	2; 3 in adverse weather
Walking Time	Allow 4½ hours
Maps	OS 1:50 000 Landranger sheet 79, Hawick & Eskdale, Langholm
	Forestry Commission – Scotland, Craik Forest Walks & Cycle Trails
Accommodation	All facilities available in Hawick
Parking	Craik Forest, signposted 'Park & Picnic Areas', by Craik village

For those with an affinity for matters historic, reivers' cries can still be heard on the 'soughing' (old Scots for sighing) wind, for in the 14th and 15th centuries these parts were in the front line of reiver ('patriot' or 'plunderer') country.

A burnside, hillside, drove road walk, through the mature working forest of Craik, on well-waymarked paths in company with the thriving indigenous flora and fauna. In particular look out for deer, red squirrels and otters. Views far and near open out between and above Crib Law's coniferous cloak, and on the remote fells above lonely, ethereal Borthwick Water.

Craik Forest drapes the rippling hills to the west and south of the valley of Borthwick Water, a tributary of the River Teviot that runs through the Border mill town of Hawick. Craik village, our starting point, lies 11 miles (17.5km) southwest from Hawick via the B711 and the unclassified Borthwick Water road (signposted 'Craik Forest'). Access from the Ettrick Valley, by Tushielaw, is via the B711 to Greenbank, there to join the Craik Forest road southwest.

The Route Start from the waymarked car park and picnic site south of Craik village, where maps are displayed. Our guiding colours are orange for the Crib Law walk and pale blue for the Aithouse Burn shared section leading to Wolfcleuch Waterfall. After descending from the summit of Crib Law with our orange markers, we link up with the purple waymarks of the drove road walk and later, for the final stages, with the pale blue of Aithouse Burn – three guides for our circular journey.

Walk southwest from the car park into and through, for a short distance, a dark stand of established conifers alongside **Borthwick Water**. At the forest ride ahead turn right, ascending northwest via the seat-lined pathway to emerge left onto a wide forest road running west. After 220yds (201m) our guiding waymarks direct us right, i.e. overall north, via a grassy alleyway back into the conifers, soon to cross a forest road to continue ahead, descending into the gully that carries busy, winding Aithouse Burn from the western summit slopes of Hog Knowes. When the dancing waters of the burn are met, swing left, walking along the burnside initially west. (Look out for small landslips underfoot.)

Borthwick Water This delightful river valley winds northeast and east from Craik, below Crib Law, through a series of low, grass-clad hills to join the River Teviot at Goldielands a few miles west of the mill town of Hawick. The river is steeped in blood and tales of the Border reivers, in which the family name Scott constantly occurs. For example, the ballad 'Jamie Telfer o' the Fair Dodhead':

> Warn Wat [Scott] o'Harden and his sons,
> Wi' them will Borthwick Water ride.

Wolfcleuch Waterfall

Walk west and north alongside the 'true right' bank of Aithouse Burn, where a forest road to the right, shored up by tons of boulder stones, comes into view through the trees. Continue west with the burn, over bridges and a clear, cambered path, lit with shafts of sunlight in the right conditions, to arrive at a parting of the orange Crib Law walk and the pale blue Aithouse Burn and Wolfcleuch Waterfall walk. Once over the bridge onto the true left bank of the burn turn left, i.e. north-west, alongside the burn for several hundred yards to cross yet another footbridge. Swing left, i.e. west, with the pathway into the narrow confines of a side-gully containing adventurous Wolfcleuch Burn and the spectacular twin cascades of Wolfcleuch Waterfall. Return to the Crib Law walk and rise left to join the wide forest road.

Turn left, ascending north with a series of wide sweeps between the shoulder of Grey Hill and the domed saddle of Crib Law 1391ft (424m) and, to the north, Hog Knowes 1345ft (410m). As a small roadside quarry is passed, and in spite of the omnipresent conifers, there is an ever-increasing feeling of space and far-distant views approaching. On the left the remains of an old corrugated iron and wooden shed are passed, and a Crib Law waymark just beyond on the right indicates a pathway leaving the road to zigzag northeast–south-east–northeast. This well-constructed angled track, known as Crib Law Climb, is shared with a mountain bike route and quickly and efficiently brings you to a fine **viewpoint** looking south and east from Crib Law's summit. Continue northeast with the wide track for approximately 230yds (210m), and with the orange waymark swing left for an angled contour north along the eastern summit slopes of tree-clad Hog Knowes that

Crib Law viewpoint Views are to the north over the valleys of Ettrick, Yarrow and Tweeddale, and northeast to the Eildon Hills. East reveals the border line ridge from Peel Fell and Carter Bar to the distant Hogs Back of Muckle Cheviot. Southeast are the badlands of Liddesdale – the reivers' retreat. South looks over Teviot Head towards Langholm, while southwest reveals Eskdale. Western and northwestern views are of the challenging Moffat Water Valley, Tweedsmuir Hills and Manor Hills.

finally descends northeast to the source of Dirthope Burn. From here it wriggles overall southeast to join a forest road, part of the purple **drove road** walk.

Drove roads Along these commercial arteries came the drovers and their Border cattle. Raised and grazed in sheltered grassy valleys such as Borthwick Water and Teviotdale, cattle and drovers would walk along these quiet ways from the Border hills to the hungry markets of northern England. These routes avoided, where possible, border customs posts such as those at Hawick and Moffat.

At this point we turn sharp right, and with the gently descending roadway walk west then southeast and south for ¾ mile (1.2km) to leave the roadway, left, at the orange and purple waymarks leading south, parallel with the forest road. Eventually we reach and cross Aithouse Burn, and with the musical waters on our left begin a particularly pleasing sylvan journey east and southeast on grassy paths, crossing the forest road once, beside fine broadleaves, rush beds and frog ponds, as the undulating countryside unfolds. Pass by Craik House and its nearby water chute, then a strip of lime, sycamore, acer, and some unusual broadleaves, including a group of spiked and thorny 'Siberian crab', to Craik village, the information board and toilets, then the car park and picnic site.

Ettrick – east to Gamescleuch Hill (Walk 31)

CHAPTER 3

ETTRICK FOREST

Ettrick Water and its winsome offspring, Yarrow Water, flow sweetly northeast through roughly parallel valleys, from Ettrick Head and Loch of the Lowes, to join together before running into the Tweed north of Selkirk. The twin glens are surrounded by a circlet of hills bounded by the old county boundary of Selkirkshire. In profile the rounded and grass-covered hills resemble a herd of sleeping elephants, though the steep slopes that form the eastern wall of Moffat Water Valley no doubt give another impression to walkers gazing up with some trepidation to the 1500ft (457m) rise from the A708.

Access to Ettrick Forest is good, however, for unlike the Cheviots these hills are bisected by two rivers along whose banks a narrow ribbon of well-surfaced road runs into the very heart of this delightful area. A minor inconvenience to free access onto the upper slopes is the acres of close-planted conifers in both glens, and in particular in upper Ettrick. The Forestry Commission and the private woodland owners do, however, permit walkers to use forest access roads and forest rides.

While containing no dramatic Munroes, or even Corbetts, there are nine hills over 2000ft (610m) in Ettrick Forest: Herman Law, Andrewhinney Hill, Bell Craig, Bodesbeck Law, Capel Fell, Croft Head, Loch Fell, Wind Fell and Ettrick Pen, and six tops over 2000 feet: Trowgrain Middle, Mid Rig, White Shank, Smidhope Hill, Loch Fell West and Hopetoun Craig – a total of 15 summits over 2000 feet. Nine of the 15 are covered in the walks in this chapter. On the heights the paths vary, ranging from distinct and good underfoot, to the faintest of sheep traces, and on some sections they are nonexistent. Navigation is rarely a problem, however, in spite of there being a sameness about the summits and a lack of waymarks and signposts. The summits and most of the walk routes are linked by regional, county, and parish boundary stone dykes and fences which make first-class navigational aids.

Not having to refer constantly to the guidebook or the map enables the walker to enjoy the wide and varied surroundings of Ettrick Forest, ranging from the distant riot of the Ettrick and Yarrow hills, to the charm and kindly folds of the twin valleys of Ettrick Water and Yarrow Water, with the added bonus of the two sparkling jewels in the crown of Yarrow – St Mary's Loch and Loch of the Lowes. These are quiet hills where walks can be completed in total isolation. They also remain rich in wildlife, both furred and feathered, and are exceedingly well populated by our woolly friends.

Entry into the area is easily gained by a short drive (maximum 25 miles (40km)) from Moffat, Langholm, Hawick, Selkirk, Galashiels or Innerleithen. Accommodation and refreshments can be obtained at hotels and inns around St Mary's Loch, Ettrickbridge and Tushielaw, with bed-and-breakfasts dotted along the two valleys, as are the occasional caravan and campsites (with wild camping possible in the upper reaches of Ettrick Water). There is also a youth hostel at Broadmeadows (the first in Scotland) 4 miles (6.4km) west of Selkirk, and a small bothy on the Southern Upland Way at Over Phawhope (Walks 34, 35 and 36).

Public transport runs through the Yarrow Valley on the Moffat–St Mary's Loch–Selkirk service. The Ettrick Valley is not so well served, Selkirk to Ettrickbridge End being the only service. Timetables are available from bus stations and tourist information centres in Moffat and Selkirk. Post buses can also be utilised in both valleys.

THE WALKS

Walk 28 is a fine introduction to the Yarrow Valley and the surrounding hills, good underfoot with extensive views from the broad and walkable ridges. From these ridges the route of Walk 29 gives the walker the first sight of St Mary's Loch, then leaves the valley floor to visit two pele towers, returning alongside musical and historic Douglas Burn. For convenience and beauty, the next three walks all start and finish on the narrow isthmus between St Mary's Loch and Loch of the Lowes. Walk 30 encircles St Mary's Loch, visiting the old kirkyard of St Mary's and many other points of interest. This is a gentle lochside walk for all seasons. Walk 31 starts as a lochside walk over the isthmus of St Mary's Loch and Loch of the Lowes, before ascending the high ground to the east then descending into the Ettrick Valley. After a visit to fascinating Ettrick Kirk, it's over the hills again to return to St Mary's Loch, 'That's the way for Billy and me' (in the words of the poet James Hogg). Walk 32 takes the route much used by Sir Walter Scott and James Hogg, when they travelled from Tibbie Shiels Inn to Tushielaw by the Ettrick, quaintly known as the Captain's Road.

The next two walks and two variations leave the lower slopes and ascend to the highest summits in the Ettrick Forest. Walk 33 covers the ridge between the dramatic east wall of Moffat Water Valley (referred to in the first paragraph of the introduction to this chapter) and the picturesque head of Ettrick Water, from where the whole of the Ettrick Horseshoe (Walks 34, 35 and 36) can be seen. These are high-level walks of varying lengths, with views that surprise the visitor to the Borders, comparing favourably with some of the best in Britain.

WALK 28 – In Search of an Army's Pay Chest

Yarrowford, Minchmoor Road, Wallace's Trench,
Brown Knowe, Broomy Law, Three Brethren,
Broadmeadows, Yarrowford

Distance	8½ miles (13.7km)
Height Gain	1378ft (420m)
Start/Finish	Yarrowford, GR 407300, on the A708 4 miles (6.5km) west of Selkirk
Grade	2 or 3
Walking Time	5 hours
Maps	OS 1:50 000 Landranger sheet 73, Peebles, Galashiels & Selkirk, Tweed Valley
Accommodation	Selection at Selkirk and Yarrowford, youth hostel at Broadmeadows
Parking	Parking at Yarrowford by the village hall

This introductory walk to the charm of Yarrow Water and its photogenic surrounds is all things to all walkers. Although the pathways are good and distinct, walking boots are recommended, and if the walk is contemplated in winter or in adverse weather conditions, a map and compass are advisable.

The Route Broadmeadows and Yarrowford lie side by side on the A708 some 4 miles (6.5km) west of Selkirk, involving a picturesque drive past **Foulshiels Farm** and **Newark Tower**. At Yarrowford leave the A708 at the right turn past the telephone

Steeped in the past, with the promise of lost treasure somewhere along the way, this walk, which includes a section of the Southern Upland Way, is indeed tempting.

Foulshiels Farm Three-quarters of a mile (1.2km) east of Broadmeadows is the birthplace of the African explorer Mungo Park (1771–1806), a man whose exploits moved Dr Livingstone to write: 'For actual hardship undergone, for dangers faced, and difficulties overcome, Mungo Park stands without a rival.' A statue to this redoubtable pedestrian stands proudly in Selkirk (Chapter 5).

Newark Tower Opposite Foulshiels, on the south bank of the Yarrow, stands 'Newark's stately tower'. Completed in 1423, 'New Werk', as opposed to its predecessor 'Auld Wark', was originally a royal hunting seat. The royal arms are high on the west wall.

box, signposted 'Public footpath to Innerleithen by Minchmoor' to reach the parking at the red village hall.

From the village hall walk north past houses and a row of garages to the left, before ascending a waymarked stepped way leading to what was a corridor of oak and beech alongside a coniferous plantation, rising to the corner of

Hangingshaw wood.

It is 2 miles (3.2km) from the woodside corner along Minchmoor Road to Wallace's Trench. Initially the track swings northwest and follows the woodside, rising through a series of gates to a ridge between Hangingshaw Burn and Gruntly Burn, eventually to leave the trees and zigzag onto the open fell to the north on what is a fine and invigorating ridge walk. As

Hangingshaw In the tower, now long gone, dwelt the outlaw Murray. A pond or well in the vicinity of Hangingshaw wood is said to be the repository of a lost pay chest belonging to Montrose's army, defeated at Philiphaugh. Many have searched, but as yet none has been successful. Has the spring known as Katythirsty Well, by the side of Minchmoor Road, 164yds (150m) southeast of the southern end of Wallace's Trench, been searched?

Wallace's Trench This is a single trench 300yds (274m) long and 4ft to 5ft (1.2 to 1.5m) deep, with a raised embankment on the west side 4ft to 5ft (1.2 to 1.5m) high. The exact significance of the trench is not clear, and it must have been constructed well before the lifetime of Sir William Wallace. However, it is said that this is where Wallace waited in 1297 for the fighting men of the Borders to join his cause.

height is gained, Minchmoor Road swings northwest as **Wallace's Trench** is approached.

A small stone marker with the words, 'Wallace's Trench 300 yards' – now difficult to decipher – is close by the track on the right, and signals the start of this distinct trench and earthwork that slashes the hillside to the north. Follow the trench to the cairned, far-seeing panoramic summit of Brown Knowe 1718ft (524m), turning right before the fence onto the dirt-and-stone **Southern Upland Way**, once an old drove road. From Brown Knowe follow the (thistle) waymarked track and path in an easterly direction, over sweeping Whitehope Rig alongside its thin line of conifers, for the next 3 miles (4.8km). The

The Southern Upland Way A continuous long-distance coast-to-coast path, opened in 1984. It goes from Portpatrick on the west coast to Cockburnspath on the Berwickshire coast, covering a distance of 202 miles (325km) (see Chapter 5).

The old drove road to Broomy law

This is a fine rooftop ridge walk, with extensive views of the Yarrow Valley to the southwest and the Tweed Valley to the northeast, and Three Brethren providing an appropriate climax.

triple peaks of the Eildon Hills beyond Broomy Law, and the summit and three distinctive cairns of **Three Brethren** 1523ft (464m), our destination, are prominent. ◀

> **Three Brethren** This prominent hill stands to the northwest of Selkirk and is crowned by three large identical cairns, each 9ft (2.7m) tall and 6ft (1.8m) in diameter at the base, hence the name Three Brethren. Each cairn marks the boundary of the estates of Yair, of Philiphaugh, and the burgh of Selkirk. The 'Brethren' are visited on the first Tuesday of June during Selkirk's colourful Common Riding festivities, when the marches are ridden and the colours are 'cast'.

From Three Brethren pass through the small single gate and descend south through the heather, not on the Southern Upland Way, but on the right-hand pathway to the right of the fence, walking as far as a track/pathway crossroads ½ mile (0.8km) below. Turn right, i.e. west, at the crossroads onto a damp, distinct path that loses height and crosses Long Philip Burn before its heathery ascent southwest over the northern saddle of Foulshiels Hill. The valley of the Yarrow opens up to the southwest, its silver river jinking between fold after fold of rolling hills, and fading into the distant Manor range. Continue descending for ½ mile (0.8km) to the woodside by the track, here to turn right and circle the north end of the trees, by crossing a wet and boggy pasture, to the gate at the northwest corner of the wood. A waymark and a path through the mixed woods, alongside a burn then above a cleuch, lead to Broadmeadows Youth Hostel (the first in Scotland, in 1931, and now run during summer by volunteers), and onto a farm road that twists west and south for 1 mile (1.6km) to Yarrowford below.

Yarrowford in Yarrow Valley

WALK 29 – Pele Towers and an Italian Balloonist

Dryhope, Blackhouse, Craig Douglas, Dryhope

Distance	5½ miles (8.8km)
Height Gain	400ft (122m)
Start/Finish	The Southern Upland Way departure from the A708 at GR 273244
Grade	1
Walking Time	3 hours
Maps	OS 1:50 000 Landranger sheet 73, Peebles, Galashiels & Selkirk
Accommodation	Inns around St Mary's Loch and bed-and-breakfasts along the Ettrick Valley
Parking	Small layby at GR 273244, or lochside laybys several hundred yards west

So many, infinitely more capable than I, have in prose and verse sung the praises of this valley of the Yarrow. By walking its highways and byways the traveller can appreciate the romance of its legends and the beauty of its waters.

This walk returns to its starting point either as a triangular – one-third is on a roadside verge – or a there-and-back journey to Blackhouse. Well-marked paths allow the walker to appreciate the relics of yesteryear alongside loch and surrounding hills.

The Route Dryhope Tower stands a few hundred yards north of the A708 at the east end of St Mary's Loch and 15¼ delightful miles (24.5km) west of Selkirk. The walk starts at the Southern Upland Way crossing GR 269242, marked by a stile, a short distance east from the entrance to Dryhope farm. From this point proceed north, with Dryhope farm on the left and **Dryhope Tower** ahead. When the wallside pathway reaches its nearest point to the crumbling tower, turn right after crossing the stile and follow the clear track between Ward Law and South Hawkshaw Rig (with its prominent cairn). After about ½ mile (0.8km) the farm track swings left and follows Dryhope Burn in its deep gully. Our route carries on, however, as directed by a Southern Upland Way marker, northeast onto a grassy

Dryhope Tower This massive little pele tower, 10yds (9.1m) by 7yds (6.4m), with walls 3ft (0.9m) thick, was the birthplace in 1550 of Mary the Flower of Yarrow, bride of Auld Wat Scott of Harden. As if the tenancy of a Scott of Auld Wat's calibre was not enough, the tower was also home to another brigand of great notoriety. Dick of Dryhope (Driupp) Armstrong (mentioned in 'The Ballad of Kinmont Willie') also dwelled within its walls. With a Scott and an Armstrong as residents, it all proved too much for James VI, who in 1592 ordered Dryhope Pele to be demolished. Later it was rebuilt, but today it stands roofless and open, home only to birds and vermin.

In 1784 an Italian balloonist 'dropped in' to Dryhope Tower. Believing St Mary's Loch to be the North Sea, he attempted an emergency landing, losing a flag, some rope and an anchor. Never ones to miss an opportunity, the Borderers cut up the flag for handkerchiefs.

Dryhope Tower

path passing below the cairn and by a circular sheep stell to a multiple split in the path.

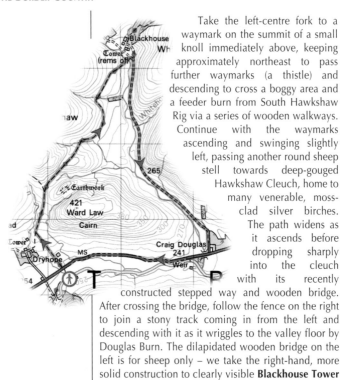

Take the left-centre fork to a waymark on the summit of a small knoll immediately above, keeping approximately northeast to pass further waymarks (a thistle) and descending to cross a boggy area and a feeder burn from South Hawkshaw Rig via a series of wooden walkways. Continue with the waymarks ascending and swinging slightly left, passing another round sheep stell towards deep-gouged Hawkshaw Cleuch, home to many venerable, moss-clad silver birches. The path widens as it ascends before dropping sharply into the cleuch with its recently constructed stepped way and wooden bridge. After crossing the bridge, follow the fence on the right to join a stony track coming in from the left and descending with it as it wriggles to the valley floor by Douglas Burn. The dilapidated wooden bridge on the left is for sheep only – we take the right-hand, more solid construction to clearly visible **Blackhouse Tower** north of the burn.

Blackhouse Tower Yet another aged pele tower, now totally ruined, this one was built in the late 1600s. It was a Douglas stronghold, whose most famous son, James Douglas, known as Black Douglas, cunningly captured Roxburgh Castle by disguising his forces as black oxen. Blackhouse Tower was the scene of the events so poignantly described in the ballad 'The Douglas Tragedy'. At the farm of Blackhouse the poet James Hogg (the Ettrick Shepherd) was shepherd from 1790 to 1800, during which time he experienced the violent blizzard of 1794, described by Hogg in *Blackwood's Edinburgh Magazine* of July 1819.

Douglas Burn Legend has it that the stones high on the fell (now buried under a thick pall of Sitka spruce) mark the site of the demise of Lady Margaret Douglas's seven brothers and her father, all of whom fell under the irresistible sword of her lover, who also perished in the dispute. The burn is named after the House of Douglas.

Nestling in the confluence of **Douglas Burn** and Craighope Burn, and below the steep side of Whitehope Rig 1587ft (484m), stand the few remains of Blackhouse Tower, close by the working farm of Blackhouse. Once across Douglas Burn turn right and follow the farm track (a Scottish public right of way from Craig Douglas to Peebles) south for 2 miles (3.2km) to Craig Douglas. The winding track keeps close to the burn, which supports a profusion of **birdlife** and wild flowers. The farm of Craig Douglas is white and tidy as it stands close by the A708, with its milestone on the south side of the road. Turn right onto the roadside verge, which is followed west for 1½ miles (2.4km) through the scenically pleasing Yarrow Valley to the Southern Upland Way crossing at Dryhope.

Peewits Also known as lapwings or plovers, these delightful summer visitors grace the fells with their distinctive cry of 'pee-weet'. Past masters of the broken wing or broken leg technique, which is immediately used as a diversionary tactic should an unwanted visitor approach their nest, yet they are fearless in driving off predators who encroach into their territory. The *pièce de résistance* is without doubt the synchronised aerobatics of the flock, flying with such speed and precision they surely have no equal in the bird kingdom.

For all its comic antics and synchronised flying displays, the peewit has not always been a popular bird in the Borders, for it was the 'wailing cry' (so described by James Hogg) of the plover when disturbed on these deserted fells that often led the dragoons to the sorely persecuted Covenanters.

WALK 30 – Fair St Mary's and Literary Giants

Tibbie Shiels Inn, St Mary's Loch, Bowerhope, St Mary's Kirkyard, Cappercleuch, James Hogg Monument, Tibbie Shiels Inn

Distance	7½ miles (12.1km)
Height Gain	200ft (61m)
Start/Finish	Tibbie Shiels Inn, south end of St Mary's Loch, GR 240205
Grade	1
Walking Time	4 hours
Maps	OS 1:50 000 Landranger sheet 73, Peebles, Galashiels & Selkirk
Accommodation	Accommodation, plus limited camping and refreshments, are available at various establishments between the two lochs
Parking	Off-road at the T-junction between St Mary's Loch and Loch of the Lowes

If you are averse to roadside verge walking, the journey can be accomplished as a there-and-back from Tibbie's to the bridge over Yarrow Water at the loch's northern tip, or alternatively arrange to be collected at the bridge.

St Mary's Loch, 3 miles (4.8km) long, is the largest and most picturesque loch in the Borderland. Crescent shaped and narrow, it nestles beneath steep-sided hills, some conifer clad, offering the pedestrian a level walk of scenic excellence. Rich and varied in bird- and plant-life, the walk can be enjoyed at a leisurely pace. Navigation and conditions underfoot do not present any problems, and in summer trainers can be worn. For those of you who value solitude, may I suggest a clear crisp day from December to March.

The Route St Mary's Loch lies alongside the A708 18 miles (29km) southwest of Selkirk, at the head of the fascinating Yarrow Valley. Start the walk from **Tibbie Shiels Inn**, a quaint hotchpotch of whitewashed buildings sheltered by a few trees of venerable age, on the southern tip of the loch. Walk though the car park and pass through the gate, signposted 'St Mary's Loch Sailing Club

Tibbie Shiels Inn 'Tibbie's' is the famous watering hole between St Mary's Loch and Loch of the Lowes so beloved by the literary giants of the past: Sir Walter Scott and James Hogg. Born in Ettrick in 1782, Tibbie Shiels lived in the cottage from 1823. Her husband, Robert Richardson, a shepherd and mole catcher, died the following year, but this determined women turned the cottage into a welcoming haven for wayfarers who journeyed through the valleys of Yarrow and Moffat Water. The present bar, it is said, held 13 small box-beds, rather like nocturnal coffins, and no doubt just as unhealthy!

members only', to the lochside, passing in front of the sailing clubhouse. The trail soon reaches a path alongside the east bank of St Mary's Loch. This path, containing several stiles – that allow passage for dogs – is part of the Southern Upland Way and provides constant reflective views over the loch. It is waymarked for the entire 3 miles (4.8km), with the only habitation being the farm of **Bowerhope**, situated below the steep northern flank of Bowerhope Law 1570ft (478m), some 2 miles (3.2km) from the starting point. ▶

The walk is a pleasant mix of old established coniferous and deciduous trees, but not so the hillside above, which lies blanketed under acres of barely acceptable Sitka spruce.

Reflective St Mary's – Summerhope Burn below Oxcleuch Rig and Watch Law

Bowerhope Pronounced 'beer-op', the farmhouse kitchen at Bowerhope in the early 1800s had such a low ceiling it caused the room to be perpetually full of smoke, yet farmer Sandy Cunningham is quoted as saying, 'Ministers may talk o' Heevin' as they like; commend me to Bowerhope; I cud tak a tack (lease) o't to a' eternity.' One recent farmer bred and reared llamas, hiring the surplus males as pack animals to Southern Upland Wayfarers.

The northern end of the loch, feeding Yarrow Water, is crossed by a bridge leading northwest to the A708. At this point turn left to follow the shoreline west-southwest towards Cappercleuch. After approximately 1 mile (1.6km), at GR 256235, leave the waterside to cross the road on the right, signposted **'St Mary's Kirkyard'**, an

interesting diversion and a peaceful place from which to view the loch. The climb is sharp, but seats are thoughtfully provided. Return as far as the broad grassy track running through the bracken and parallel to the road, turn right and walk west on this quiet and scenic path until the narrowing road is reached. Care is needed until the village hall is passed and the wide and open bridge across Megget Water is crossed.

South from Megget Bridge the route is shared with the internal combustion engine. There is, however, a wide grass verge and a shoreline that can be used, with exceptional views of the never-ending charm of **St Mary's Loch**.

St Mary's Kirkyard Destroyed by fire in 1557 by a group of fractious Scotts who unsuccessfully pursued a Cranston to the sanctuary within, St Mary's Kirk has never been rebuilt. The old kirk stood at the northwest corner of the present graveyard, and in memory of the Covenanters who often had only a blanket for shelter, a Blanket Preaching is held each year on the last Sunday in July. Seldom used today, the kirkyard allows but the few privileged families of Brydon, Scott, Anderson, Armstrong and Grieve to rest within its stone walls.

St Mary's Loch

> What boon to lie, as I now lie,
> And see in silver at my feet
> Saint Mary's Lake, as if the sky
> Had fallen 'tween those hills so sweet.
> *Alexander Anderson*

One-and-a-half miles (2.4km) south of Megget Bridge, overlooking the old bridge between the two lochs, stands a memorial to **James Hogg, the Ettrick Shepherd** (1771–1835). Visit the statue and read the verse. From this tribute to Hogg it is but a short step east over the narrow bridge to Tibbie Shiels.

James Hogg, the Ettrick Shepherd Born at Ettrick Hall, a grand name for a rather damp little cottage (its walls fell down around 1830), Hogg is without doubt the greatest poet to spring from Border soil, and his fine memorial (by Andrew Currie, 1860) is placed above the junction of the lochs. On the scroll in the shepherd's left hand is the poem, 'He Taught the Wandering Winds to Sing.'

> Oft had he viewed, as morning rose,
> The Bosom of the Lonely Lowes:
> Oft thrilled his heart at close of even
> To see the dappled vales of heaven,
> With many a mountain moor and tree,
> Asleep upon Saint Mary.

The James Hogg Memorial

WALK 31 – 'That's the Way for Billy and Me'

Tibbie Shiels Inn, Southern Upland Way to Scabcleuch, Ettrick Kirk, Pikestone Rig, Loch of the Lowes, Tibbie Shiels Inn

Distance	10½ miles (16.9km)
Height Gain	1550ft (472m)
Start/Finish	Junction of the two lochs alongside the A708, GR 238205
Grade	3
Walking Time	6½ hours
Maps	OS 1:50 000 Landranger sheets 73, Peebles, Galashiels & Selkirk, and 79, Hawick & Eskdale
Accommodation	Available at the southern end of St Mary's Loch, plus refreshments
Parking	Junction of the two lochs alongside the A708, GR 23820

An invigorating figure-of-eight fell walk that encompasses two valleys, the Yarrow and the Ettrick, utilising sections of the Southern Upland Way.

The adventure, with ascents of 1850ft (564m), is graded 3 because care is needed with navigation on the return journey (take a map and compass).

The Route With the James Hogg memorial directly behind, walk over the small stone bridge to the east and join the Southern Upland Way at **Tibbie Shiels Inn**.

This walk includes a ramble through classic Border hill scenery, and follows Scabcleuch Burn on its journey to visit the birthplace and burial place of James Hogg, the Ettrick Shepherd.

Tibbie Shiels Inn When widowed in 1824, Isobella (Tibbie) Shiels took in gentlemen lodgers to support herself and her six children, the first lodger being Robert Chalmers, researching his book *The Picture of Scotland*. A small active woman with an essential sense of humour, Tibbie prophetically said, 'Folk a' ken me best as Tibbie Shiels, and I dare say when I'm deid and gone this place will still be ca'ed Tibbie Shiels's.' Today memorabilia from that bygone age decorate the inn, including a picture of Tibbie herself, complete with accompanying ghost – seen only by those with the second sight, or those who have imbibed well but not too wisely!

The Southern Upland Way below Peniestone Knowe

Continue east past Crosscleuch, ascending steadily southeast then south along the undulating farm road for approximately 1 mile (1.6km). Here the way leaves the broad track, turning half-right at the corner of Berry Wood onto a narrow path (waymarked with the thistle) between two established coniferous plantations. The path, wet in places, is now quite distinct and well waymarked on its way south, on the southern flanks of Earl's Hill, to a wooden bridge leading to the sad ruins and ailing conifers of **Riskinhope Hope**. On the valley floor by Whithope Burn the path is somewhat wet and boggy underfoot, but once it climbs west with the waymarks from Riskinhope Hope, and contours Pikestone Rig south above the glaciated U-shaped valley, on a wide pathway to below the summit of Peniestone Knowe 1807ft (551m), conditions improve.

Riskinhope Hope 'Hope' means 'a sheltered valley', thus making this valley the valley above Riskinhope. Sadly, like so many of its kind in these high hills, the farm of Riskinhope Hope, which stands at the southern end of the Loch of the Lowes, is but a grey and decaying ruin.

Ettrick Kirk A new Kirk of Ettrick was built in the early 16th century, though the present church dates from 1824. A severe yet compelling building, it remains 'a preaching kirk', with its pulpit and sounding board surmounted by a dove. The kirk is closely linked to the unbending Calvinism of the Reverend Boston, 'Boston of Ettrick', a minister whose hellfire sermons swelled the congregation from 57 in 1710 to 777 in 1731. From far and wide they came, no doubt on the same paths as are included in this guide.

In its churchyard lie the earthly remains of James Hogg, the Ettrick Shepherd, Tibbie Shiels, who died in her 95th year, and William Laidlaw, whose headstone tells us, 'Here lyeth William Laidlaw, the far famed Will of Phaup, who for feats of Frolic, Agility, and Strength, had no equal in his day.' Will of Phaup was Hogg's grandfather, and the last man in Ettrick to speak to fairies.

Close by the kirk, east towards the school, stands another monument, commemorating the birthplace of the Ettrick Shepherd.

> Where the pools are bright and deep,
> Where the grey trout lies asleep,
> Up the river and o'er the lea,
> That's the way for Billy and me.
> 'A Boy's Song', by James Hogg

Continue south to the col ahead from which the Ettrick Horseshoe (Walks 34, 35 and 36) – a semicircle of 2000ft (610m) summits ringing Ettrick Head – can be seen to the southwest. Note also the stile and signpost to the left on the col, for this point is to be met on the return journey. The path now descends southeast. Keep to the right of the two paths, waymarked with a thistle, and follow Scabcleuch Burn (a foul name for a fine burn) for 1⅓ miles (2.1km) to the farm of Scabcleuch and a narrow metalled road.

Turn left when the road is met and leave the Southern Upland Way to meander east for ¾ mile (1.2km) to the peace of **Ettrick Kirk** on the left, surrounded by trees and guarded by constantly crowing rooks. West of the church pass by gated Craighill farm on the path signposted 'St Mary's Loch' leading northwest,

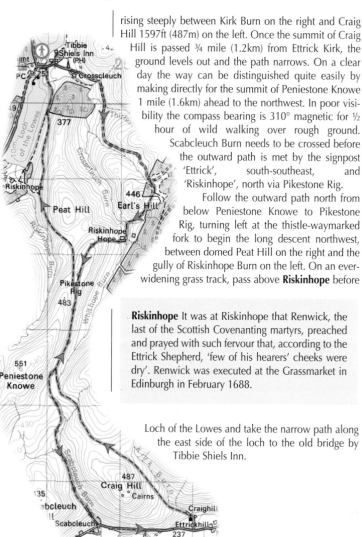

rising steeply between Kirk Burn on the right and Craig Hill 1597ft (487m) on the left. Once the summit of Craig Hill is passed ¾ mile (1.2km) from Ettrick Kirk, the ground levels out and the path narrows. On a clear day the way can be distinguished quite easily by making directly for the summit of Peniestone Knowe 1 mile (1.6km) ahead to the northwest. In poor visibility the compass bearing is 310° magnetic for ½ hour of wild walking over rough ground. Scabcleuch Burn needs to be crossed before the outward path is met by the signpost 'Ettrick', south-southeast, and 'Riskinhope', north via Pikestone Rig.

Follow the outward path north from below Peniestone Knowe to Pikestone Rig, turning left at the thistle-waymarked fork to begin the long descent northwest, between domed Peat Hill on the right and the gully of Riskinhope Burn on the left. On an ever-widening grass track, pass above **Riskinhope** before

Riskinhope It was at Riskinhope that Renwick, the last of the Scottish Covenanting martyrs, preached and prayed with such fervour that, according to the Ettrick Shepherd, 'few of his hearers' cheeks were dry'. Renwick was executed at the Grassmarket in Edinburgh in February 1688.

Loch of the Lowes and take the narrow path along the east side of the loch to the old bridge by Tibbie Shiels Inn.

WALK 32 – A Drovers' Way

Tibbie Shiels Inn, Captain's Road, Thirlstanehope, Tushielaw, NW on B709 to GR 275201, Berry Wood, Tibbie Shiels Inn

Distance	12 miles (19.3km)
Height Gain	1660ft (506m)
Start/Finish	Isthmus between St Mary's Loch and Loch of the Lowes, GR 239205
Grade	3
Walking Time	7 hours
Maps	OS 1:50 000 Landranger sheets 73, Peebles, Galashiels & Selkirk, and 79, Hawick & Eskdale
Accommodation	Accommodation and refreshments at the start, the halfway point and the finish
Parking	Either side of the A708, alongside the isthmus of Loch of the Lowes and St Mary's Loch before the bridge and Tibbie Shiels Inn

There are no navigational problems, and good waymarked paths, tracks and roads along this route, although sections in the coniferous plantations between Fall Law and Cowan's Croft can be very wet underfoot after heavy rain. The even spread of the 1660ft (506m) ascent make this walk seem much shorter than it actually is.

The Route From the entrance to Tibbie Shiels Inn the road is signposted Southern Upland Way. Follow this road east past Crosscleuch, climbing overall south-east to the north side of Earl's Hill. At this point, by the corner of Berry Wood, a directional post 'Public footpath to Hopehouse by the Captain's Road' indicates a split in the route. Take the indicated **Captain's Road** right, shared for a short distance with the Southern Upland Way on the narrow path alongside the conifers, to the southeast as far as a second signpost, 'Hopehouse, Captain's Road'.

A circular walk from the Yarrow Valley to the Ettrick Valley and back, a route often taken by Scott and Hogg, and much favoured by drovers.

181

The Captain's Road Thomson's 1824 map of Selkirkshire lists 'the Captains Road' from St Mary's Loch to Tushielaw as a drove road, linking it into the chain of drove roads running south from Peebles, through the glen of the Douglas Burn and Dryhope (Walk 29), via St Mary's Loch (Walk 30), and south from Tushielaw alongside Rankle Burn to the valley of the Teviot at Hawick.

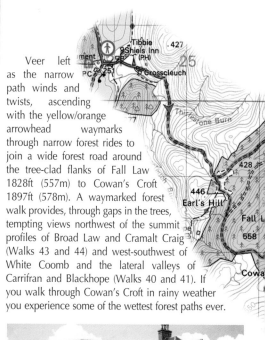

Veer left as the narrow path winds and twists, ascending with the yellow/orange arrowhead waymarks through narrow forest rides to join a wide forest road around the tree-clad flanks of Fall Law 1828ft (557m) to Cowan's Croft 1897ft (578m). A waymarked forest walk provides, through gaps in the trees, tempting views northwest of the summit profiles of Broad Law and Cramalt Craig (Walks 43 and 44) and west-southwest of White Coomb and the lateral valleys of Carrifran and Blackhope (Walks 40 and 41). If you walk through Cowan's Croft in rainy weather you experience some of the wettest forest paths ever.

Tibbie Shiels Inn

Fortunately the 'paddy field' paths are only several hundred yards long before you burst out of the conifers at the head of Hopehouse Burn Valley.

In the 3½ mile (5.6km) journey from Tibbie Sheils Inn to the floor of the Ettrick Valley, this isolated, descending side-valley is one of the highlights of our walk, providing, as we descend the Captain's Road southeast and east-southeast, fine profiled views of the ridged border line from Peel Fell on the right, Carter Fell (Walk 16), centre, and Rubers Law (Walk 25) on the left. The twin track is good, the isolation is complete and the

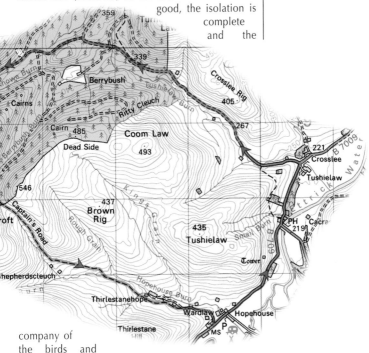

company of the birds and sheep just right as the pathway descends past a series of glacial deposits, known as 'kames', before contouring the left-hand valley slopes to take us past

Tushielaw Inn by Ettrick Water

and above the ageing buildings of Shepherdscleuch and its relatively new stone road leading to Thirlestanehope farm.

Cross this new road to continue on the grassy, surrounded by rushes in places, Captain's Road to cross Yoke Burn, keeping Hopehouse Burn and the white farmhouse of Thirlstanehope below and to the left. Leave the fellside and join a tarmac lane east and south to meet the B709 at Wardlaw. Shepherdscleuch Cairn and Hopehouse Burn winding down to Thirlstanehope is a particularly pleasing sight.

Thirlestane Tower Today Thirlstane Tower is a ruin, cut to stubble height by the severe arm of the Earl of Hertford as he slashed his infamous swath through the Borders in 1544 and 1545. The pele tower belonged then to Sir John Scott, whose descendant Lord Napier of Ettrick (motto 'Readdy, ay Readdy') has his seat in nearby Thirlestane, a mansion built in the early 1800s.

At the B709 at Wardlaw turn left. **Thirlestane Tower** lies 1 mile (1.6km) to the right, and note the milestones on this road – they appear every ½ mile (0.8km)! Follow the road northeast and north for nearly 2 miles (3.2km) to the junction of **Tushielaw**, a scenically pleasing road passing an ancient pele tower and the sloping bridge straddling Ettrick Water by Tushielaw Inn, a suggested refreshment stop.

Tushielaw Tushielaw also has its ruined pele tower, this one being the stronghold of Adam Scott of Tushielaw, King of the Thieves. Folklore has it that Adam was hanged from a branch of his own ash tree within his tower's walls. Facts never quite make such a good story: he was executed in 1530 in Edinburgh for taking blackmail. Reivers such as Adam Scott perfected the protection racket, spawning the word 'blackmail'.

At the road junction by Tushielaw farm take the left fork west, and then northwest along a narrow minor road for 3 miles (4.8km) to the col at GR 275201. The conifer-surrounded climb is gradual, nevertheless there is much to please the eye en route. Swing left onto a forest track, signposted 'Vehicles at drivers own risk', to walk west and then southwest for 1½ miles (2.4km) to join the outgoing Captain's Road by Earl's Hill at the corner of Berry Wood, and return to Tibbie Shiels Inn.

WALK 33 – 'A Glacialist's Walk'

Potburn, Longhope Burn, Bught Hill, Bell Craig,
Andrewhinney Hill, Bell Craig, Bodesbeck Law,
Bodesbeck Col, Potburn

Distance	8¾ miles (14km)
Height Gain	1496ft (456m)
Start/Finish	Potburn turning circle, GR 188093
Grade	3; 4 in poor visibility
Walking Time	6 hours
Maps	OS 1:50 000 Landranger sheet 79, Hawick & Eskdale
Accommodation	The nearest facilities, plus refreshments, are between Ettrick and Tushielaw
Parking	Limited parking on the vergeside rim of the turning circle north of Potburn

For most of its length this walk traverses the eastern rim of the valley of Moffat Water, providing an eagle's-eye view into the most dramatic example of a glaciated U-shaped valley within the Border Country.

Choose a day when the cloud is high and the air is clear for this walk along the Bodesbeck Law–Andrewhinney Hill ridge, high above the glaciated valley of Moffat Water and picturesque upper reaches of Ettrick Water. This is a classic walk of its kind, justly graded 3, that includes three summits of over 2000ft (610m) and two above 1940ft (591m), though once height is attained there are no severe ascents on the ridge. Paths and tracks are mostly distinct and good underfoot, though it is recommended that boots, adequate clothing, a map and compass, together with water and a snack, be taken. Do not forget the camera and a spare roll of film, as the all-embracing views from the ridge summit are perhaps the most varied, extensive and interesting in the guide.

The Route From Selkirk the 24 mile (39km) drive alongside Ettrick Water is a picturesque and pleasant journey, initially via the B7009 to Tushielaw, then with the narrowing B709 road to Ramseycleuch, where a narrow road with passing places, signposted 'Ettrick', forks to the right. A further 7 miles (11.3km) west and southwest brings us to the end of the public road above the deserted farmhouse of South Potburn below the Ettrick Horseshoe.

From this 'back door' turning circle starting point, 1200ft (366m) above sea level, surrounded to the south by a continuous ring of conifer-cloaked Border hills, we begin our ascent to the highest point of this classic border ridge – Andrewhinney Hill. Pass through the gate, waymarked 'Bodesbeck Law, Ettrick Horseshoe' on the northwest edge of the turning circle, leading onto a forest track west. After several hundred yards a second finger post directs us ahead, ascending for 20 minutes between coniferous plantations, north and northwest, with Longhope Burn out of sight on our left. Now on the open grass-covered fell, we continue ascending via a series of zigzag twin tracks between Bushie Law and Pot Law that lead to the flatter ground of Bught Hill's eastern spur. It's an enticing section as we travel approximately west with our route for the day unfolding with every step. Cairned Bodesbeck rises on our immediate left, and then ahead and to the right the rippling ridge culminates in the domes of Bell Craig 2047ft (624m) and beyond to the mass of Andrewhinney Hill 2221ft (677m).

The twin track/pathway swings half-left to ascend Bodesbeck Law, while directly ahead our guiding, crumbling regional boundary wall with its adjoining fence can

The turning circle above Potburn

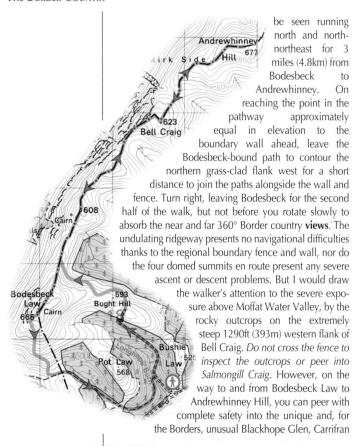

be seen running north and north-northeast for 3 miles (4.8km) from Bodesbeck to Andrewhinney. On reaching the point in the pathway approximately equal in elevation to the boundary wall ahead, leave the Bodesbeck-bound path to contour the northern grass-clad flank west for a short distance to join the paths alongside the wall and fence. Turn right, leaving Bodesbeck for the second half of the walk, but not before you rotate slowly to absorb the near and far 360° Border country **views**. The undulating ridgeway presents no navigational difficulties thanks to the regional boundary fence and wall, nor do the four domed summits en route present any severe ascent or descent problems. But I would draw the walker's attention to the severe expo-sure above Moffat Water Valley, by the rocky outcrops on the extremely steep 1290ft (393m) western flank of Bell Craig. *Do not cross the fence to inspect the outcrops or peer into Salmongill Craig.* However, on the way to and from Bodesbeck Law to Andrewhinney Hill, you can peer with complete safety into the unique and, for the Borders, unusual Blackhope Glen, Carrifran

Far-seeing views In the eastern quadrant the England–Scotland border line can be followed from Peel Fell to the Cheviot, with its northern outliers of Rubers Law and Hownam Law clearly visible, as are the tops of the more northerly, freestanding Eildon Hills by Melrose. The valley of Moffat Water provides spectacular views southwest to the market town of Moffat and the pleasing Lowther Hills.

From Bodesbeck Ridge, looking north to Andrewhinney Hill

Glen and highland Loch Skeen, adorned with mountains such as Saddle Yoke, Carrifran Gans, White Coomb and Lochcraig Head, the guardian of Loch Skeen, source of Tail Burn and the thunderous Grey Mare's Tail waterfall. All are met in Walks 37 to 41.

Flat-domed and grassy **Andrewhinney Hill**, the highest hill on our route, also provides spectacular sightings of the Grey Mare's Tail, should it be in spate, and provides a fine halfway house before setting off back to Bodesbeck Law 2173ft (662m). The faint path continues south-southwest in a somewhat haphazard fashion, rising

---

Andrewhinney Hill A fine vantage point from which to appreciate the views and scotch the rumour that everything south of the Highlands is flat, for not only do the Southern Uplands qualify in height as mountains, they also qualify in certain areas as perfect examples of the mountain form, small in size but beautifully proportioned.

and falling according to the whim of each summit. With Moffat Water 1500ft (457m) below, the summit of Bell Craig, with its rocky outcrops and severe drops above Salmongill Craig, is all too soon passed, as are the two small unnamed summit mounds of 1850ft (564m) and 1992ft (707m) ¾ mile (1.2km) or so south of Bell Craig. Next is the wallside approach to the dominant, cairned grandstand of **Bodesbeck Law** above Capplegill in Moffat Water Valley – an ideal spot to rest and enjoy a break.

Bodesbeck Law Bodesbeck Law stands guard over Bodesbeck farm, as in James Hogg's poem, 'Brownie of Bodesbeck'. To the north and northwest deep and dramatic Blackhope Glen lies imprisoned by Saddle Yoke, Saddle Craigs, Hart Fell and Swatte Fell (Walk 41). To the southwest the narrow glen of Moffat Water unfolds with a patchwork of in-bye fields as the town of Moffat is approached, and below the occasional 'Dinky toy' crawls ant-like along the hairline of the road. South and east Ettrick Water gathers strength as it breaks free from the three-sided grip of the Ettrick Horseshoe, White Shank, Capel Fell, Wind Fell and Ettrick Pen (Walks 34, 35 and 36).

The steep descent south from Bodesbeck Law continues to be guided by the stone dyke and fence of the regional boundary to the col below, meeting a bridlepath from the Ettrick Valley, the outward pathway of the Ettrick Horseshoe, Walk 34. At this point turn left to descend east between various coniferous plantations. The gated track forks twice – always take the left-hand fork – then the invariably damp forest track ends at Longhope Burn. Cross the burn – easily fordable – and immediately turn right at the finger post of our outward journey, descending to the turning circle above Potburn, our starting point.

WALK 34 – The Ettrick Horseshoe

Potburn, Bodesbeck Col, White Shank, Capel Fell, Ettrick Head, Wind Fell, Hopetoun Craig, Ettrick Pen, Over Phawhope, Potburn

Distance	10 miles (16.1km)
Height Gain	2265ft (690m)
Start/Finish	Potburn, GR 188093
Grade	3; 4 in adverse weather
Walking Time	6 hours
Maps	OS 1:50 000 Landranger sheet 79, Hawick & Eskdale
Accommodation	Campsite between Ettrick village and Tushielaw, where there is an inn, GR 303177; bed-and-breakfasts and self-catering accommodation sprinkled along Ettrick Valley
Parking	Potburn, GR 188093, available on the edge of the turning circle

The Ettrick Horseshoe – a high-level trek to be savoured when the sun is warm on the back and the winds have lost winter's bite – covers six summits of 2000ft (607m) plus. Steep in places but never hazardous, this circular walk treads paths that at lower levels are good and distinct, but on the heights little more than sheep traces through tussock grass, and in some stretches almost nonexistent. However, navigation is simplified by the regional boundary stone dyke and fence that runs for the entire length of the horseshoe. Walking boots and correct clothing are essential, as are map and compass, together with a camera to record the upland solitude of these Borderland hills.

The solitude of the Border landscape can be fully appreciated on this high-level route.

The Route The 24 mile (39km) drive from Selkirk along the banks of Ettrick Water is a pleasant experience, especially in spring and autumn. First on the B7009 Selkirk to Tushielaw, then the B709 to Ramseycleuch, where a narrow road with passing places, signposted 'Ettrick', forks to the right. Follow this road west and southwest for 7 miles (11.3km) to the end of the public road at South Potburn, GR 188093.

To Bodesbeck col

From the starting point of the walk at GR 188093, 1200ft (366m) above sea level, an unbroken horseshoe of mountains rises high above the coniferous tide mark, an indication that this promises to be a challenging walk of quality. Pass through the right-hand gate, waymarked 'Bodesbeck Law, Ettrick Horseshoe', onto the forest road leading west. After several hundred yards fork left at the finger post to ford Longhope Burn onto a grassy path running between the trees. Walk southwest and then west, climbing steadily, passing two gates and a circular sheep stell (keep to the right at the fork). Bodesbeck col 1555ft (474m), with its dilapidated gate at the regional boundary, is reached after 40 minutes. To the right stands the summit of Bodesbeck Law, to the left White Shank.

Leave the track at the col and follow the stone dyke left, i.e. south, to the immediate skyline, from where it zigzags west across an almost pathless hillside, later to swing left, i.e. south, at the summit of Fauldside Hill 1858ft (566m), before rising steadily to White Shank 2035ft (620m). Do not at any point on this walk doubt the accuracy of the boundary wall/fence as your guide – keep it in sight and to hand all the way to Ettrick Pen 2270ft (692m). During the ascent of White Shank, which should be reached 1½ hours from the start, stop and look west across Moffat Water Valley to the exciting view of rock in the dramatic glen of Blackhope (Walk 41). The way from White Shank over Capel Fell 2223ft (678m) to Ettrick Head, though something of a switchback, is never dull. First, Smidhope Hill 2111ft (643m), where the guiding wall is replaced by a fence that swings left to the summit. At the gate on the summit descend, with the fence on our right, southeast to Ettrick Head 1700ft (518m). This stretch is perhaps the wildest and most desolate of the walk, with deep and dark ravines scouring the rounded hillsides to the south, and ahead a black mass of peat loitering with intent at the foot of steep-sided Wind Fell 2180ft (664m).

The Southern Upland Way intersects the route at Ettrick Head, with the heartening notice 'Welcome to Borders Region' prominently displayed. Ahead the ascent

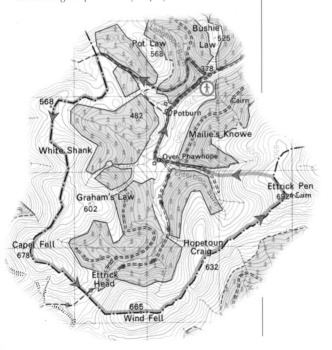

To Ettrick Head and Wind Fell

The approaches to Ettrick Pen are marked by a clutch of well-constructed cairns, although the summit cairn is somewhat untidy.

of Wind Fell 2180ft (664m) requires some determination, due to the absence of paths and the initial crossing of the peat, but once attained it marks the start of another fine ridge walk. Continue northeast for nearly 2 miles (3.2km) over Hopetoun Craig 2075ft (632m) to Ettrick Pen, at 2270ft (692m) the highest point on the walk. This section offers fine views on all sides, particularly south to Eskdalemuir. ◄

Leave the summit cairn of Ettrick Pen and the guiding fence for an adventurous hike of over ½ mile (0.8km), descending the open fell of Ettrick Pen's west ridge. On a clear day the line of descent is towards the summit of White Shank, 2 miles (3.2km) to the west. In poor visibility descend on a compass bearing of 282° magnetic. The ridge and the shoulder are not difficult to negotiate, and the marker to aim for is an old tin shed by Entertrona Burn. From the tin shed descend to the valley floor and the bothy at Over Phawhope (a bed for the night if required).

The Southern Upland Way is met at the bothy and followed across the wooden bridge via abandoned Potburn to the turning point on the public road, GR 188093.

WALK 35 – By Forest and Fell over Ettrick Pen

Potburn, Over Phawhope, Ettrick Head, Wind Fell, Ettrick Pen, Over Phawhope, Potburn

Distance	6 miles (9.7km)
Height Gain	1170ft (357m)
Start/Finish	Potburn turning circle, GR 188093
Grade	3
Walking Time	4 hours
Maps	OS 1:50 000 Landranger sheet 79, Hawick & Eskdale
Accommodation	A campsite is situated between Ettrick village and Tushielaw (inn, accommodation and refreshment) on the B709, GR 303177; bed-and-breakfasts are also sprinkled along Ettrick Valley
Parking	Potburn, GR 188093, on the edge of the turning circle

This variation of Walk 34 enables the walker to sample a valley walk (a section of the Southern Upland Way) to the watershed at Ettrick Head, yet still experience the exhilaration and visual pleasure of the high ridge by walking one half of the Ettrick Horseshoe. Conditions underfoot for this hike are mainly along farm or forest roads, with 2½ miles (4km) on the open fell.

The Route From the turning point at GR 188093, take the wide farm road south to South Potburn, clearly visible ahead. Continue to follow the road to the wooden bridge and the bothy of Over Phawhope. A few yards past the bothy the forest road swings right at Entertrona Burn and continues south, ascending the valley for 1¼ miles (2km) to Ettrick Head. On all sides coniferous plantations mask the rolling hillsides, though clearings have been left by the banks of fledgling Ettrick Water. Once clear of these dark woodlands the waymarked Southern Upland Way to Ettrick Head on the regional boundary is distinct and most welcome.

The walk is visually pleasing, very photogenic, and offers a high interest factor.

Over the stile and sharp left, first circumnavigate the deep peat, and then ascend the steep flank of Wind Fell 2180ft (664m), using the ever-present boundary fence as a guide. The ridge walk northeast from the summit of Wind Hill, via the craggy top of Hopetoun Craig 2075ft (632m), to the majestic cairn on Ettrick Pen 2270ft (692m), is 2 miles (3.2km) of pedestrian pleasure. Keep an eye open for the selection of cairns on the approach to Ettrick Pen.

Leave the large cairn and make for the trackless open fell due west. Use the peak of White Shank, 2 miles (3.2km) across the Ettrick Valley, as a marker, and in poor visibility a bearing of 282° magnetic. Descend the western ridge to a tin hut on Entertrona Burn where a good wide track is met. This pathway descends sedately west to Over Phawhope bothy, an opportunity for a break and a look at the visitors' book before returning north on the farm road to Potburn and our starting point at the turning circle.

Potburn to Over Phawhope

WALK 36 – An Eagle's Eye View of the Moffat Water Valley and the Tweedsmuir Hills

Potburn GR 188093, Over Phawhope, Ettrick Head, Capel Fell, White Shank, Bodesbeck Col, Potburn

Distance	7 miles (11.3km)
Height Gain	1123ft (342m)
Start/Finish	Potburn turning circle, GR 188093
Grade	3
Walking Time	4 hours
Maps	OS 1: 50 000 Landranger sheet 79, Hawick & Eskdale, Langholm
Accommodation	A campsite is situated between Ettrick village and Tushielaw (inn, accommodation and refreshment) on the B709, GR 303177; bed-and-breakfasts and self-catering accommodation are sprinkled along the Ettrick Valley
Parking	Potburn turning circle, GR 188093

This walk is for the enthusiast who for various reasons has limited time or energy at his or her disposal, but who nevertheless has the urge to go just that little bit further. Take a map, if only to identity the tempting walks to the northwest of and beyond Moffat Water Valley, involving the 'honeypots' of Carrifran Glen and White Coomb, or Saddle Yoke, Hart Fell Craig and Black Craig above the gouged glen north of Capplegill.

This tempting half-day aperitif has good conditions underfoot, but walking boots are nevertheless recommended.

The Route Start the ramble at GR 188093 and take the route to the stile at Ettrick Head as described in Walk 35. At the regional boundary, having crossed the stile, do not immediately turn right and leave the Southern Upland Way, but continue south for ½ mile (0.8km) to gaze into the jaws of Selcoth Burn on the southern flanks of Capel Fell. Retrace your steps to the stile and turn left to follow the fence as it climbs 520ft (158m) to the summit of Capel Fell.

Smidhope Hill

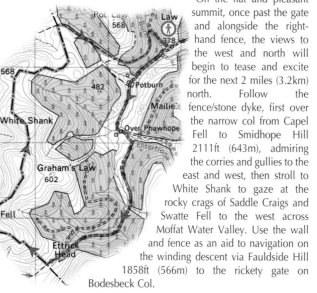

On the flat and pleasant summit, once past the gate and alongside the right-hand fence, the views to the west and north will begin to tease and excite for the next 2 miles (3.2km) north. Follow the fence/stone dyke, first over the narrow col from Capel Fell to Smidhope Hill 2111ft (643m), admiring the corries and gullies to the east and west, then stroll to White Shank to gaze at the rocky crags of Saddle Craigs and Swatte Fell to the west across Moffat Water Valley. Use the wall and fence as an aid to navigation on the winding descent via Fauldside Hill 1858ft (566m) to the rickety gate on Bodesbeck Col.

The gate on the col straddles the track from upper Ettrick Valley, so turn right and descend east through two gates, keeping to the left forks at any dividing of the ways. The path enters another collection of conifers and ends abruptly at Longhope Burn. Ford the burn to join another wide forest road to the right. One more gate and 300yds (274m) returns the walker to the starting point at the turning circle, GR 188093.

Col to White Shank, Capel Fell and Ettrick Pen

To Saddle Yoke and Black Craig (Walk 41)

CHAPTER 4

THE TWEEDSMUIR HILLS

Within the environs of the Tweedsmuir Hills lie two distinctive groups of mountains, the Moffat Hills and the Manor Hills, which between them form the western bastion of the Scottish Border country covered in this guide.

THE MOFFAT HILLS

Neatly enclosed in a triangle of rivers and roads, these fascinating hills offer an impressively compelling landscape, particularly when viewed from the A708 that winds through Moffat Water Valley. It is from this steep-sided glen that the wild lateral valleys of Blackhope, Carrifran and the Grey Mare's Tail (Walks 37 to 41) curve gracefully and seductively northwards, offering an enticing invitation to the walker. These glaciated intrusions, penetrating deep into the central plateau, are ringed by spectacular stretches of broken rocky crags, loose shale and scree, and divided by sharp and narrow grassy ridges. Steep cliffs and boulder-strewn slopes in excess of 1000ft (305m) emphasise the plunging nature of the southeastern section of these hills.

In addition to glaciated glens, the Moffat Hills contain gorges and gullies, some exposed for all to see, the more interesting remaining hidden in dark and secretive hillsides. Two lochs, Loch Skeen 1700ft (518m) and Gameshope Loch 1850ft (564m), are situated high in the range, while at lower levels the narrow reservoirs of Talla and Megget securely lock the northern boundaries of the group.

Contained in the Moffat Hills are four mountains over 2500ft (762m) – White Coomb, Hart Fell, Lochcraig Head and Molls Cleuch Dod – together with two tops that exceed that height, Firthope Rig and Great Hill. There are six hills over 2000ft (610m) – Under Saddle Yoke, Swatte Fell, Cape Law, Garelet Dod, Erie Hill and Whitehope Heights, and nine tops – Nickies Knowe, Carrifran Gans, Saddle Yoke, Carlavin Hill, Nether Coomb Craig, Falcon Craig, Lairds Cleuch Rig, Garelet Hill and Din Law.

This isolated and lonely area is so devoid of human habitation that not one road or farm track entering these hills completes its journey to emerge at the other side. The few isolated hill farms that populate the region are only to be found on the extremities. The landscape of the Tweedsmuir Hills is rich in wildlife – ravens, ring ouzels and red grouse inhabit the higher fells, while herons, dippers, grey wagtails and sandpipers favour Moffat Water and the lower burns. Feral goats, foxes, otters, feral mink, mountain hares and the occasional deer can all be found. Limestone-loving plants are present at lower levels, while the upper ground is covered by acid-loving plants such as heaths and heather. On wet and badly drained cols, ubiquitous peat hags lurk, with half-hidden wet-holes innocently covered by bright-green feather-bed moss. The roads ringing the area are the A708 St Mary's Loch to Moffat, the A701 Moffat to Tweedsmuir, and the unclassified road running from Tweedsmuir via Talla and Megget reservoirs to St Mary's Loch.

THE MANOR HILLS

Rising north of the Moffat Hills, these hills are wild and exposed on their eastern and southern flanks, though this severity is tempered on the west and north by the unmistakable beauty of the Upper Tweed Valley, the intriguing Manor Water Valley, and that of Quair Water. The range consists of an upland sprawl of lumpy, rounded grassy summits joined together by broad ridges that run willy-nilly over the entire plateau. Lacking the form and character of the more dramatic Moffat Hills, they have one great virtue – gentle slopes. With dry conditions underfoot and boundary fences and dykes to aid navigation, the miles can be traversed with some ease and not a little aplomb. The main ridge runs north from Cramalt Craig to flank and overlook the nine miles of Manor Valley, while the more shapely ridges of the massif descend in graceful curves to the Tweed between Drumelzier (pronounced 'drum-eelier') and Cademuir Hill, south of Peebles.

If height is an attraction, this massif contains some of the highest mountains in southern Scotland, and certainly the highest in the Border region. There are two mountains over 2700ft (823m), Broad Law and Cramalt Craig, with one over 2600ft (792m), Dollar Law, and one top, Fifescar Knowe. Ten hills exceed 2000ft (610m) – Dun Rig, Pykestone Hill, Glenrath Heights, Middle Hill, Black Law, Talla Cleuch Head, Stob Law, Drumelzier Law, Birkscairn Hill and Greenside Law, with six tops in excess of 2000ft – the Scrape, Blackhouse Heights, Clockmore, Hunt Law, Taberon Law and Deer Law.

Lochs and rocks are minimal, Loch Eddy being the only stretch of water of any note, though the southern boundary is restrained by St Mary's Loch and the manmade reservoirs of Megget and Talla. Rock and scree can be found at Polmood Craig on the north face of Broad Law, the small but picturesque Bitch Craig at Manorhead, and also at Juniper Craig below Preston Law.

The Manor Hills are encircled by roads, the A701 Tweedsmuir to Drumelzier, the B712 to Peebles and the A72 to Innerleithen, where a right turn onto the B709 travels south to join the A708 to St Mary's Loch, with an unclassified single-track road leading west via the reservoirs of Megget and Talla to Tweedsmuir.

Peebles, Innerleithen, Moffat and Selkirk provide the widest variety of accommodation for the Tweedsmuir Hills, ranging from hotels to camping and caravan sites. Inns and small hotels are found at St Mary's Loch, Tweedsmuir and Mountbenger, with a selection of bed-and-breakfasts scattered along the roads surrounding the hills. Scotland's first youth hostel is situated at Broadmeadows, 4 miles (6.4km) west of Selkirk.

Public bus services are none too frequent. Details can be obtained at the bus stations in Peebles, Innerleithen and Selkirk, and from local tourist information centres. Post buses run to the more remote regions, invariably early in the day.

THE WALKS

With not one Munro in the area the hills are not bagged to death by the relentless tramp of the feet of 'tickers', and as a result seekers of solitude can find just that. Walk 37 visits two fine waterfalls, and Walks 38 and 39 climb past the thundering falls of the Grey Mare's Tail to venture onto the high plateau, giving a bird's eye view of Loch Skeen, the black loch 1700ft (518m) above sea level. For the more adventurous, Walk 39 adds a steep rock scramble in the narrow confines of Midlaw Burn Gorge. Continuing in the energetic mood, Walk 40 treks into Carrifran Glen below the dramatic face of Raven Craig, ascending to the highest summit in the Moffat Hills, White Coomb. Having sighted the graceful, narrow curving ridge of Saddle Yoke from Carrifran Gans, Walk 41 will have become imprinted on the walker's mind. The high-level circuit of the wild and precipitous Blackhope Glen over Saddle Yoke, Hart Fell and Swatte Fell is in my opinion the finest of Border journeys. Walk 42's entry into the Moffat Hills is from the northern extremity of the range, via the mysterious glen of Gameshope, to a ridge carrying four 2500ft (762m) mountains.

Walk 43 introduces the Manor Hills by ascending the gentle slopes of the highest mountain in the range, Broad Law 2754ft (839m), before Walk 44 visits the second highest, Cramalt Craig 2723ft (830m). The ascent of both is cushioned by starting the walk from 1483ft (452m). Walk 45 starts in Manor Water Glen beyond Langhaugh, ascending above Kirkhope Burn to stride along the Thief's Road from Long Grain Knowe to Pykestone Hill, returning via the eyrie of Posso Craig. Walk 46 is through the delightful glen of Quair Water, with secluded Loch Eddy at its head, then over the heather-clad hills of Blake Muir to Traquair Parish Church by Kirkhouse.

WALK 37 – Two Dramatic Waterfalls

*Grey Mare's Tail, Tail Burn, Infant Moffat Water,
Dob's Linn, Grey Mare's Tail*

Distance	3 miles (4.8km)
Height Gain	100ft (30.5m)
Start/Finish	Grey Mare's Tail car park alongside A708, Moffat Water Valley, GR 187145, 10 miles (16.1km) northeast of Moffat, 24 miles (36.6km) southwest of Selkirk
Grade	1
Walking Time	2 hours
Maps	OS 1:50 000 Landranger sheet 79, Hawick & Eskdale
Accommodation	Accommodation and refreshments around St Mary's Loch
Parking	GR 187145, off-road under the auspices of National Trust Scotland

Two very different waterfalls are seen on this short walk.

Situated barely 1 mile (1.6km) apart, the cascades of the Grey Mare's Tail and Dob's Linn, southwest from white-washed **Birkhill Cottage** on the watershed via **Birkhill Pass**, differ vastly in appearance. This there-and-back walk embraces both waterfalls and introduces the walker to the classic glaciated valley of Moffat Water. This is a relatively short walk, mainly on the valley floor alongside Dob's Linn Burn. Walking boots with good gripping soles are recommended as the way is stony underfoot, and if photography is of interest the morning light provides the best shots of both waterfalls.

Birkhill Birkhill Cottage is a solitary and lonely house by the side of the A708 near the summit of Birkhill Pass 1108ft (338m), considered by many to be the finest border pass of all. From here the water that flows north and east runs into the North Sea at Berwick, and the southerly flow of water runs into the Irish Sea via the Solway Firth. The cottage carries a plaque: 'Birkhill Cottage, where between 1872 and 1877 Charles Lapworth recognised the value of Graptolites, as a clue to the geological structure of these hills. Erected by Scottish Geologists in 1951.'

Birkhill Pass

The Route A pathway leads north-northwest from the car park, with Tail Burn on the right and the steep flanks of Upper Tarnberry glowering above left. The visible pathway to the right, beyond and above Tail Burn and the white waters of the **Grey Mare's Tail**, is for another day, Walks 38 and 39. Our path ascends gradually for approximately 1/3 mile (535m) to view the thundering foot of the falls, but a barrier prevents further passage, *for danger lies ahead and under no circumstances attempt to gain closer views*. Return to the car parks, from where the walk to Dob's Linn begins.

The Grey Mare's Tail This spectacular waterfall, with its 200ft (61m) drop, falls through one of the most striking examples of a hanging valley in the south of Scotland. During the ice age a large glacier gouged a much deeper channel into the Moffat Water Valley than did the smaller side-glaciers, forming a step that left the resultant Tail Burn hanging. It took the route of least resistance, hence the eye-catching Grey Mare's Tail.

205

To Dob's Linn

The gorge entrance of Dob's Linn requires several crossings of the rock-filled burn – take care if using wet rock as stepping stones; I found that walking poles assist passage.

Exit southeast from the car parks onto the A708, turn left and cross the bridge walking northeast. Once over, leave the road left into the stone-strewn and grass-clad strip that runs north-northeast between the A708 and the sheer eastern slopes of Bran Law, and through whose centre wriggles the infant **Moffat Water**. Sheep trods between burn and road provide passage for the short and pleasant 1¼ mile (2km) to the narrow, rock-strewn entrance of Dob's Linn. ◄

Moffat Water When ice covered the country a main and swiftly moving glacier gouged out what is now Moffat Water glen, and was fed by smaller lateral glaciers. Large quantities of sand, clay and rocks were dumped at the side of the main glen and in the side-valleys, and these 'kames' can be seen today as vegetation-covered mounds.

The multiple and severe gullies of **Dob's Linn** appear unexpectedly. The first gully on the left has a constant burn running into it (feeding Dob's Linn), with a few stunted trees clinging precariously to the sheer rim. *On no account must ascents or descents be attempted into the cleuchs.* Keep close to the burnside as the steep slopes on all sides are composed of crumbling and unstable shale, made more so with half-hidden wet patches. The majestic five falls and slides of Dob's Linn are now in full view, and also of interest are the rocks and plants in the surrounding gullies. ▶

Look out for a herd of feral goats that frequents Dob's Linn and surrounding fells.

Dob's Linn While not as awesome as the Grey Mare's Tail, the five falls and water slides of Dob's Linn are just as dramatic, and perhaps more picturesque, as they slide down the exposed face of two sheer slabs of rock. The geologist Charles Lapworth contributed greatly to our understanding of geological time with his work around Dob's Linn. He made a special study of fossilised 'graptolites', small, plankton-eating animals that lived some 300 million years ago on the surface of ancient seas, their remains becoming incorporated in the sediments of these seas to produce the sandstones and shales from which the present day landscape was formed.

The linn also provided a secure hideaway, or refuge, in the form of a tiny sheiling above the five gullies and a cave in the linn, for two prominent Covenanters, David Dun and Halberd Dobson, known locally as Davie Din and Hab Dob, to escape the persecutions of the servants of John Graham of Claverhouse, Viscount Dundee, a zealous suppressor of the Covenanters. Legend has it that one day the devil sought to drive the two Covenanters over the linn to their deaths below. They, however, fashioned a cross from a nearby mountain ash, and with aid from their bible they pitched the devil himself over the linn. The old dialect verse says it all:

> For Hab Dob, an Davie Din,
> Dang the Diel owre Dob's Linn.
> Habby held him grif an' grim
> Davie threush him liff an' limb.

Return to the car park below the Grey Mare's Tail via the outward route along Birkhill Pass, a pleasant 1¼ miles (2km) southwest alongside the infant Moffat Water.

Dob's Linn, the Moffat Hills

WALK 38 – Dark and Deep Loch Skeen

*Grey Mare's Tail (car park), Tail Burn, Loch
Skeen, Lochcraig Head, Firthybrig Head, Loch
Skeen, Grey Mare's Tail (car park)*

Distance	7 miles (11.3km)
Height Gain	2024ft (617m)
Start/Finish	Grey Mare's Tail car park, Moffat Water Valley, GR 187145
Grade	3
Walking Time	5 hours
Maps	OS 1:50 000 Landranger sheet 79, Hawick & Eskdale
Accommodation	A selection available in Moffat and around St Mary's Loch
Parking	Two pay car parks on the north side of the A708, GR 187145

A steeply ascending path leads the walker above the spectacular falls of the Grey Mare's Tail to begin, via steep pathways, grassy tracks and occasional forays through peat hags, an elevated circuit of the dark and rather secretive Loch Skeen.

The items of interest for this walk, highlighted in bold, are described fully in Walk 39.

The Route From the A708 Moffat to Selkirk road, at GR 187145 (very popular in summer with coach trips), take the stepped path to climb steeply up the flank of Bran Law, north of the **Grey Mare's Tail**. Above the falls the path winds northwest alongside Tail Burn, then through a rather desolate area of glacial pimples, to the foot of **Loch Skeen**. Before the loch, at the point where Midlaw Burn runs into Tail Burn from the left, a faint and narrow trace through the heather leaves the main path on the right to ascend over a glacial mound. Take this heathery trace north for ½ mile (0.8km), to the angle in the fence, leading north to Lochcraig Head.

Exhilarating but never hazardous, the walk requires mountain walking footwear and clothing, and in adverse weather or poor visibility a map and compass are essential.

By the Grey Mare's Tail northwest to Loch Skeen

Over Loch Skeen to Lochcraig Head

Loch Skeen is now several hundred yards to the west, i.e. left, with the steep face of Lochcraig Head a cruel mix of bare rock and sheer scree to the north. Further west a stark ridge from Firthybrig Head combines to give the loch its reputation as 'a gloomy tarn'. On reaching the fence turn left and follow the path north for 1 mile (1.6km), ascending steeply for 800ft (244m) to the flat grassy summit of **Lochcraig Head** 2625ft (800m), the zenith of the walk.

From this point the elevated circuit of Loch Skeen begins, first west along the regional boundary fence and wall to Firthybrig Head 2504ft (263m), taking care not to stray too close to the rim of the rocky crag on the left. At the summit of Firthybrig Head swing south for 300yds

Loch Skeen surrounded by glacial deposits

(274m), then leave the guiding fence to cross an open fell southeast, i.e. left, to join the rock-strewn ridge, Mid Craig 2208ft (673m), that encloses the western banks of Loch Skeen. Rather ragged along the top but with a good path, the ridge descends sharply at its southern tip to join and ford Tail Burn at the out-fall from Loch Skeen (easy in summer but troublesome in winter). A well-constructed path leaves Loch Skeen behind and marches southeast to join the outward path above the Grey Mare's Tail. Descend slowly for the last mile (1.6km) to the car park at the side of the A708. The views of glaciated Moffat Water Glen, with its spectacular waterfalls and steep-sided Bodesbeck Ridge opposite, are indeed breathtaking.

WALK 39 – A Waterfall, a Loch, a Gorge and Surrounding Summits

Grey Mare's Tail, Loch Skeen, Midlaw Burn Gorge, Donald's Cleuch Head, Firthybrig Head, Lochcraig Head, Tail Burn, Grey Mare's Tail

Distance	7 miles (11.3km)
Height Gain	2154ft (657m)
Start/Finish	Grey Mare's Tail car park, Moffat Water Valley, GR 187145
Grade	4
Walking Time	6 hours
Maps	OS 1:50 000 Landranger sheet 79, Hawick & Eskdale
Accommodation	A selection available in Moffat and around St Mary's Loch
Parking	Two pay car parks on the north side of the A708, GR 187145

This is a variation of Walk 38 for those who relish the challenge of a rocky cleuch (gorge) scramble, followed by an elevated circuit of Loch Skeen.

Midlaw Burn Gorge rises 250ft (76m) from mouth to head, and involves rough walking, crossing Midlaw Burn at least six times. The ascent out of the gorge involves a scramble up a stone chute. Sections of rough and pathless terrain, plus passage through the gorge, gives this walk a difficulty rating of 4. On a clear day navigation is not difficult, nevertheless it is advisable to carry map and compass, and essential to wear the right gear. This is a very photogenic walk.

The Route The start and initial ascent, from the car parks at GR 187145, takes the stepped path climbing steeply north-northwest up the western flank of Bran Law. Above, the **Grey Mare's Tail** path and Tail Burn level out through a rather desolate area of heather-clad glacial pimples, to the southern foot of **Loch Skeen**. Ford Tail Burn – flat stones aid passage – to ascend with the distinct, at times waterlogged, path to the western ridge

While embracing all the scenic grandeur of Walk 38, this walk, with its accompanying waterslides, goes 'just that little bit further', for in the cleuch and on some sections of open fell there are no definite paths.

The Grey Mare's Tail A waterfall of outstanding size and power, and a tourist attraction of some note, the Grey Mare's Tail is named after the grey mare in Robert Burns's poem, 'Tam O'Shanter'. A statistic for the rock climber – two climbing routes up each side of the waterfall were pioneered by Edinburgh climbers during the severe winter of February 1969, in a climb of 450ft (137m).

Loch Skeen Set in a wild and desolate moor pimpled by glacial deposits and ringed by rocky mountain crags of some presence, Loch Skeen, lying at 1700ft (518m), is ¾ mile (1.2km) from north to south, its dark waters sinking to a depth of over 25 fathoms, or 150ft (46m). Loch Skene (19th-century spelling) was visited by Sir Walter Scott (which part of the Borders was not?) who, with his companion and their horses, was caught in the folds of a clinging mist. 'As we were groping through a maze of bogs the ground gave way, and down went horse and horsemen pell-mell into a slough of peaty mud and black water, it was no easy matter to get extricated.' Today the traveller has the talisman of the guidebook to help him on his way, and the walker can be assured that on a fine day the loch is a jewel in the crown of the Moffat Hills.

above Loch Skeen. Three-quarters of a mile (1.2km) after crossing Tail Burn a large boulder is met at the 1900ft (579m) contour line. At this boulder turn left on a bearing of 280° magnetic into a wilderness peppered with hummocks of glacial debris. Progress is easier if the 1900ft contour is maintained to the mouth of **Midlaw Burn Gorge** (it's the larger one on the right), ½ mile (0.8km) west of the boulder.

Midlaw Burn Gorge The upper reaches of Midlaw Burn Gorge 2250ft (686m) contain several spectacular water slides, shooting down huge slabs of rock. The stony scramble of 250ft (76m), ascending with Midlaw Burn, is not often offered to the mountaineer in these well-rounded and fully clothed hills.

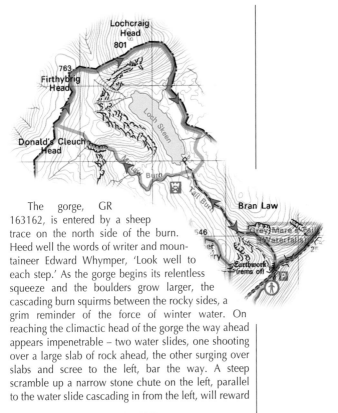

The gorge, GR 163162, is entered by a sheep trace on the north side of the burn. Heed well the words of writer and mountaineer Edward Whymper, 'Look well to each step.' As the gorge begins its relentless squeeze and the boulders grow larger, the cascading burn squirms between the rocky sides, a grim reminder of the force of winter water. On reaching the climactic head of the gorge the way ahead appears impenetrable – two water slides, one shooting over a large slab of rock ahead, the other surging over slabs and scree to the left, bar the way. A steep scramble up a narrow stone chute on the left, parallel to the water slide cascading in from the left, will reward

Midlaw Burn Gorge in winter's grip

215

the experienced and determined mountaineer. An ascent via the waterfall ahead should be ignored. If conditions are not perfect for the ascent up the stone chute, i.e. excess water or ice, retrace your steps to the second curve in the burn and ascend the easier south side, i.e. right, to the top rim. Should this climb not be acceptable, return to the mouth and ascend on the south rim to above the head of the gorge at GR 161163.

From this point, on a compass bearing of 280°, tramp over the open fell for ½ mile (0.8km) to reach the fenced dyke at Donald's Cleuch Head 2510ft (765m). On this flat and indistinguishable summit, GR 156164, turn immediately right and follow the helpful fence north for ½ mile (0.8km) to Firthybrig Head 2504ft (763m). Here the guiding fence turns sharp right, i.e. east-northeast, to descend to a peat-clad col before ascending steeply to the flat peak of **Lochcraig Head** 2625ft (800m). ◄

> The summit of Lochcraig Head must surely be one of the most noble grandstands in the Tweedsmuir Hills.

Lochcraig Head A fine, flat-topped mountain, capped in short grass and strewn with scattered sandstone, whose exposed rocky south face drops dramatically for 400ft (122m) to the north shore of Loch Skeen. Third in height of the Moffat Hills, it provides a superb grandstand from which to view the surrounding peaks of the Southern Uplands.

The descent turns right, i.e. south, with the stone dyke, and is so abrupt that care is needed for the next ¾ mile (1.2km). In poor visibility always keep the dyke/fence in sight, for the south face of Lochcraig Head is dangerously precipitous. Once level ground is reached, the path by the fence is a mixture of peat and heather, with Loch Skeen now only 100–200yds (91–183m) to the right. Halfway along the loch the fence swings left, i.e. southeast, and it is here a thin path leaves the fence to continue south over heather-covered mounds for ½ mile (0.8km), to join the path and Tail Burn at the southern end of Loch Skeen. The luxury of a good path is the walker's reward as it descends with the picturesque and noisy Grey Mare's Tail.

Walk 40 – 'A Walk on the Wild Side' – 9000 Years Ago

Carrifran, Carrifran Burn, Corrie of Gupe Craig, White Coomb, Carrifran Gans, Carrifran

Distance	7 miles (11.3km)
Height Gain	2355ft (718m)
Start/Finish	Carrifran car park, GR 159116, on the A708 2½ miles (4km) southwest from the Grey Mare's Tail
Grade	4
Walking Time	5 hours
Maps	OS 1:50 000 Landranger sheet 79, Hawick & Eskdale
Accommodation	Moffat and St Mary's Loch provide the nearest facilities
Parking	Limited – a small off-road car park, gate marked 'CARRIFRAN', a few yards north of the bridge that marks the combined start of our walk and also a shorter, more recent one, the Carrifran Wildwood Walk, instigated by the Borders Forest Trust

The hidden glen of Carrifran, second of the three lateral glaciated valleys that grace the Moffat Hills, digs deep into the central plateau, providing a fine valley walk culminating in serious wild walking/scrambling out of the valley floor to the summit of White Coomb, the highest mountain in the range. Conditions underfoot vary, from wide farm tracks to narrow sheep traces with a steep burnside scramble (in places) through the upper reaches of these hills, and a steep descent from Carrifran Gans. Mountain clothing must be worn, and a map and compass carried, together with food and drink. A camera is recommended. Should the burnside ascent from the corrie northwest of Gupe Craig en route to White Coomb not appeal to you, I would suggest a return via the outward valley-floor route, which rejoins the waymarked path of the short Carrifran Wildwood Walk (see p.218) and provides an alternative, interesting return to the car park.

A fine valley walk with a scramble up to White Coomb.

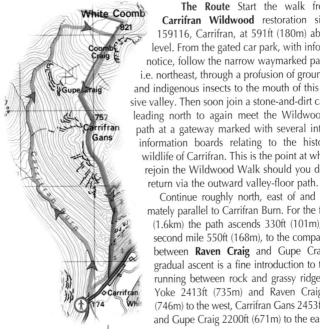

The Route Start the walk from the **Carrifran Wildwood** restoration site, GR 159116, Carrifran, at 591ft (180m) above sea level. From the gated car park, with information notice, follow the narrow waymarked path right, i.e. northeast, through a profusion of ground cover and indigenous insects to the mouth of this impressive valley. Then soon join a stone-and-dirt cart track leading north to again meet the Wildwood Walk path at a gateway marked with several interesting information boards relating to the history and wildlife of Carrifran. This is the point at which you rejoin the Wildwood Walk should you decide to return via the outward valley-floor path.

Continue roughly north, east of and approximately parallel to Carrifran Burn. For the first mile (1.6km) the path ascends 330ft (101m), for the second mile 550ft (168m), to the compact corrie between **Raven Craig** and Gupe Craig. This gradual ascent is a fine introduction to the glen, running between rock and grassy ridge, Saddle Yoke 2413ft (735m) and Raven Craig 2247ft (746m) to the west, Carrifran Gans 2453ft (748m) and Gupe Craig 2200ft (671m) to the east.

Carrifran Wildwood At the head of the glen, fringing the rocky heights of Raven Craig, lie the peaty wastes of Rotten Bottom. It was here that a hill walker found a prehistoric bow that can now be seen in the Museum of Scotland in Edinburgh. Rotten Bottom's peat also gave scientists a cornucopia of preserved seeds and plant fossils, the richest haul within Scotland, that enabled them to date and tabulate the biological life of the area.

Raven Craig These dramatic cliffs rise for 500ft (152m) at the head of the glen, and coupled with Priest Craig form a formidable barrier of rock stretching for 1 mile (1.6km). Home to the peregrine falcon and the raven, these crags are the result of lateral glacial activity.

When the twin track peters out, continue using the 'true left', i.e. east, bank of Carrifran Burn, and at a fork by a coned cairn, swing right to follow the deer-fenced main burn north-northeast. With its series of water slides as a guide, clamber north, ascending steeply with care alongside the burn. At the 2000ft (610m) contour the steep incline thankfully levels off, with the rounded bulk of **White Coomb** 2694ft (821m) rising ½ mile (0.8km) ahead. In good visibility leave the burn, turn half-right, i.e. northeast, and make an easy ascent across the open fell to the summit. Should conditions be poor with limited visibility, continue to follow the burn to its source, and when a fence/dyke is met, turn right to follow it east-southeast to the summit.

Fenceside descent from Carrifran Gans

White Coomb White Coomb is spacious on top, providing an excellent vantage point from which to admire the entire panorama of the Southern Uplands and the Border hills. Its western aspect slopes gently and easily to three outliers, but not so to the north and east, where the descent is sudden and precipitous at Rough Craigs and Coomb Craig.

Below White Coomb, 1 mile (1.6km) to the south-southwest, the flat and green top of **Carrifran Gans** is easily reached on a path that drops to the dividing col then rises gently to the twin-cairned summit. The descent south, 1½ miles (2.4km) from Carrifran Gans, is straightforward, albeit steep in places. It drops 1880ft (573m) to the road below, with the final leg following a boundary fence of patchy woodland, apparently suffering from an attack of 'arboreal alopecia', to join the farm track and the Wildwood Walk. ▶

Keep an eye open for the herd of **feral goats** that dwells on these slopes.

Carrifran Gans Carrifran Gans (is the word from the Greek 'ganos', meaning 'brightness'?) provides spectacular views of the glen below and the twin cones of Saddle Yoke on the opposite ridge. Its western flank drops dramatically, and in poor visibility is dangerous to approach. Two small cairns a hundred or so yards apart adorn the summit, each appearing to be higher than the other.

Feral goats Outcasts from the domestic scene, these semi-wild goats roam the Border hills and Southern Uplands. Running in small herds of around 20, poor feeding and severe winters tend to keep the numbers low (though their diet is now supplemented by tourists' debris around the Grey Mare's Tail car park). They can also be seen near Dob's Linn (Walk 37) and Black Craig (Walk 41).

North to Raven Craig

WALK 41 – On the Edge of Blackhope's Glacial Glen

Capplegill, Saddle Yoke, Raven Craig, Hartfell Rig, Hart Fell, Swatte Fell, Black Craig, Capplegill

Distance	10 miles (16.1km)
Height Gain	2245ft (684m)
Start/Finish	Blackhope Cottage, Capplegill, GR 147098
Grade	4
Walking Time	Between 5 and 7 hours
Maps	OS 1:50 000 Landranger sheet 78, Nithsdale & Annandale
Accommodation	Available in Moffat and around St Mary's Loch, plus fish and chips
Parking	Limited space available on the A708 verge at the east end of Blackhope Cottage

An impressive and challenging high-level walk. As an example of mountain scenery it may lack a little in height, but it certainly lacks nothing in form. This adventure has its hardest slog in the first 2 miles (3.2km) in the initial ascent of 1945ft (593m), the remaining 8 miles (12.9km) involving only a minor ascent of 500ft (152m).

In places this is a high-exposure walk, so be prepared.

The Route Capplegill, a white and tidy farm 5½ miles (8.8km) northeast of the market town of Moffat, stands by the A708. Take care when parking your vehicle on the narrow, twisting A708, and do not block access to Blackhope Cottage's garage or the field gate. The initial 2 mile (3.2km) climb begins by the five-bar gate a few yards east of the whitewashed cottage. Follow the track north for 200yds (183m) to a round sheep shelter on the right. Immediately beyond swing right, leaving the main track to pass the stone stell and reach a stile in the fence to the east. Once over the stile the sharp, bracken-clad sloping shoulders to **Saddle Yoke** rise to the north, nearly 2 miles (3.2km) ahead and 1900ft (579m) above, and the serious business of the climb to the summit of Saddle

Conditions and time spent sightseeing, taking photographs, birdspotting or other high-level activities determine the length of time taken on the hill.

Yoke 2413ft (735m) begins. Initially, paths are at best faint and thin, though if the north bearing is adhered to the trace becomes more distinct as height is gained and a second stile is met. On reaching the grass-covered peak, the Siamese twin of **Under Saddle Yoke** can be seen. The ascending, descending, ascending path up to and over the narrow and windy col is distinct and quite safe, with fine views west to Upper Coomb Craig and into the valley floor and snaking Blackhope Burn, though this section is not recommended for vertigo sufferers.

Saddle Yoke and Under Saddle Yoke The twin peaks of Saddle Yoke are something of a rarity among the rounded, flat-topped hills of Tweedsmuir. Joined by a narrow and quite exciting little ridge, these steep-sided mountains, with their distinctive and pointed peaks, still remain grass clad. Saddle Yoke is named only on the 1-inch OS map, and Under Saddle Yoke, the higher of the twins, is named only on the OS 1:50 000 sheet. To capture the most effective and dramatic photographs of the sweeping ridges that circumnavigate this glen it is wise to harness the morning light.

From the twin peaks walk north to a fork in the trace. Take the right-hand path to cross a flat and wet plateau northeast above the rim of the cliffs of **Raven Craig**. Proceed northeast to an unnamed summit 2247ft (685m) above Raven Craig, bisected by the regional boundary fence/dyke. Turn left at the fence, and using it as a guide follow it first north and then west-southwest, through heather and hag, passing hardly noticed Hartfell Rig 2432ft (739m), for 2½ long miles (4km) to the summit of **Hart Fell** 2651ft (808m), marked by a rather small and untidy shelter cairn.

Raven Craig These hills are designated by Nature Conservancy as being of special interest. Keep an eye open for ravens, buzzards, peregrine falcons and red grouse. By the lower burns herons, ring ouzels, dippers, wagtails and sandpipers can be seen. Mammals include mountain hares, foxes, otters, feral goats, and now feral mink are spreading.

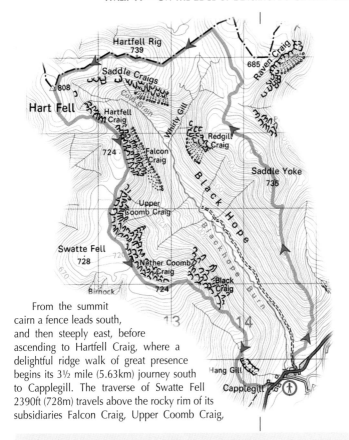

From the summit cairn a fence leads south, and then steeply east, before ascending to Hartfell Craig, where a delightful ridge walk of great presence begins its 3½ mile (5.63km) journey south to Capplegill. The traverse of Swatte Fell 2390ft (728m) travels above the rocky rim of its subsidiaries Falcon Craig, Upper Coomb Craig,

Hart Fell The second highest of the Moffat Hills, giving pole position to White Coomb by a mere 44ft (13m), Hart Fell is a hill of many flat ridges that rewards the walker with far-reaching views. In clear and crisp air, over the silvery waters of the Solway Firth, the peaks of the northern English Lakes signal a greeting, and one winter's day, through air of great clarity, I had the good fortune to see the snow-capped summit of Ben More 3852ft (1174m), 85 miles (137km) north.

Feral goats below Saddle Yoke

Nether Coomb Craig and Black Craig. A path that ranges between 2373ft (723m) and 2150ft (655m) is in places perilously close to the edge of the crags, but provides the walker (with a head for heights) with maximum views of Blackhope Valley and Whirly Gill. At Falcon Craig and Black Craig the path is perhaps too close to the edge, and in strong winds should be avoided by retreating well to the west.

On the descent from Black Craig the trail grows faint as a burn on the right is met. Cross the burn and make for a gate/stile in the electric fence ahead. Descend steeply south-southwest on a grassy path above the farm of Capplegill, turning left onto a broad farm track. When the steading is reached turn left onto the A708 to return to Blackhope Cottage.

WALK 42 – A Walk of Two Halves – Equally Appealing, Distinctly Different

Talla Water Bridge, Games Hope Glen, Great Hill, Donald's Cleuch Head, Firthybrig Head, Molls Cleuch Dod, Talla Water Bridge

Distance	8 miles (12.9km)
Height Gain	1700ft (518m)
Start/Finish	A small layby/parking space, GR 143201, above Talla Water bridge
Grade	3 or 4
Walking Time	5 hours
Maps	OS 1:50 000 Landranger sheets 72, Upper Clyde Valley, 78, Nithsdale & Annandale, and 79, Hawick & Eskdale
Accommodation	St Mary's Loch and Tweedsmuir; also refreshments
Parking	Alongside the narrow road between Megget and Talla reservoirs there is a small parking space (6–8 cars) at GR 143201

The first 3½ miles (5.6km) are confined within the initially narrow, wild and lonely glen of Games Hope; the second half, after a steep ascent of Great Hill, is an explosion of Southern Upland scenery and solitude. Pathways vary from good to faint, drouthy (dry) to damp. A compass and map are needed in poor visibility and weatherproof clothing is essential for winter walking.

The Route Starting at the parking point, cross the stone bridge that straddles Talla Water to descend west, on the steepest public road in the Borders, for ½ mile (0.8km) to the mouth of Games Hope Glen by Talla Linnfoots farm. Talla Reservoir lies below, curving gracefully northwest.

When **Games Hope Burn** is reached a five-bar gate on the left marks the entrance to the glen. The farm track south is wide, generally easy underfoot although stony in places, with the fascinating burn hurrying by on the right and savage boulder fields covering the sides of Carlavin Hill.

Along this walk it is possible to see the routes – or parts of the routes – of at least 14 other walks in this book.

225

After 1½ miles (2.4km) you reach the collapsing cottage of Gameshope, on the other side of the burn, in the process of partial restoration in 2004 (note the 1987 photograph).

Games Hope Burn For the first ½ mile (0.8km) or so Games Hope Burn remains a rather ordinary mountain stream, but once beyond the point where the boulder-strewn hillsides close in a transformation takes place. From a gurgling, benign stream, it changes into a brawling torrent, surging as if in panic from linn (waterfall) to linn in a matter of seconds. On all sides the air is filled with a symphony of running water. Higher still, as the valley opens out, the burn changes again, murmuring softly here and there as if reluctant to disturb the solitude.

Ahead a corrugated fodder store marks an indistinct trace south alongside the wet 'true right bank' (the east side) of the burn, soon to meet and pass by a rocky defile. For the next mile (1.6km), initially prone to wetness underfoot, the valley floor widens, and then for the first time since leaving Gameshope farm, past the confluence of Donald's Cleuch Burn, the walking is better if the burnside route is abandoned. Walk south-southeast, i.e. diagonally across the plateau, passing the occasional peat hag, and after 200yds (183m) a quad-bike track is met. Turn right and follow the track south as far as a broken fence – a small wooden sheep pen and a metal fodder shed lie close by to the south.

Gameshope Cottage, before restoration, by Games Hope Burn

Above to the left, i.e. east, is the rounded two-tier dome of **Great Hill** 2541ft (774m), its fence posts (broken wire entangled underfoot) aiding navigation for the sharp climb of 750ft (229m) that can take ¾ hour. ▶

The summit marks the start of 2 miles (3.2km) of far-seeing solitudinous ridge walking. Follow the dilapidated fence line southeast to the col below. At its lowest point turn east, i.e. left, and leave the posts to join a pathway above **Donald's Cleuch**. Three-hundred-and-fifty yards (320m) ahead another fence with an accompanying stone wall (both in need of repair) is met. Turn left,

West from Great Hill over Gameshope Loch

The climb to the summit of Great Hill reveals a bundle of hill views and small Gameshope Loch west to the Lowther Hills, plus many of the walks described in this book.

Great Hill The panorama from Great Hill is as follows. South: the hogsback of Hart Fell and the black crags of Swatte Fell, with the cones of Under Saddle Yoke and Saddle Yoke probing dramatically skywards, and the flattened bulk of White Coomb to the left. East: Donald's Cleuch Head, Firthybrig Head and Lochcraig Head. North: Molls Cleuch Dod masks the giants of the Manor range. West: Gameshope Loch, an elevated expanse of water with not one tree growing within sight; above it the ridge of Garelet Dod and Garelet Hill.

Donald's Cleuch A wild and inhospitable place that spawns the burn of the same name. 'Donald' refers to the Reverend Donald Cargill, minister of the Barony Church, Glasgow, who in 1665, deprived of his living for denouncing the Restoration, and fearing for his own safety, fled to these lonely and rugged hills. Here, it is said, the Reverend Donald laid low for many months, well hidden from John Graham of Claverhouse, the scourge of the Covenanters, and his prying dragoons. Heaven help them all, should they have been afoot on these mountains during winter's icy blast.

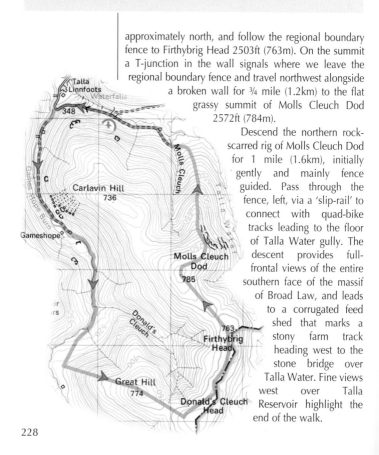

approximately north, and follow the regional boundary fence to Firthybrig Head 2503ft (763m). On the summit a T-junction in the wall signals where we leave the regional boundary fence and travel northwest alongside a broken wall for ¾ mile (1.2km) to the flat grassy summit of Molls Cleuch Dod 2572ft (784m).

Descend the northern rock-scarred rig of Molls Cleuch Dod for 1 mile (1.6km), initially gently and mainly fence guided. Pass through the fence, left, via a 'slip-rail' to connect with quad-bike tracks leading to the floor of Talla Water gully. The descent provides full-frontal views of the entire southern face of the massif of Broad Law, and leads to a corrugated feed shed that marks a stony farm track heading west to the stone bridge over Talla Water. Fine views west over Talla Reservoir highlight the end of the walk.

WALK 43 – Broad Law, the Borders' Highest Mountain

Megget Stone, Fans Law, Cairn Law, Broad Law, Wylies Burn Head, Cairn Law, Megget Stone

Distance	6 miles (9.7km)
Height Gain	1304ft (398m)
Start/Finish	East fromTalla Water bridge, GR 143201
Grade	2
Walking Time	3½ hours
Map	OS 1:50 000 Landranger sheet 72, Upper Clyde Valley
	OS Pathfinder 471, Tweedsmuir
Accommodation	Food and accommodation are available at St Mary's Loch
Parking	Limited parking for cars above and east of Talla Water bridge

Broad Law, at 2754ft (840m) the highest summit in Border country, is an easy-to-ascend mountain that unfortunately has very little apart from the views to excite the explorer. The walk starts at 1450ft (442m) above sea level, which leaves a relatively easy ascent of only 1304ft (398m) for the entire 6 miles (9.7km). Paths when dry, and navigation, present no problems, though do show the highest mountain in the range and your feet some respect by wearing your walking boots.

The Route Walk east for ½ mile (0.8km) to the cattle-grid at the regional boundary close by the **Megget Stone** and a solitary, summer-time-resident Portaloo. To the left, i.e. north, a continuous boundary fence staggers north-west over the flank of Fans Law to ascend overall north for 2 miles (3.2km) to the domed summit of Broad Law.

From Fans Law the boundary marker swings west and then northwest to the halfway grandstand of Cairn Law 2353ft (717m). Cairn Law, its upper reaches scattered with well-constructed cairns, directs the walker north alongside the fence for a gentle 1¼ mile (2km) ascent to the flat and wide western summit of **Broad Law**,

Unlike the wild corries and rocky crags of the Moffat Hills, the Manor's residents are generally composed of gentler slopes that favour an easy passage for the hill walker.

The items of interest for this walk, highlighted in bold, can be found in Walk 44.

229

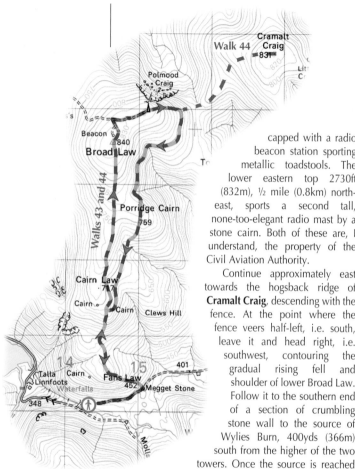

capped with a radio beacon station sporting metallic toadstools. The lower eastern top 2730ft (832m), ½ mile (0.8km) north-east, sports a second tall, none-too-elegant radio mast by a stone cairn. Both of these are, I understand, the property of the Civil Aviation Authority.

Continue approximately east towards the hogsback ridge of **Cramalt Craig**, descending with the fence. At the point where the fence veers half-left, i.e. south, leave it and head right, i.e. southwest, contouring the gradual rising fell and shoulder of lower Broad Law. Follow it to the southern end of a section of crumbling stone wall to the source of Wylies Burn, 400yds (366m) south from the higher of the two towers. Once the source is reached and passed, continue contouring south via sheep tracks over the grass- and, in places, heather-clad fell. After ½ mile (0.8km), with the guiding fence of our ascent visible right and roughly parallel, we pass the source of Score Burn on the left to reach the slight bump of Porridge Cairn 2519ft (768m). From this point the

From Fans Law to Talla Reservoir

prominent Shepherds' Cairn on the southern shoulder of Cairn Law, our next destination, can be seen.

Walk south-southwest on a carpet of fine grass or definite sheep trods to the cairn on the southern shoulder. This ridge is a fine and airy place to walk, providing the wonderful feeling of solitude so characteristic of these hills. There are intriguing views south beyond the cairn through the narrow, glacial, gouged defile below the rock-scarred summit of Molls Cleuch Dod to the domed summit of White Coomb. The descent from cairned Cairn Law is overall south and then southeast, via the regional boundary fence of our ascent, to the Megget Stone, cattle-grid and road leading west over Talla Moss to the car parking space above Talla Water bridge.

WALK 44 – Broad Law plus Cramalt Craig

*Broad Law, Cramalt Craig, Porridge Cairn,
Cairn Law, Megget Stone*

Distance	9 miles (14.5km)
Height Gain	1954ft (596m)
Start/Finish	East from Talla Water bridge, GR 143201
Grade	3
Walking Time	5 hours
Maps	OS 1:50 000 Landranger Sheet 72, Upper Clyde Valley
	OS Pathfinder 471, Tweedsmuir
Accommodation	Food and accommodation are available at St Mary's Loch
Parking	Limited parking for cars above and east of Talla Water bridge

This extension of Walk 43 rewards the energetic.

An extension of the Broad Law ascent (see map Walk 43), this route involves an additional 3 miles (4.8km) of walking, plus an ascent of 650ft to the second highest summit in the Manor Hills.

The Route The journey to the mast on the lower summit of **Broad Law** is a carbon copy of Walk 43, and from this point the distinct top of Cramalt Craig with its large cairn can be seen to the northeast. When

Broad Law It is said the summit can be traversed 'with a sleeping babe in a push chair', so flat is it and so smooth the path. This may be so, but it is still worth the effort to walk the wide fells of this slumbering giant, especially after a light dusting of snow. On a more romantic note, the spring known as Gedde's Well, gushing from the western heights of Broad Law, is reputed to be the spot where 'the Wizard Merlin was wont to rest'. In 1891 Broad Law was the first mountain to be climbed by the newly formed Scottish Mountaineering Club.

An alternative 10½ mile (16.9km) round trip can be made, from near Tweedsmuir, west-northwest, in the upper Tweed Valley, past Hearthstane on a waymarked, somewhat tedious, vehicular and forest track, to the CAA's summit communications constructions and towers.

descending east from Broad Law, keep close to the angled fence and do not stray left, as the precipitous cliffs of Polmood Craig lurk unseen to the north. The fence that has been a constant guide descends steeply to, and crosses, a damp and peaty area before rising sharply northeast over Middle Hill to **Cramalt Craig** 2727ft (831m) 1½ miles (2.4km) away.

Cramalt Craig The second highest of the great Manor Hills, connected to the third, Dollar Law 2681ft (817m), by a fine flat ridge that forms the western ridge (see Walk 45) of that most picturesque of valleys, Manor Water. A ridge that can be walked from Megget to Peebles, some 19 miles (30.6km) or so, by following the regional boundary and then a parish boundary. With such fiscal and spiritual guidance, who would not be encouraged to venture forth to Peebles.

On the summit the large cairn provides that little extra height from which to view the entire range of the Manor Hills, for it is at this point that we must turn and begin the return journey. Descend on the path of ascent as far as the col below Broad Law and Cramalt Craig, and from the lowest point of the col ascend west-southwest with the fence to the point at which it veers half-left, i.e. south, then see the last two paragraphs of Walk 43 for the return route to the **Megget Stone**. This variation extends Walk 43 by 1½ hours into a pleasant 5 hours.

The Megget Stone Standing some 3ft (0.9m) high, the Megget Stone rests just south of the cattle-grid. Although it bears some indistinct markings, e.g. 'Tweed', it appears to have no greater claim to fame than that of a simple boundary mark.

WALK 45 – A Walk through Time

*Langhaugh, Old Kirkhope, Long Grain Knowe,
Pykestone Hill, Posso Craig, Langhaugh*

Distance	6½ miles (10.5km)
Height Gain	1654ft (504m)
Start/Finish	Manor Water Valley, GR 199307
Grade	3; in adverse weather or poor visibility, 4
Walking Time	4 hours
Maps	OS 1:50 000 Landranger sheet 72, Upper Clyde Valley
	Harvey 1:40 000 Peebles, Manor Hills & St Mary's Loch
Accommodation	Wide selection of refreshments and beds in Peebles
Parking	GR 199307, for 6 vehicles in a layby between the white cottage and the bridge over Newholm Hope Burn

This is a walk that provides superb views in an area steeped in history – in the footsteps of the ancient 'Gadeni' (Scottish Celts), the Romans, Gaels, Picts and Angles. Norsemen named the burns, and the Wizard Merlin was stoned to death alongside 'Powsayl' – Powsail (willows) Burn.

Manor Water Valley is a picturesque valley typical of these parts, benign and welcoming on the valley floor, gaunt and forbidding on the surrounding tops and ridges. It cannot be ignored. The walk circumnavigates valley, hill and ridge. Underfoot the tracks, paths and traces are clear and mainly dry, though some sections, such as above Old Kirkhope and the summit of Posso Craig, test the lungs.

Boots and mountain clothing are recommended, and in poor visibility a map and compass.

The Route Leave the A72 1½ miles (2.4km) west of Peebles to enter Manor Water Valley (signposted 'Manor and Manorhead'). Travel south along the narrow unclassified road for 7 miles (11.3km) to GR 199307, a few hundred yards past the white buildings of Langhaugh on the left. A solitary white cottage at GR 199307 marks the start of the walk.

Take the farm track leading southwest to Old Kirkhope, and immediately the appetite is whetted. Posso Craig rises steeply to the right, with the domes of Pykestone Hill 2418ft (737m) and Long Grain Knowe 2308ft (703m) covering the skyline ahead. And if that's not enough, the mysterious **Font Stone** on its ancient plot comes into view on the right.

The Font Stone Standing in a field, right of the track to Kirkhope, is the site of the ancient Kirk of St Gordian, now scarcely visible save for its grass-covered foundations and the levelled ground. At its side stand the Font Stone (2ft across and hollowed out) and its guardian granite cross, embellished with interwoven decorations and inscribed 'Sanct Gordiani'. Headstones are also present, their inscriptions masked with grey lichen.

The Font Stone

Three-quarters of a mile (1.2km) from the start we meet a multiple sheep stell adjacent to the deserted cottage of Old Kirkhope, backed by a bracken-clad mound serrated by several paths or tracks. Skirt the buildings via a track on the north side to cross the rickety footbridge over tree-lined Kirkhope Burn to the wall-lined foot of the bracken-clad mound. Ascend west via the right-hand farm track – it's the one that zigzags, as opposed to a direct, lung-bursting assault to the summit. The pathway or track now has Kirkhope Burn and its feeder burns below and to the north, our right, and a post-and-wire fence immediately left. Our grassy track, ascending over a series of shoulders towards the heather line, continues overall west after it leaves the left-hand

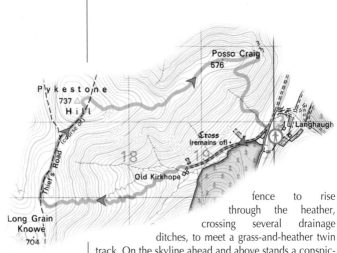

fence to rise through the heather, crossing several drainage ditches, to meet a grass-and-heather twin track. On the skyline ahead and above stands a conspicuous stone cairn (marked on Harvey's map) which is met and passed via a series of westbound zigzags to the col between cairn-clad Long Grain Knowe, on the left, and twin-domed Grey Weather Law (hopefully not living up to its name!) on the right, i.e. north. The distance to the col between these two summits, from Old Kirkhope, is 1½ miles (2.4km).

Once the ridge is breasted bear right, i.e. approximately north, to the initially well-defined and -cairned twin track known as the **Thief's Road**, close to the parish boundary fence. The way continues rising and falling alongside the fence, at a brisk pace, by peat hags, for 1¼ miles (2km) to a relatively large fenceside trig point marking the flat-domed, stone-strewn summit of **Pykestone Hill**. ◀

Pykestone Hill is distinguished by an extensive scatter of spear- or pike-headed stones protruding skywards.

The Thief's Road Just as it sounds – a way used in the past to drive 'borrowed' cattle along. It is well above the prying eyes of the valley floor, but was later to be used as a legitimate drove road.

Pykestone Hill The summit of a four-pointed star whose outliers, Long Grain Knowe, Den Knowes Head, Breach Law and Posso Craig, radiate to the four points of the compass, and whose twin top, the Scrape, stands guard to the north. No doubt its name was derived from the sharp and pointed 'pike-headed' stones found in profusion on the summit.

Pykestone Hill summit and trig point

It includes a cairn to the east that acts as a marker directing to the ridge leading east to Posso Craig, a favourite for swooping swifts in search of summer flies, soaring raptors in search of bigger game, and curious, upstanding hares.

From the trig point on Pykestone Hill, face the cairn to follow a sometimes faint double track east and finally northeast for ¾ mile (1.2km), descending

237

From Posso Craig over North Wood Hill into Manor Water Valley

steadily on the all-revealing, narrowing ridge to Posso Craig. To the north is the black and severe gully of Posso, and beyond the picturesque patchwork of Manor Valley, while to the south lies the more gentle, confined glen of Kirkhope. Continue to lose height as the ridge swings northeast, i.e. left, and the summit of **Posso Craig** 1859ft (567m) with its three piles of stones is approached. It's a delightful spot from which to view Manor Valley 1000ft (305m) below, but do take great care. *Do not venture past the large, well-made cairn standing on the northern rim of the summit – beyond, the rock drops dramatically to the valley floor.* From above the cairn, circle and descend southeast and then southwest around Posso Craig, dropping rapidly, using narrow though clear sheep traces to reach the valley floor at the white cottage, GR 199307.

Posso Craig The watchdog of Manor below whose rocky eastern cliffs stands the Ship Stone, cliffs referred to in Scott's *Bride of Lammermuir* as the source of hunting hawks. It is a place to sit and ponder, and to admire Manor Valley and the central valley 'hump', or 'knoll', of Castlehill, site of a 1734 school which cost £191-7s-6d (Scots).

WALK 46 – Benign Surroundings Hide a Dark and Dangerous Past

Traquair Parish Church by Kirkhouse, Orchard Mains, Glen House, Glenshiel Banks, Peat Hill, Blackhouse, Southern Upland Way, Blake Muir, Traquair Parish Church

Distance	10 miles (16.1km)
Height Gain	1450ft (442m)
Start/Finish	By Kirkhouse, GR 321335
Grade	3
Walking Time	5½ hours
Maps	OS 1:50 000 Landranger sheet 73, Peebles, Galashiels & Selkirk
	OS 1:25 000 Explorer 337, Peebles & Innerleithen
Accommodation	Traquair and Innerleithen provide accommodation and refreshment
Parking	Off-road car park at the south end of Traquair Parish Church – avoid Sunday

A colourful walk, particularly in spring and autumn, that combines the sylvan beauty of Quair Water Glen with the invigorating, far-seeing solitude of the waymarked Southern Upland Way over the Blake Muir ridges of the Tweedsmuir Hills.

The Route Start the walk at white-walled **Traquair Parish Church** by Kirkhouse, on the B709 1 mile (1.6km)

The history of John Porteus of Glen House, passed en route, is a reminder of more turbulent times.

Traquair Parish Church A kirk has stood on this spot since the early 1500s, the present one having been built in 1778 and altered in 1821. The outside staircase is of interest (its like can be seen at Ettrick Kirk, Walk 31), as are the many gravestones emblazoned with a skull and crossbones, and the graves headed with a single, unmarked river boulder. The roadside wall of the church bears a memorial plaque to blacksmith Alexander Brodie of Traquair (died 1811) who invented 'the register stoves and fire hearths for ships' as used by the Royal Navy.

239

south of Traquair village. Walk northeast with the narrow road for 150yds (137m) or so to a left-hand junction signposted 'Glen House 1¾ miles, Orchard Mains'. Turn left, i.e. west, and cross the bridge over Quair Water to the tidy farm buildings of **Orchard Mains**. Follow the quiet country lane southwest and then west for 1 mile (1.6km) to reach the arched main gates of

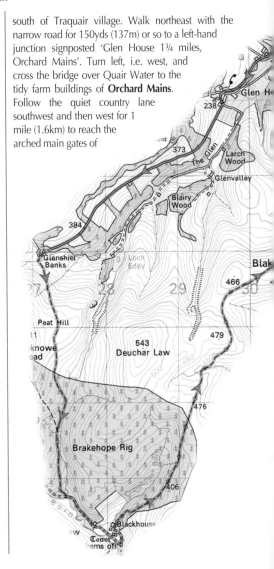

Glen House, a journey that presents a colourful canvas of birch, bracken and heather, which when last walked were resplendent in their autumnal cloaks. At this point the tree-lined right fork winds southwest to the rear of Glen House. When the metalled road ends, just past a cottage and kennels, a notice saying 'Private' refers only to motorised vehicles – the route from Glen House to Glenshiel Banks is a pedestrian right of way. Turreted, half-hidden Glen House is passed on the left, as are two cottages and a farmsteading on the right, before swinging right at the fork to follow the ascending farm track southwest for two very pleasant miles (3.2km), passing coniferous strip plantations and pastures. Note to the left, i.e. south, the dramatic narrow side-gully of Glendean Banks and the shimmering waters of Loch Eddy, before the two cottages (one in use, the other a ruin) at Glenshiel Banks.

Orchard Mains The farm buildings, in particular the barn by the roadside, are well worth an inspection. At the road end leading to the farm a red Victorian letterbox, embossed 'Letters Only, VR', can be seen.

Glen House The original house was the birthplace of one Captain John Porteous, whose infamous order to the city guard of Edinburgh to open fire on the crowd at a public hanging in 1736, killing four, led to him being tried and sentenced to death. He was granted a pardon by Queen Caroline, and this act so incensed the populace that they broke John Porteous out of the tollbooth and hanged him from a street sign, breaking his neck. Another Porteous from these parts (no doubt an antecedent) gained infamy by slaughtering 16 captive troopers from Cromwell's army in cold blood. An historian recorded it thus, 'did cut off numberis of the Englishes, and seased thair pockettis and horssis'.

Loch Eddy below Glendean Banks

Pass through a five-bar gate ahead to the heather-clad flanks of Peat Hill 1550ft (472m). To the west, i.e. right, the rounded, cairn-topped summit of Dun Rig 2433ft (742m) can be seen, the highest top of this section of the Manor Hills. Once through the gate three faint pathways are visible – take the centre one and ascend Peat Hill south-southeast. This steady, wet-in-places climb affords fine views below and to the north of the picturesque glen of Quair Water. On the highest point of the shoulder on Peat Hill, a single post indicates the now descending path that continues to the edge of an extensive coniferous plantation. From Glenshiel Banks to the woodside boundary fence is 1 mile (1.6km).

Once over the grassy, heather-and-rush-clad brow of Peat Hill, descend south to the conifers below. Enter the plantation ride that cloaks Brakehope Rig, walking on a forest path for approximately 1 mile (1.6km) to join a forest road running southeast with Douglas Burn (Walk 29), breaking cover before Blackhouse and its crumbling tower (Walk 29) to join the Southern Upland Way. Swing left, i.e. northeast, past Blackhouse to enter the conifers once more above Craighope Burn. After 1 mile (1.6km) the district boundary is crossed at the plantation edge as the Southern Upland Way continues north-northeast for nearly 4 miles (6.4km) over Blake Muir to Traquair Parish Church.

Cross Yellow Mire Burn, keeping it on the right, before taking the path on the left to the marker post (a thistle) ahead. From this post the path to Blake Muir 1532ft (467m) is overall north, and shortly before the summit the way broadens out into a distinct track. The moorland crossing to Blake Muir reveals some fine views northeast and east of the folding ridges of Minch Moor, Brown Knowe and the outstanding cairns topping Three Brethren (Walks 23 and 28).

Follow the ridge north with fine views over Fethan Burn to Glen House, descending steadily between embankments, alongside a fence, to the western corner of a lone plantation. Two more stiles are crossed as the way runs alongside a stone dyke, swinging northeast to descend to the B709 close to the car park of Traquair Parish Church.

Traquair Parish Church

CHAPTER 5

LONG DISTANCE WALKS AND TOWN TRAILS

Four long-distance paths pass through the Borders: the Pennine Way, the Alternative Pennine Way, the Southern Upland Way and St Cuthbert's Way, with a fifth, the Borders Abbeys Way, that is contained within the Border country. The Pennine Way is covered by a wide selection of guides, including one for the Alternative Way. The less publicised Southern Upland Way has fewer, although all are readily available from bookshops, outdoor shops and public libraries. Booklets with local information describing the town trails are also available from tourist information centres. It is intended, therefore, to give only the briefest of descriptions in this chapter, in the hope that the appetite for walking these long-distance paths and the town trails will be stimulated further.

The Pennine Way

This high-level walk, waymarked with an acorn sign, was created in 1965. Stretching 270 miles (434km) north from Edale in Derbyshire, it traverses the backbone of England to complete its last 29 miles (46.5km) on the windswept ridges of the Cheviot Hills to Kirk Yetholm, the Borders, Scotland. Ten walks in Chapter 1 tread this long-distance path, although only six travel its well-worn way for any appreciable distance.

The Schil and Cheviot's north face from Corbie Craig

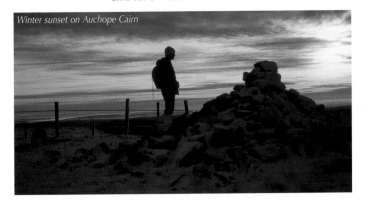
Winter sunset on Auchope Cairn

Maps   OS 1:50 000 Landranger series, sheets 74 and 80
Publication *The Pennine Way Companion*, by A Wainwright
(Frances Lincoln, 2004)

From Byrness in Redesdale to Kirk Yetholm in Roxburghshire, there are 27 high-level miles (43.4km) – 29 long miles (46.5km) if the summit of the Cheviot is included. The way zigzags and undulates with the national boundary fence for most of the journey, and never passes shelter save for two small wooden refuges on the slopes of Lamb Hill and Auchope Cairn. It is a testing walk, only to be undertaken in a single trip by fit and experienced walkers. Given good weather and clear skies, the rewards are high. Endless folds of grass- and heather-clad hills surrounded by the patchwork of the Northumbrian coastal plain and the Tweed Valley reward the walker tenfold. In recent years much of the sting has been taken out of some of the more sadistic sections, with the construction of wooden walkways and slabbed stone pathways across the peaty wastes.

The Alternative Pennine Way

This walk of 268 miles (431km) from Ashbourne in Derbyshire to Jedburgh in Scotland is the invention of Denis Brook and Phil Hinchliffe. It takes an easier walking line than the original, with accommodation available at every stage.

Maps   OS 1:50 000 Landranger series, sheets 74 and 80
Publication *The Alternative Pennine Way*, by D Brook and P Hinchliffe
(Cicerone, 1992)

The route approaches the Borders from Nenthead, via Allendale Town, Haltwhistle, and over Hadrian's Wall to Falstone and Kielder, then through the forest to Byrness and so to Jedburgh, with an optional extension to Melrose.

The Southern Upland Way

Extending for 202 miles (325km) on Scottish soil, it runs from Portpatrick on the west coast to Cockburnspath on the east coast. Opened in 1984, it is Scotland's first long-distance path to run from coast to coast. Although not as rugged as the West Highland Way (Scotland's most popular long-distance path), the Southern Upland Way climbs to heights that exceed any point on the West Highland Way. Eighty-five-and-a-half miles (138km) of this well-waymarked path (thistle logo) enters the Borderland at Ettrick Head, by the 'Welcome to Borders Region' sign, and finishes at Cockburnspath on the Berwickshire coast.

Several of its most picturesque and interesting sections are incorporated into a selection of the walks in this guide, in Chapters 2, 3 and 4. In all a total of nine walks in the guide cover sections from Ettrick Head to Yair Bridge.

Maps	OS 1:50 000 Landranger series, sheets 67, 73, 74 and 79
Publication	*A Guide to the Southern Upland Way*, by David Williams (Constable and Co. Ltd)

By Berry Wood to Captain's Road

North from Blake Muir to rainbow-lit Glen House

The eastern section of this coast-to-coast long-distance walk enters the area at Ettrick Head, a wild and lonely col 1700ft (518m) above sea level. The way covers lonely hills, romantic glens and that oft-praised loch, St Mary's, in addition to the banks of the silvery Tweed. It is a quiet route, with no problematic navigation, that draws the intrepid traveller ever onwards. In the words of James Hogg, 'That's the way for Billy and me'.

From the exposed col of Ettrick Head the way descends northeast into the shelter of Ettrick Water Valley, Walks 35, 36, 31. The twin jewels of Loch of the Lowes and St Mary's Loch are included in Walk 30, and the open fells to Dryhope and Blackhouse are described in Walk 29. A climb northeast to the fine ridge of Blake Muir, Walk 46, leads to the village of Traquair, also the start of Walk 23. Walk 28 includes the summit of Three Brethren, from where Walk 22 takes the wayfarer down to the River Tweed at Yair Bridge.

St Cuthbert's Way

A Borders walk of 62½ miles (101km) dedicated to a seventh-century Borderer, Saint Cuthbert. It starts from Melrose Abbey, passing east and south-east through the Tweed Valley into the Cheviots, utilising sections of Dere Street, an old Roman road, to Yetholm and Wooler. Then onward through the fertile valleys of north Northumberland, passing St Cuthbert's Cave, to the charismatic tiny island of Lindisfarne – Holy Island – where Cuthbert served as Bishop of Lindisfarne.

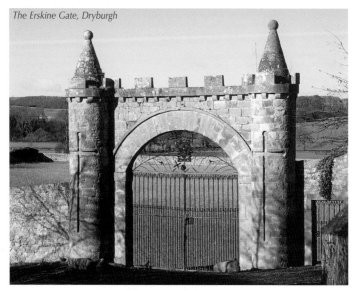

The Erskine Gate, Dryburgh

| **Maps** | Although shown on the latest OS Explorer OL16 and Landranger sheet 75 maps, it is Harvey's St Cuthbert's Way map, complete with marked route, guidelines and useful information, that is the most convenient |

We meet this increasingly popular Borders long-distance way, waymarked with a Celtic cross, in Walks 1, 4, 5, 6, 20, 21 and 24.

The Borders Abbeys Way

A circular walking route of 65 miles (105km) which, when finally completed, will connect the four sadly ruined Borders abbeys of Kelso, Jedburgh, Melrose and Dryburgh, and the prominent Borders towns of Hawick and Selkirk. Travelling highways, byways and riverbanks in the dales of Teviot and Tweed, the Borders Abbeys Way is waymarked with an A superimposed on a W.

Maps   OS OL16, OS Landranger sheets 73, 74, 79 and 80

This pleasing walk through the centuries is encountered in Walks 18, 20, 21 and 25.

Berwick-upon-Tweed

Exploring Berwick – Berwick Visitors Guide No. 4, and *The Tweed Estuary Circular Walk*, published by the Berwick Ramblers, are available from local tourist information centres. *Exploring Berwick* contains two trails, the first a complete circuit of the unique town walls, while the second embraces the fascinating streets of the old town. The Tweed Estuary Trail is a 5½ mile (8.8km) circular walk providing fine views of this historic town and its three bridges, built 1634–1928.

Berwick changed hands no less than 14 times in its turbulent past, and was under English control in the second half of the 1500s when the construction of the town walls began. At that time they represented the most advanced design known to military engineers, but due to the Union of the Crowns in 1603 the walls never experienced shot or shell fired in anger.

The Wall Trail begins at Meg's Mount on the north wall, including Cumberland Bastion and Brass Bastion – turn south past Cow Port and Windmill Bastion to King's Mount. The bastions all have two 'flankers', while the mounts have only one (a flanker is a protected gun emplacement allowing fire along the face of the wall). From the east wall the views are to the sea and the river mouth, a fact reflected in the names of points of interest along the route: Pier Gate, Fishers Fort, Shore Gate and Quay Walls. From Quay Walls the walls pass by the Old Bridge and the Royal Tweed Bridge to return to Meg's Mount.

Roxburgh Viaduct (Borders Abbeys Way)

The Street Trail also starts at Meg's Mount, and travels south into the main shopping street with the town hall, built in 1761, resplendent at its foot. From the town hall walk into Church Street, leading north to the Parade, the parish church (without a spire) and the barracks (containing the Regimental Museum of the King's Own Scottish Borderers, the Borough Museum and Art Gallery with Berwick's Burrell Collection). South of the barracks Ravensdowne leads to Palace Green, Bridge Street and Quay Walls. An interesting end to the walk is to cross the old bridge to Tweedmouth, returning via the Royal Tweed Bridge.

The Tweed Estuary Circular Walk is a three-hour circular walk embracing both banks of the Tweed estuary, with fine views of Berwick and its surrounds, in particular the Royal Border Bridge (a railway bridge) with its elegant arches, designed and built by Robert Stephenson and opened in 1850 by Queen Victoria.

Kelso

Kelso Town Trail, available from the local tourist information centre, contains three walks through the ancient market town, each telling a historical, ecclesiastical and trading story. The town, of some 6500 inhabitants, stands by two rivers, the Tweed and the Teviot, and proudly boasts two castles and an abbey. Kelso is renowned for its livestock sales, the Border Union Agricultural Show, the Dog Show, and in the recent past its fine floral displays. The walks start and finish in the picturesque cobbled square at the town's centre.

The Abbey Walk includes the abbey, an interesting bridge by James Rennie, a riverside walk and the octagonal old parish church.

The Market Walk Starting south of the town hall by a group of Georgian houses, it travels along Woodmarket to the Coalmarket (an area of the town where coal mined south of Berwick-upon-Tweed was sold), turning into Horsemarket to return to the square.

The Upper Town Walk This walk leaves the square on the north side, passing the fine facade of the library, the old ragged school (initially a school for children of the poor), two churches and the old Kelso dispensary, established in 1777. Return to the town centre via the banks of the Tweed and Cunzie, which was either the town mint or the place from where coins were distributed.

Jedburgh

The *Jedburgh Town and Surrounds* walks booklet is available from the local tourist information centre.

The royal burgh of Jedburgh (granted by King William the Lion 1143–1214), now home to 4200, had its origins 3000 years ago. It grew in stature and importance with the founding of its Augustinian abbey in 1138 – an abbey that was sacked and rebuilt many times before its final demise under the sword of the Earl of Hertford in 1545. But centuries of repeated destruction failed to quell the spirit of 'Jethart', and destruction has slowly given way to construction, although some of the more macabre happenings from the past are still remembered, such as the game of 'handba'. This was a form of coarse rugby played by the 'uppies and the doonies' of the town. The original 'bas' were said to be the severed heads of English soldiers, which were then thrown and kicked around the streets. The annual contest takes place every February.

Contained in the walks booklet is a map of this compact town, showing in detail points of interest along the way. The trail starts at the market place, passes Newgate (once a prison with a condemned cell), and goes to the visitors' centre of Jedburgh Abbey. After completing a tour of the abbey, walk up Castlegate, passing Bonnie Prince Charlie's house and Abbey Close, to reach Castle Jail. Return to the market place and travel north through High Street to Mary Queen of Scots' house, a fine example of a 16th-century fortified Border house. Continue to the riverside for examples of buildings that supplied the town's water, housed the burgh's pipers, and to see the town's defences.

Melrose

A Walk Around Melrose describes walks around the town, complete with comprehensive maps, and is available from the local tourist information centre.

Melrose, dominated by the distinctive triple peaks of the Eildon Hills (Walk 21), was first settled by the ancient tribe of Selgovia some 2000 years ago, later to be followed by the Romans at Trimontium (camp of the three hills). Centuries later the Celtic Christians established a monastery at Mailros (a bare headland) where Cuthbert, a local shepherd, was to start his monastic life. In 1136 King David founded the Cistercian abbey, the ruins of which bear sad witness to the deeds of the Earl of Hertford who, in 1545, reduced this most humorous of abbeys to the building you see today. The humour is supplied by the many fine carvings and gargoyles seen on the skyline, such as a pig playing the bagpipes. Priorwood Gardens, close by the abbey, features an 'Apple Orchard through the Ages', and flowers suitable for drying. During the 18th century the town was famous for the fine linen it produced, and in 1883 the game of rugby sevens was introduced to the world by Ned Haigh, a local butcher.

The Inner Circle Walk starts at the abbey car park and encompasses Abbey Street, the market square, High Street and Buccleuch Street. It includes the market cross (1645), the town hall, the corn exchange, the George and Abbotsford Hotel and Leslie House, before returning to the abbey and its most interesting museum.

The Outer Circle Walk also starts at the abbey car park, to follow the route of the Inner Circle Walk as far as the High Street. Pass St Mary's Preparatory School and the famous Greenyards, home of Melrose Rugby Football Club (once a post-glacial lake, later rough grazing and an area for selling sheep), to reach higher ground and the parish church. To the east is the Chain Bridge, circa 1826, allowing foot traffic to cross to and from Gattonside, passing the Melrose Motor Museum before returning to the starting point.

Galashiels

Two small guides with maps, *Galashiels Old Town Walk* by Ian M Miller, and *Walks in Gala Countryside* by B and M E Lennox, are both available from the local tourist information centre.

Galashiels, a town of some 14,000 souls, is steeped in the woollen trade. The Galashiels Manufacturers' Corporation, founded in 1776, spun the motto, 'We Dye to Live and Live to Die'. So highly thought of is the Scottish College of Textiles, based in the town, that in 1991 it became a college of Heriot Watt University, Edinburgh.

Galashiels Old Town Walk is a compact stroll around the tight-knit perimeter of the old town of Gala, a settlement dating from the 15th century. It embraces Old Gala House, on the site of the original manor house, Gala Town Cross, Gala Parish Church and Scott Aisle. Galashiels, invariably referred to throughout the Borders as Gala, appears to have escaped the extremes of violence experienced by other Borders towns in centuries past, though the area known as 'Whitchyknowe' witnessed the firing of 'whitches' in both the 16th and 17th centuries.

Start at Old Gala House, now a museum and exhibition centre, then walk to Scott Park (the site of New Gala House, built 1876, demolished 1985). The route then proceeds along Scott Crescent, past the towering spire of St Pauls, to the Gala Town Cross (circa 1599). A walk along Elm Row, Tea Street (by Whitchyknowe) and Glebe Street, all rich in local history, brings the walker onto Church Street and the former St Peter's School. At this point the way turns sharply left to explore Gala Aisle and the old burial ground of Galashiels (a list of grave markings can be obtained from Old Gala House).

Leave the kirkyard by Bow Butts (an ancient archery practice ground) to reach the modern centre of the town, marked with statues of Sir Walter Scott, Robert Burns and Clapperton's 'Border Reiver', and turn left to return to Old Gala House and light refreshments in the Pringle Room.

Walks in Gala Countryside gives the visitor a taste of the Border hills and the silvery waters that enfold the town of Galashiels. The walks start from the public golf course, Mossilee and Hollybush Road, and are easily identified from 'The Little Map of Gala'.

South of the town the terrain is relatively hilly and the walks utilise a section of the Southern Upland Way long-distance path, covering the banks of the Tweed and the highest hill around Gala, Meigle Hill. East via the Gala Water Valley could test the stamina of the walker, but this is compensated for by the thoughtful route suggested and the many items of interest along the way – items such as one of the three Pictish brochs (a circular drystone tower) found in the Borders.

The walks to the west of Gala Water are both varied and testing, taking the walker to the lesser-known corners of the steep-sided hills and quiet valleys that lock this proud mill town well and truly into the centre of the Borders.

Selkirk

The booklet *The Ring o' the Toun* is full of fascinating facts about and illustrations of Selkirk and is available from the local tourist information centre.

Selkirk in Anglo-Saxon means 'church in the forest', so the present name cannot have been in use before the 700s. Since then the town grew slowly and, as with all Border towns, not always peacefully, with life centred around the market place now identified as 'the Ring o' the Toun'. A triangle of streets – Kirk Wynd, Back Row (no reference to the rugby team) and High Street – complete the ring, and are all included in the town trail. In the 19th century Selkirk expanded rapidly when the woollen trade boom hit the ancient burgh. With the aid of this booklet the rich history of Selkirk and its characters comes very much alive, and at no time more so than during the annual celebrations of Common Riding week during July.

The Ring o' the Toun Trail begins and ends as all good town walks should, in the market place. First it goes to West Port, turning right to Kirk Wynd and then to Back Row, past the impressive Mungo Park memorial in High Street, which it follows to the equally charismatic statue of Fletcher (the soul of Selkirk) at the Flodden memorial. Here the walk turns to retrace its steps along High Street to the market place (with Sir Walter Scott in the centre). Leave the market place and walk down Galashiels Road as far as the sheriff's court and the Old Jail, then return to the starting point in the market place. This is a walk that tells many stories of 'Souters' (natives of Selkirk) great and small, of Walter Scott and Mungo Park, of Dr Lawson and Johnny Souter, James Hogg, and the Duke of Wellington (not a Souter).

Hawick

The informative booklet *Walks Around Hawick* is available from Hawick's tourist information centre and describes 12 walks in and around the town. It also contains a map and a fund of local details.

Hawick, the largest of the Scottish Border towns, is the undisputed capital of the Border knitwear industry. Unlike many of the other Border towns, Hawick is perhaps not steeped so thoroughly in history and blood, yet in the words of Madge Elliot, town provost, 'It is obvious this is a Mosstroopers Town.' The first written record of Hawick is in a 12th-century book about St Cuthbert, and the town was used extensively for many centuries as a staging post by cattle drovers. Hawick rose to prominence after Bailie John Hardie (1722–1800) brought the first knitting machines to the town, thus completing the triumvirate essential for a successful knitwear industry: sheep, water and machinery.

The town walks are circular, beginning and ending at the tourist information centre. They and the out-of-town walks follow well-defined paths and country lanes, with the routes well described. A selection includes the following.

Park, Trim-Track, Woods and Wilton Dean. A walk of 2½ miles (4km) close to the town centre, taking 1 hour to complete, but more enjoyable and longer in duration if the activities in the park are enjoyed and extended to the burgh boundary.

Loan, Crumhaughhill, Goldielands Tower. A longer walk this time, covering 4½ miles (7.2km) into the country and passing the 16th-century Border pele tower of Goldielands, once the property of the Scotts of Buccleuch.

Loan, Vertish Hill, Williestruther Loch. Yet another out-of-town ramble of 4½ miles (7.2km), this time over the 'Cornets Chase', used in the Common Riding ceremonies.

Stirches, Dykeneuk, Whitehaugh, Wilton Dean. This walk embraces the peace of the Border countryside and enables the walker to enjoy prominent Borders landmarks such as Rubers Law.

APPENDIX 1
Glossary

Local Terms And Names

Bell	Hill
Berwick cockles	Very strong mint sweets
Bield	Shelter, from the elements
Blaeberry	Bilberry, small purple edible berry
Burn	Small stream
Cairn	Pile of stones or standing stone; route or burial site marker
Champian	Level, open country
Clag	Wet cloud or mist that suddenly envelops summits
Cist	Stone coffin
Clarts or clarty	Adhesive mud, or muddy
Cleuch or cleugh	Narrow gully with burn (spellings as per OS maps)
Col	High saddle, lowest part of ridge between two summits
Common riding	Riding town boundaries, an annual Border festival
Corrie	Cirque, or glaciated hollow, in a mountainside
Craig	Rocky crag or outcrop
Cushat	Wood pigeon
Deer-hair	Coarse grass on wet upland areas
Dod	Surveyors' marker or pole; also a derivation of the name George
Doo	Town pigeon
Drouthy	Dry
Dyke	Drystone wall or manmade trench
Feral goat	Wild goat descended from domestic stock
Gimmer	Ewe (sheep)
Glar	Mud
Glebe	Church land, for grazing or cultivation
Glidders	Scree (Northumbrian)
Haugh	Flat ground by water
Hawick balls	Strong, round mint sweets
Heugh	Sharp-ended hill

Hole	Hollow
Hope	Sheltered valley
Jethart snails	Mint-flavoured sweets
Kames	Glacial debris or ridges
Ken	Know or understand
Knowe	Small hill
Law	Hill
Leat	Water running to a mill
Linn	Waterfall or waterslide
Loch	Lake
Lochan	Small lake
Lough	Small lake (Northumbrian)
Mosstrooper	A brigand in the border country of England and Scotland in the mid-17th century
Neb	Nose
Nolt	Cattle
Peewit	Lapwing or plover
Reiver	Cattle rustler, or entrepreneur!
Rig	(local spelling with one 'g', see OS maps of the area) Ridge
Rill	Small burn or stream
Scotch mist	Low cloud and very wetting drizzle
Scotsman's heids	Cotton grass, favours wet conditions
Scree	Loose rocks or shale on a hillside
Sea haar	Cold sea mist or fog
Shiel	Summer grazing, or a small hut on such ground
Sike	Stream
Spreat	Species of rush
Steading	Farm buildings or yard
Stell	Round stone sheep shelter (Northumbrian)
Strath	Broad flat river valley
Swire	Neck of land
Syke	See 'sike'
Troots	Trout
Trow	Trough
Trows	Little valleys
Tup	Ram (entire male sheep)
Vennel	Alley
Whaup	Curlew
Wight	Robust or manly

Local Pronunciations

Alwinton	al-inton
Berwick	ber-rik
Bowerhope	bier-op
Buccleuch	buck-loo
Hawick	hoy-ik
Hownam	hoo-num
Haugh	hoff or hock
Jedburgh	jed-boro, known locally as Jethart
Cleuch	clook
Cleugh	clook
Lough	loff

APPENDIX 2
Bibliography

A Short Border History, Francis Hindes Groome (J & J H Rutherford, 1887)

Exploring Scotland's Heritage, Lothians and the Borders (Her Majesty's Stationery Office, Edinburgh, 1996)

Highways and Byways: In the Border, Andrew and John Lang (Macmillan and Co., London, 1913, reprinted 1914 and 1929)

Homes and Haunts of Sir Walter Scott, George G Napier (J MacLehose & Sons, Glasgow, 1897)

The Life of Sir Walter Scott, Lockhart (University Press of the Pacific, 2002)

A Pennine Way Companion, A. Wainwright (Frances Lincoln, 2004)

Southern Upland Way, David Williams (Constable and Co. Ltd, London, 1989)

St Cuthbert's Way, Roger Smith and Ron Shaw (Scottish Borders Council, 1997)

The Border Line, James Logan Mack (Edinburgh, 1926)

The Borders, F R Banks (B T Batsford, London, 1977)

The Corbetts & Other Scottish Hills Scottish Mountaineering Club Hillwalkers' Guide (2nd edition, 2002)

The Drove Roads of Scotland, A R B Haldane (David & Charles, 1952)

The Steel Bonnets, George MacDonald Fraser (Akadine Press, 2001)

Walks in the Cheviot Hills (Northumberland County Council, National Park and Countryside Department, Hexham, 1986)

APPENDIX 3
Useful Information

ACCOMMODATION

Lists and bookings, together with a Book-a-Bed-Ahead scheme, plus details of transport, Border abbeys, castles, ancient monuments, museums and galleries, visitors' centres, gardens, crafts, leisure and recreation, and 'what's on' can be obtained from the Scottish Borders Tourist Board, ☎ 0870 6080404; written enquiries, Scottish Borders Tourist Board, Shepherds Mill, Whinfield Road, Selkirk TD7 5DT. Website: **www.visitscottishborders.com**

VISITOR INFORMATION CENTRES

Open all year:
Jedburgh, Murrays Green TD8 6BE
Kelso, Town House TD5 7HF
Melrose, Abbey House TD6 9LG
Peebles, High Street EH45 8AG

Open April to end October:
Eyemouth, Auld Kirk TD14 5JE
Hawick, Drumlanrig's Tower TD9 9EN
Selkirk, Halliwells House TD7 4BL

NORTHUMBRIA TOURIST BOARD

Aykley Heads, Durham DH1 5UX Tel 0191 375 3000
Tourist Information Centre, 106 Marygate, Berwick-upon-Tweed TD15 1BN
☎ 01289 330733
Tourist Information Centre, The Cheviot Centre, 12 Padgepool Place, Wooler NE71 6BL
☎ 01668 282123

SCOTTISH YOUTH HOSTELS

Broadmeadows, Old Broadmeadows, Yarrowford, Selkirk
☎ 0870 004 1107 or 01750 76262
Coldingham, The Mount, Coldingham Sands, Coldingham
☎ 0870 004 1111 or 018907 71298
Kirk Yetholm, The Green, Yetholm ☎ 0870 004 1132 or 01573 420631
Melrose, Priorwood, Melrose ☎ 0870 004 1141 or 01896 822521

ENGLISH YOUTH HOSTELS

Area Office, Bowey House, William Street, Newcastle upon Tyne NE3 1SA
☎ 0191 284 7473
Byrness, 7 Otterburn Green, Byrness, Otterburn ☎ 01830 520425
Wooler, 30 Cheviot Road, Wooler ☎ 01668 281365

TRANSPORT

Air
Edinburgh International Airport, Turnhouse, Edinburgh ☎ 0131 333 1000
Newcastle International Airport, Woolsington, Newcastle upon Tyne
☎ 0870 122 1488

Rail
National Rail Enquiries ☎ 0845 748 4950 for Berwick, Edinburgh and Carlisle

Road, Long Distance
National Express Ltd, sales and enquiries ☎ 0870 580 8080
Scottish Citylink Coaches Ltd, bookings and enquiries ☎ 0870 550 5050

Local Services
Timetables and fare details available from:
Scottish Borders Council, Newtown St Boswells, Melrose TD6 0SA
☎ 01835 825200
First, Customer Services, all enquiries ☎ 08708 72 7271
Munro's of Jedburgh 01835 862253
IDM Travel, Wooler 01668 281578
Royal Mail (post buses), enquiries ☎ 08457 740740

MISCELLANEOUS ADDRESSES

Countryside Ranger Service, Scottish Borders Council, Harestanes, Ancrum
☎ 01835 830281

Forestry Commission, Scottish Borders Forest District, Weavers Court, Forest Mill, Selkirk TD7 5NY ☎ 01750 721120

Mountaineering Council of Scotland, 4a St Catherine's Road, Perth PH1 5SE
☎ 01738 638227

National Trust for Scotland, Priorwood Gardens, Melrose ☎ 01896 822965, regional office: Northgate House, 32 Northgate, Peebles ☎ 01721 722502

Northumberland National Park, Eastburn, South Park, Hexham NE46 1BS
☎ 01434 605555

Ordnance Survey Customer Helpline, Romsey Road, Southampton, SO16 4GU (a range of local OS maps is available from outdoor shops and newsagents)

Scottish Widlife Trust, 115 High Street, Galashiels ☎ 01896 755516

Scottish Rights of Way and Access Society, 24 Annandale Street, Edinburgh EH7 4A
☎ 0131 558 1222

Scottish Youth Hostels Association, 7 Glebe Crescent, Stirling FK8 2JA
☎ 01786 891400

Woodland Trust, Westgate, Grantham, Lincs NG31 6LL

Mountain rescue service and the police – dial 999 (freephone)

Borders General Hospital NHS Trust, Huntlyburn, Melrose TD6 9BS
☎ 01896 825500 or 0800 374277

WEATHER FORECASTS

Newcastle Meteorological Office, Newcastle Weather Centre, for the Cheviot Hills ☎ 0845 300 0300

All meteorological enquiries covering the Border country ☎ 0870 900 0100

Weathercall, Borders ☎ 09068 505 3 22 (10-day) or 0870 600 4242

Daily forecasts, Radio Borders, FM 96.8

Daily forecasts, Border Television, Teletext page 152

ITV Scotland and Borders Channel 3, daily forecasts Monday–Friday

BBC Radio Scotland, FM 93.5, regular forecasts throughout the day; hill walkers' forecast Saturday 07.03 hrs

BBC1 Scotland, daily forecast 18.55 hrs Monday–Friday, hill walking forecast 18.55 hrs Friday

BBC1 and 2, Ceefax pages 401, 402 and 403

BBC Radio Scotland FM, hill walkers' forecast Friday 19.30 hrs, Saturday and Sunday 07.03 hrs.

APPENDIX 4: Summary of Walks

Walk	Distance miles (km)	Time (hrs)	Grade	Start	Finish
1	7 (11.3)	4–4½	3	Old Yeavering cottages (GR 924304)	Old Yeavering cottages
2	8½ (13.6)	5½–6	4	E of Langleeford	E of Langleeford
3	10 (16.1)	6	3/4	Upper Harthope Valley	Linhope Spout (GR 953225)
4	5 (8)	2½	2	Halterburn Valley (GR 840277)	Halterburn Valley
5	8 (12.9)	4–4½	2/3	Halterburn Valley (GR 840277)	Halterburn Valley
6	8 (12.9)	4	2	Halterburn Valley (GR 840277)	Halterburn Valley
7	8 (12.9)	6	4	Cocklawfoot (GR 853186)	Cocklawfoot
8	7½ (12.1)	4½	2/3	Cocklawfoot (GR 853186)	Cocklawfoot
9	10¾ (17.3)	7	3/4	Cocklawfoot (GR 853186)	Cocklawfoot
10	7 (11.3)	4	2/3	Cocklawfoot (GR 853186)	Cocklawfoot
11	7 (11.3)	4–5	2/3	Hownam village	Hownam village
12	7 (11.3)	4	2/3	Greenhill (GR 788177)	Greenhill
13	8 (12.9)	4½–5	3	Heatherhope Reservoir (GR 808167)	Heatherhope Reservoir
14	10½ (16.9)	6–6½	2/3	Towford (GR 761132)	Towford
15	10 (16.1)	5	2/3	Pennymuir (GR 755144)	Pennymuir
16	6¼ (10.1)	4	2/3	Carter Bar (GR 698068)	Carter Bar
17	5½ (8.8)	3½	2	St Abbs (GR 919673)	St Abbs
18	10½ (16.9)	5	2	The Junction, Kelso (GR 724335)	The Junction, Kelso

Walk	Distance miles (km)	Time (hrs)	Grade	Start	Finish
19	3½ (5.6)	2½	1	Smailholm village	Smailholm village
20	4¾ (7.6)	3	1	Scott's View (GR 594342)	Mertoun Bridge (GR 609320)
21	4¾ (7.6)	3	3	Melrose Abbey	Melrose
22	7½ (12.1)	5	2/3	Peel (GR 436349)	Peel
23	10 (16.1)	5½–6	2/3	Traquair village	Traquair village
24	4 (6.4)	2½	1	Harestanes (GR 641245)	Harestanes
25	5 (8)	3	2	Denholm	Denholm
26	10¼ (16.5)	6	4	B6399 road (GR 510979)	B6399 road
27	8 (13)	4½	2/3	Craik village CP (GR 348080)	Craik village CP
28	8½ (13.7)	5	2/3	Yarrowford (GR 407300)	Yarrowford
29	5½ (8.8)	3	1	A708 SUW (GR 273244)	A708 SUW
30	7½ (12.1)	4	1	Tibbie Shiels Inn (GR 240205)	Tibbie Shiels Inn
31	10½ (16.9)	6½	3	By A708 (GR 238205)	By A708
32	12 (19.3)	7	3	St Mary's L/L of the Lowes (GR 239205)	St Mary's L/L of the Lowes
33	8¾ (14)	6	3/4	Potburn (GR 188093)	Potburn
34	10 (16.1)	6	3/4	Potburn (GR 188093)	Potburn
35	6 (9.7)	4	3	Potburn (GR 188093)	Potburn
36	7 (11.3)	4	3	Potburn (GR 188093)	Potburn
37	3 (4.8)	2	1	Grey Mare's Tail CP (GR 187145)	Grey Mare's Tail CP
38	7 (11.3)	5	3	Grey Mare's Tail CP (GR 187145)	Grey Mare's Tail CP
39	7 (11.3)	6	4	Grey Mare's Tail CP (GR 187145)	Grey Mare's Tail CP
40	7 (11.3)	5	4	Carrifran (GR 159116)	Carrifran
41	10 (16.1)	5–7	4	Capplegill (GR 147098)	Capplegill
42	8 (12.9)	5	3/4	Talla Water Burn (GR 143201)	Talla Water Burn

Walk	Distance miles (km)	Time (hrs)	Grade	Start	Finish
43	6 (9.7)	3½	2	E of Talla Water bridge (GR 143201)	E of Talla Water bridge
44	9 (14.5)	5	3	E of Talla Water bridge (GR 143201)	E of Talla Water bridge
45	6½ (10.5)	4	3/4	Above Langhaugh (GR 199307)	Above Langhaugh
46	10 (16.1)	5½	3	By Kirkhouse (GR 321335)	By Kirkhouse at church CP

CP = car park

Grade or degree of difficulty

1 Good path, moderate ascent, no navigational problems.
2 Distinct path, steeper ascents, longer walk.
3 Paths rough in places, ascent 2000ft, exposed in places.
4 Few paths, ascent 2400ft plus, exposed, compass needed.

NOTES

NOTES

NOTES

LISTING OF CICERONE GUIDES

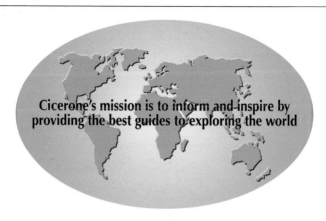

Cicerone's mission is to inform and inspire by providing the best guides to exploring the world

Since its foundation over 30 years ago, Cicerone has specialised in publishing guidebooks and has built a reputation for quality and reliability. It now publishes nearly 300 guides to the major destinations for outdoor enthusiasts, including Europe, UK and the rest of the world.

Written by leading and committed specialists, Cicerone guides are recognised as the most authoritative. They are full of information, maps and illustrations so that the user can plan and complete a successful and safe trip or expedition – be it a long face climb, a walk over Lakeland fells, an alpine traverse, a Himalayan trek or a ramble in the countryside.

With a thorough introduction to assist planning, clear diagrams, maps and colour photographs to illustrate the terrain and route, and accurate and detailed text, Cicerone guides are designed for ease of use and access to the information.

If the facts on the ground change, or there is any aspect of a guide that you think we can improve, we are always delighted to hear from you.

Cicerone Press
2 Police Square Milnthorpe Cumbria LA7 7PY
Tel:01539 562 069   Fax:01539 563 417
e-mail:info@cicerone.co.uk   web:www.cicerone.co.uk

CICERONE